Faith and Resistance in the Age of Trump

Faith and Resistance in the Age of Trump

Miguel A. De La Torre, editor

ORBIS BOOKS
Maryknoll, New York

ORBIS ✪ BOOKS
Maryknoll, New York 10545

Fathers and Brothers
MARYKNOLL™
TOGETHER IN GOD'S MISSION OF MERCY

Founded in 1970, Orbis Books endeavors to publish works that enlighten the mind, nourish the spirit, and challenge the conscience. The publishing arm of the Maryknoll Fathers and Brothers, Orbis seeks to explore the global dimensions of the Christian faith and mission, to invite dialogue with diverse cultures and religious traditions, and to serve the cause of reconciliation and peace. The books published reflect the views of their authors and do not represent the official position of the Maryknoll Society. To learn more about Maryknoll and Orbis Books, please visit our website at www.maryknollsociety.org.

Library of Congress Cataloging-in-Publication Data

Names: De La Torre, Miguel A., editor.
Title: Faith and resistance in the age of Trump / Miguel A. De La Torre, editor.
Description: Maryknoll : Orbis Books, 2017. | Includes bibliographical references and index.
Identifiers: LCCN 2017014044 (print) | LCCN 2017024566 (ebook) | ISBN 9781608337125 (e-book) | ISBN 9781626982475 (pbk.)
Subjects: LCSH: Christianity and politics—United States—History—21st century. | Trump, Donald, 1946—Public opinion.
Classification: LCC BR516 (ebook) | LCC BR516 .F28 2017 (print) | DDC 277.3/083—dc23
LC record available at https://lccn.loc.gov/2017014044

Dedicated to Lillian
from her "tío,"
hoping our words
and more important our praxis
leave you a more just and peaceful world
to inherit.

Contents

Contributors

Special gratitude is offered to the following contributors for literally dropping everything so as to participate in this project. The reader should note the book they hold in their hands was sent to the publisher a month after Trump's inauguration. Hence, this book provides a glimpse of a moment in time from the perspective of thinkers, activists, and/or participants of different religious traditions. This moment in time spans from his election, to when he placed his hand on the Bible and took the presidential oath, to the chaotic first three weeks of his administration where so much damage to basic civil justice occurred with the stroke of his executive pen. This book is a bold proclamation of why so many faith communities, specifically communities historically marginalized, are deeply concerned at the start of the Trump presidency. The reader, unlike the contributors when they penned these pages, has now lived through several months or years of the Trump administration; thus you will judge if our concerns were and/or continue to be warranted. This book also boldly declares that those often-heard and self-appointed religious leaders of this nation do not speak for the vast majority of people of faith. And neither do we. So any declaration of Trump as God's anointed, as was so often heard from more conservative alt-right ministers, is at best troubling, at worst idolatry. Again, to the following contributors who made this work possible, I offer a sincere *¡Gracias!*

Marie Alford-Harkey, is the president and CEO of the Religious Institute, a national multifaith organization promoting sexual health, education, and justice in faith communities and society. She is a Metropolitan Community Church pastor, the co-author of

Making the Invisible Visible: Bisexuality in Faith Communities, and speaks regularly on faith and sexuality in a variety of settings.

Sharon V. Betcher is an independent scholar, writer, crip philosopher, and would-be farmer living on Whidbey Island, Washington. She is the author of two academic manuscripts, *Spirit and the Politics of Disablement* and *Spirit and the Obligation of Social Flesh: A Secular Theology for Global Cities,* as well as theological essays within multiple anthologies worked through the critical lenses of ecological, postcolonial, gender, and disability studies theory.

Simone Campbell, SSS, a member of the Sisters of Social Service, is a lawyer, lobbyist, and executive director of NETWORK Lobby for Catholic Social Justice. In 2012 she organized the "Nuns on the Bus" tour to highlight social issues.

Miguel H. Díaz served under President Barack Obama as U.S. Ambassador to the Holy See and currently holds the John Courtney Murray Chair in Public Service at Loyola University Chicago. He is a theologian, prolific writer, and public speaker committed to bridging faith and public life.

Miguel A. De La Torre is professor of social ethics and Latinx studies at the Iliff School of Theology. He has served as president of the Society of Christian Ethics, has authored over a hundred articles, and published thirty-one books (five of which won national awards), and wrote the screenplay for the international award-winning documentary "Trails of Hope and Terror."

Marie Dennis is co-president of Pax Christi International, former director of the Maryknoll Office for Global Concerns, and a prime organizer of the Catholic Nonviolence Initiative. She is author or co-author of seven books, a secular Franciscan, and a member of Assisi Community in Washington, DC.

Kelly Brown Douglas is the Susan D. Morgan Distinguished Professor of Religion at Goucher College and the canon theologian at

Washington National Cathedral. Among her books are *The Black Christ, Sexuality and the Black Church,* and, most recently, *Stand Your Ground: Black Bodies and the Justice of God.*

Marvin Ellison, currently director of alumni/ae relations at Union Theological Seminary in New York, is Willard S. Bass Professor Emeritus of Christian Ethics at Bangor Theological Seminary. The founder of Maine's Religious Coalition against Discrimination, he also serves on the board of the Religious Institute and is author of *Erotic Justice: A Liberating Ethic of Sexuality, Sexuality and the Sacred: Resources for Theological Reflection* (with co-editor Kelly Brown Douglas), and *Making Love Just: Sexual Ethics for Perplexing Times.*

John M. Fife is a cofounder of the Sanctuary Movement to protect Central American refugees in the 1980s. He served as pastor of Southside Presbyterian Church in Tucson for thirty-five years and as moderator of the Presbyterian Church (U.S.A.). In retirement, he is a founding volunteer with No More Deaths and Samaritans in the Sonoran Desert borderlands.

Steven Greenberg is on the faculty of Shalom Hartman Institute of North America, the National Jewish Center for Learning and Leadership, and a founding director of Eshel, an LBGT support, education, and advocacy organization. He is the author of *Wrestling with God and Men: Homosexuality in the Jewish Tradition* and lives in Boston with his husband, Steven Goldstein, and daughter, Amalia.

Roger S. Gottlieb is professor of philosophy at Worcester Polytechnic Institute. He is the author or editor of twenty books and a hundred and fifty articles on political philosophy, environmental ethics, religious environmentalism, and contemporary spirituality, including the award-winning short-story collection *Engaging Voices.*

David P. Gushee is the author of twenty-one books, president of the Society of Christian Ethics, and president-elect of the American

Academy of Religion, and serves as Distinguished University Professor of Christian Ethics at Mercer University.

Jacqueline M. Hidalgo is associate professor of Latina/o studies and religion at Williams College. She is the author of *Revelation in Aztlán: Scriptures, Utopias, and the Chicano Movement*, and she is currently president-elect of the Academy of Catholic Hispanic Theologians of the United States.

Amir Hussain is professor of theological studies at Loyola Marymount University, where he teaches courses on Islam and world religions. His own particular specialty is the study of contemporary Muslim societies in North America. From 2011 to 2015, he was the editor of the *Journal of the American Academy of Religion*. The most recent of his six books is *Muslims and the Making of America*.

Kwok Pui-lan is the William F. Cole Professor of Christian Theology and Spirituality at the Episcopal Divinity School in Cambridge, MA, and the 2011 president of the American Academy of Religion. She is a pioneer in the postcolonial study of the Bible and theology.

Jacqui J. Lewis is senior minister at Middle Collegiate Church in New York City and host of *Just Faith* at MSNBC.com. She is an author, activist, and public theologian.

Irene Oh is associate professor of religion and director of the Peace Studies Program at George Washington University. She is the author of *The Rights of God: Islam, Human Rights, and Comparative Ethics*, as well as numerous articles, and has been elected to the boards of the Society of Christian Ethics and the Society for the Study of Muslim Ethics.

Joerg Rieger is Cal Turner Chancellor's Chair in Wesleyan Studies and Distinguished Professor of Theology, Vanderbilt University. He is the author of 130 articles and author and editor of twenty books, with translations into Portuguese, Spanish, Italian, German, Korean, and Chinese.

Santiago Slabodsky is the Florence and Robert Kaufman Chair in Jewish Studies and the associate director of the center for Race, Culture and Social Justice at Hofstra University–New York. His book *Decolonial Judaism* received the 2017 Frantz Fanon outstanding book award. He currently co-chairs the Liberation Theology unit at the America Academy of Religion, co-directs the trilingual journal *Decolonial Horizons*, and has held concurrent visiting positions in Europe, Africa, the Americas, and the Middle East.

Susan Brooks Thistlethwaite is professor of theology and president emerita of Chicago Theological Seminary. She is the author/editor of thirteen books, and has worked on two different translations of the Bible. She is a consultant to the Carter Center Scholars in Action Program to end global violence against women.

George "Tink" Tinker (wazhazhe/Osage Nation) is the Baldridge Professor of American Indian Cultures and Religious Traditions at the Iliff School of Theology in Denver. The author of several books, including *American Indian Liberation,* he is the past president of the Society for Race and Ethnicity in Religion, longtime director of the Four Winds American Indian Council in Denver, and a member of the elders' council for the American Indian Movement of Colorado.

Asante Todd is assistant professor of Christian ethics at Austin Presbyterian Theological Seminary in Austin, Texas. His research is in the area of public theology, or the ways in which theological and religious commitments impact public debate, policy, politics, and opinion. Todd's primary research focuses on the question of sovereignty in Western politics.

Jim Wallis is a *New York Times* bestselling author, public theologian, speaker, and international commentator on ethics and public life. He recently served on the White House Advisory Council on Faith-based and Neighborhood Partnerships. He is president and founder of Sojourners, and also serves as editor-in-chief of *Sojourners* magazine.

Amos Yong is professor of theology and mission at Fuller Theological Seminary. He served as president of the Society for Pentecostal Studies and has authored or edited over forty books.

Christiana Zenner is assistant professor of theology, science, and ethics at Fordham University in New York City. The author of *Just Water: Theology, Ethics, and the Global Water Crisis* and numerous articles, as well as co-editor of two volumes on sustainability and science in society, Zenner is passionate about the ethics of fresh water amid social and environmental changes, and she frequently lectures on these topics in scholarly and public venues.

Sustainability and Solidarity in the Trump Era

JIM WALLIS

In a class I taught at Georgetown this winter, we got into a lively discussion about President Trump's proposed refugee travel ban. One of my students has her law degree from Harvard and is now studying for a master's degree in public policy at the McCourt School of Public Policy, where I teach. She had been at DC airports most of the previous weekend, trying to help many of the international arrivals who had been detained. "This administration just doesn't accept the rule of law," she lamented, and said how discouraged she was feeling.

But I told her how encouraged I was just listening to her. Instead of simply focusing on a future lucrative legal career, she—along with countless other lawyers and law students—had spent a weekend trying to help all the confused and fearful people whose lives were suddenly put in jeopardy by an unexpected and badly executed order that caused chaos everywhere.

A *New York Times* article featured the large-scale response at airports across the nation, focusing on this new legal brigade. Trump's impulsive and, I would agree, lawless decision mobilized lawyers everywhere to defend "the stranger," as our Scriptures call refugees and immigrants. And that is very heartening to me.

Around the same time, I was speaking at another Jesuit school, Marquette University, during its Mission Week on Racism. My partner on the program was Bree Newsome, the young woman who famously climbed a thirty-foot flag pole on the South Carolina state capitol grounds in 2015 to remove the Confederate flag. Before that moment of international fame, Bree was an artist, filmmaker, and activist. And she has continued to be so since.

At Marquette, Bree spoke powerfully about how to make our movement of change *sustainable* by all of us doing what we do, day by day. We talked to more than a thousand students and people from the Milwaukee community who want to join a movement of resistance. As important as protest is, we both said, we have to build a movement of what we are *for* and not just what we are *against*. We must go beyond simply reacting to the crazy and dangerous things Trump says and does every day. That can be exhausting, and it is, I believe, part of his plan. As important as protest is, each of us has to also be faithful to our own calling in direct response to the crisis we face in America.

That means we need to be lawyers, artists, and activists; or teachers and students; or pastors and preachers; or service providers and advocates—workers of every kind in every vocation, all in resistance now to what we are facing in this country.

I encourage you to read the biblical passage from 1 Corinthians 12:4-31. Verses 4-11 talk about how we are each given unique gifts for unique kinds of service. Verses 14-21 give the analogy so familiar to many of us—that we are many parts, but one body. People have different God-given abilities to use for speaking, serving, caring, helping, protecting, or healing in any time and in times such as these.

Frodo, the fictional Hobbit in J. R. R. Tolkien's *Lord of the Rings*, speaks well to the situation we are now facing, and the wizard Gandalf speaks well to a biblical response:

> *"I wish it need not have happened in my time," said Frodo.*
> *"So do I," said Gandalf, "and so do all who live to see such times. But that is not for them to decide. All we have to decide is what to do with the time that is given us."*

The Trump era clearly promises to be dangerous to many people in our country: to many of our core values and institutions, to our governmental balance of powers, to the rule of law, to a free and honest press, and, seemingly, to truth itself. Many will find themselves vulnerable under our new political realities in Washington. But all of us who morally oppose what is going on and fear what is threatened have to make decisions about how and where and when we will speak and act for the things we know are right, and against the things we know are wrong.

We only have so much control over what happens in the world. As Gandalf reminds us, we don't choose the times we live in, but it's often the case that the times choose us. What that means about how we live out faith, resistance, and healing is going to be different for each of us—different gifts and callings, but all for the common good.

But confronting falsehoods with the truth is absolutely crucial, and will have to be done by all of us—not just the reporters whom we rely on to do their jobs well. So it's time for us all to stop calling the presidency of Donald Trump "unprecedented." *Dangerous* is the proper word. Attacks on the judiciary and judges who dare to disagree with him (which even his Supreme Court nominee calls "disheartening" and "demoralizing"), a continual strategy to undermine the press, protests, and polls when they disagree with him, a continual posture of conflict and bullying toward his opponents—are all the behaviors of authoritarian leaders. It is not surprising that the force of Trump's attacks have been against the press and the judiciary—primary checks and balances to his power.

Resistance from many people and places will be required now. Both Republicans and Democrats must be called to hold the president accountable; the press must be encouraged to exercise their integrity; and the judiciary must be strongly upheld to protect the rule of law. But the willingness to resist this autocratic rule will have to come from a broad and awakened citizenry. Speaking the truth and acting on behalf of what is right will require the efforts of all of us, at the deepest levels.

Preachers should preach ever more prophetically; teachers should teach formation and not just information; writers should write ever more honestly; lawyers should fight courageously for those who need their help; reporters should report the facts ever more diligently and speak the truth to power regardless of what the powers think about that; truth must overcome "alternative facts" on all of our social media; artists should make art that nurtures people and makes them think and inspires them to action. People who know about climate change should fight on climate change; people working for living wages and economic justice should keep organizing; people working for human rights, voting rights, women's rights, immigrant rights, refugee rights, and LGBTQ rights should keep defending and advocating. We all should serve those around us. We all should watch for people being left out and alone.

But even in putting our heads down and doing our work even more diligently, we can't silo ourselves off from one another; we need to stay connected, communicating with one another, and coming together for larger moments and movements of solidarity. Movements are not just events—they are made from many people doing things in their own places, and being aware that many others are acting just like they are elsewhere. If the real crises we face cause us to go deeper into our faith and to deepen our relationships, something new and powerful could come out of all of this. We confront both a danger and an opportunity.

Paul speaks to this in Corinthians when he talks about the origins of the Christian movement: "If one member suffers, all suffer together with it."

I hope this book serves you as a nurturing, connecting, and sustaining resource as we discuss the many ways faith, resistance, and healing must take shape in the Trump era. We want to support and sustain all those who are using their many callings and gifts in multiple ways to push back against bigotry, protect the vulnerable, preserve our values, stand up for the truth, and keep the faith.

We need to live and act in solidarity—together.

A Call to Resistance

JACQUI J. LEWIS

I am a Christian clergy, an African American female pastor of an almost one-thousand-member, multi-everything church on the Lower East Side of New York. It's called Middle Collegiate Church, if you'd like to find us.

We are an interesting bunch. Many races, ethnicities, sexual orientations, and gender performances. We are mostly Christian, but we are also Jews, Buddhists, Muslims, humanists, and some atheists who share our passion for justice. We sing gospel, classical, traditional hymns, some R & B, and jazz. We dance on our pews and on the pulpit. Our children both take and serve communion. Most of us believe there is more than one path to God.

All of us believe that every human being—no matter who they love, how they look, to whom they pray (or even if they do not pray at all), or how they make a living—is created in the image of God. Male and female, in the image of God, and awesomely and wonderfully made. This is the testimony of Genesis (the two creation stories there) and of the psalmist (Psalm 139 to be precise).

When Mr. Trump won the election, many of my lefty, progressive congregants were deeply hurt. Hurt that their mothers and fathers, cousins and aunties, dear friends from college and colleagues at work, along with a whole bunch of people that they did not know elected Donald Trump. They took the vote personally. Heck, so did I, to be honest. BUT we also believe deeply in the power of stories, so I created four questions to dive into the stories of our people, to "carefront" (to confront with care) our people and find out what was happening when they cast that vote. We asked:

1. Whom did you vote for? (Can't make assumptions, now can we?)
2. What did you dream would happen when you cast that vote?
3. How are you feeling now?
4. Is there anything we can do together?

These questions helped us in November. We shared them in our social networks. We came back from Thanksgiving, reporting on the difficult conversations we had, the stories we heard, and the things we learned from those who voted for the Trump/Pence administration. We were still hurt, still confused, and frankly in shock.

Now we are outraged.

The Trump/Pence administration has put billionaires in his cabinet and created an unprecedented seat at the military table for one who is a known racist and a close advisor. They are deregulating Wall Street. Many people are poised to lose their health insurance, perhaps you are among them. The sacred land that is called Standing Rock will, with the blessing of this administration, be ripped apart by a pipeline. POTUS has signed executive orders that ban Muslims from seven countries but not from nations in which he is financially invested. Our gay brothers and sisters are terrified and terrorized that they will be next.

During the first week of the Trump/Pence administration, an executive order was issued that expanded the group of immigrants considered priorities for deportation, including those without criminal records as well as those accused of crimes but not convicted. Daniel Ramirez Medina, a twenty-three-year-old Mexican immigrant who came to the United States as a child, a man with tattoos but no criminal record, was arrested Friday, February 10, in Seattle, Washington. He was but one of six hundred people arrested in one week in raids reported in eleven states.

On Friday, January 27, with the stroke of a pen, President Trump created a living nightmare for my Muslim brothers and sisters. Students unable to resume graduate studies at MIT, Stanford, and Yale. People returning to the United States after studying abroad. Grieving people fresh from the funerals of loved ones—permanent residents holding green cards. Detained for hours and sent back to their home countries. And refugees. Who spent years jumping through bureaucratic hoops. Refugees already on flights, detained at airports. A Syrian family of six, a family that has lived in a Turkish refugee camp since 2014, a family scheduled to arrive on Tuesday in Cleveland—their trip was called off. An Iranian man, who would be eligible for citizenship in November, now in limbo because he's unable to travel back to the United States.

Trump/Pence have gone after women's rights to choose a path for their own bodies. And now, *now* the targets of the "Make America Great Again" campaign are lesbian, gay, transgender, and bisexual Americans—Americans—and their constitutional rights.

I wonder now about the people who voted for this administration. How are they feeling? Do they have any sense that this administration's moves are deeply un-American? Do they fit with the so-called American dream? Do they feel safer, more secure? *And since I am a Christian, I am curious if Christians actually find these actions to be Christian?*

What I mean by that is: Do you think Jesus of Nazareth, that prophetic guy who preached that the first should be last and the last shall be first; that guy who made friends with sinners and outsiders; that guy who put women and children in the center of his ministry; that guy, that son of a God who made a stranger—an outsider, a religious minority, a Samaritan—the hero of his parable about what it means to love neighbor. Do you think *that* guy would approve of *this* behavior?

I am not an expert on the Constitution. I am clergy with several degrees related to my faith, and I am an expert on the One I follow into ministry. I am in a movement for justice and revolutionary resistance inspired by Rabbi Yeshua (Jesus' Aramaic name). You know him better as Jesus. Sometimes, I must admit, Jesus is a little niced-up for my taste. Blond. Beautiful. Harmless. Gentle.

Jesus, sadly, was "empired" when Rome made his Way the state religion.

Yeshua had a temple tantrum because of injustice, and called religious authorities a brood of vipers (Aramaic cursing, I think). Yeshua was a trouble-causing rabbi traveling around the country-side, calling people to follow him in resistance. Calling them to resist the Roman Empire, and its so-called peace. Peace enforced with sword and chariots, with high taxes and low wages. Calling them to a vision of a world they could create, calling them to shalom.

Jesus did not say one word about banning religion, about black people being inferior (curse of Cain?!?), or women being second-class citizens, or manifest destiny, or being gay, or denying people health care in all of the writings attributed to him. Not. One. Word. He did say love your neighbor as yourself. If Yeshua was teaching about neighbor love today, he might tell a story about a Muslim Samaritan. Or maybe a lesbian Samaritan. Or maybe an undocu-mented Samaritan. Someone outside of the hetero-normative Chris-tian frame. And recall that Yeshua was not a Christian; he was a Jewish rabbi. The Hebrew Scripture, our Old Testament, exhorts us to love the stranger—thirty-six times it says this—because they were once strangers, you know, in Egypt, and in Babylon.

Yeshua's life was lived in the context of empire, oppression, and subjugation. His revolution was grounded in a spiritual practice of resistance. When he saw hunger, he fed the people. When he saw sickness, he did not roll back health care programs; he healed the sick. He called women, children, outsiders, and strangers from the margins into the center. He broke cultic rules; he crossed boundar-ies. He reformed stale religion; he resisted empire.

Friends, these are hot-mess times; the empire has struck back. I heard tell recently of some gospel musicians who said that in these times we need to pray more and complain less. I think resistance is prayer.

People of faith need encouragement to cultivate a spirituality of resistance, as we seek to counter the onslaught of hatred and bigotry spilling out from the White House like a noxious poison. We need a book like this one, to sharpen our thinking, to enlarge our imaginations, to remind us that it is our moral responsibility to stand against oppression and for our neighbors. The love revolution we so desperately need is awaiting us just over the horizon. And it is not coming without us in it.

We need a primer, a guidebook, a roadmap. We need a manual on resistance in these hot-mess times.

I've been thinking hard about the possibility that maybe we had to get to a really funky, terrible, crazy, shadowy, and ominous place in order to wake up. Maybe we had to hit bottom in order to rise up. We have hit bottom, and it is dark, terrible, and frightening. We are waking up and rising up!

Did you go to any of the women's marches? Did you see the sea of people, loving, kind, inspired, chanting, singing people? Did you see the women? Called together by a couple of women. With the same idea. Collaborating, adding more women, and men, and doing a stunning thing in two hundred cities around the globe, with millions of people called to the movement, called to resist.

Called to stand for women's rights to earn what men do, to make their own choices, to not be grabbed. Called to stand for the value of black lives, immigrant lives, and refugee lives. Called to stand for Muslim lives, Jewish lives, and LGBTQ lives.

Did you see the people at the airports? Standing up for the lives of Muslims they don't know? They know this: When they come for the Muslims, they are coming next for you and for me.

And when you see the people organizing, watch for people standing for my LGBTQ brothers and sisters because they are next. And look for me, this straight, black woman in a collar. I'll be right there, raising my voice and my fist, standing up for them. Because their right to live, to love, to be who they are—this matters to me! I'll be resisting.

Right now, our new president is signing multiple executive orders to limit our freedoms. When his policies work to hurt some of us, they work to hurt all of us. This is not an easy time; this is not easy work. But work we must. We are called to be in the movement for justice. Like Rabbi Yeshua—Jesus—we are called to turn the tables; we are called to resist. Freedom is the aim of our movement. And none of us is free until all of us are free.

I am in the movement for justice inspired by Yeshua. No matter what inspires you, all voices are needed. Lift up your voice; lift up love. Turn every heart on fire for a transformation and healing of our culture. Join the resistance as an act of faith.

These essays by some of our nation's most brilliant theological minds will invite you. This primer will guide our feet while we run this race to liberty and justice for all.

¡Basta!

MIGUEL A. DE LA TORRE

In what country are beasts not bred from hatred?
—*José Martí*

A month after the 2016 election, I found myself in Cuba doing research for my next book project. One evening, while sitting at the hotel lounge, I struck up a conversation with a couple from Seattle. Eventually, the exchange turned to religion and the election of Trump. Commiserating over shots of Havana Club, the husband— a self-professed agnostic—looked me straight in the eye and told me that after an election where religious leaders supported and campaigned for a misogynist, xenophobic, adulterous, casino and strip-club owner, he "never again wanted to hear religious leaders question any politician's morality." If a tree is indeed known by its fruit, suffice to note Trump presents us with a very bare, withered stump. The same religious folks who attacked Bill Clinton for his peccadillos and who then embraced Trump during the election lost all moral authority to ever again pronounce judgment on anyone's integrity, anyone's moral fitness to be elected. As I listened to my new acquaintance, I found it difficult to argue with his logic. And yet, as a man of faith, I still believe the community of faith has something important to say about the current political situation, a crucial prophetic word that is desperately needed.

My new acquaintance's concerns about Christian support of politicians diametrically opposed to what church leaders profess to believe is a phenomenon as old as the biblical text. My own Christian tradition recounts in the last book of Holy Writ a warning concerning the "whore of Babylon." Within the New Testament's last apocalyptic entry, we are introduced to a "woman . . . drunk with the blood of God's holy people" (Revelation 17:1-6). Historically, Christian biblical exegesis associated this "whore of Babylon" with the Antichrist of Revelation, where the word "whore" had less to do with any sexual transgression and was more a reference to the act of idolatry; specifically, "whoring" the church to serve the political interests of secular rulers. Not surprisingly, much speculation swirled around whom this "whore" signified. Christian scholars mainly understood Babylon to be the Roman Empire, which engaged (until 313 CE) in the sporadic persecution of Christians.

During the Medieval Period, some reformers and critics within the Catholic Church (several of whom eventually were elevated to sainthood) equated the papacy with the whore of Babylon, specifically for internal corruption, the practice of simony, and, most importantly, political maneuvering to enhance the church's earthly power and dominion. Leaders of the Protestant movement (i.e., Luther, Zwingli, Calvin, Knox, Wesley), strengthened this association by generalizing the entire Catholic Church as corrupt, rather than providing a more complex analysis criticizing specific periods and/or popes. The pope as Antichrist, leading the Catholic Church as whore into apostasy, was not only a mainstream interpretation during the rise of Protestantism; it has remained a popular interpretation among some present-day Christians, especially fundamentalists, dispensationalists, and alt-right-leaning evangelicals.

Maintaining such an interpretation is, to say the least, highly problematic, specifically because (1) it feminizes idolatry, signifying the act of religious unfaithfulness through a sign of female sexuality; (2) it undergirds an anti-Catholic bias still present among some Protestants today; and (3) it contributes to a troublesome dispensationalist biblical interpretation fostering greater division among those deemed saved and those dismissed as damned. Nevertheless, as knotty as the sign "whore of Babylon" might be, it does raise a valid critique for a church, any church, of any faith tradition, that exchanges the radical call of justice for the status quo of oppressive social structures in hopes of obtaining political power and privilege. The cry "God is on our side" is responsible for more bloodletting in the form of crusades, wars, colonialism, and genocide than any other human-caused catastrophe. Within different societies, various faith leaders have played the "whore," falling into the temptation of tailoring a religious message to sell a political ideology, a political party, or a political candidate as ordained by God, a temptation existing for those who consider themselves among the religious right, the religious center, or the religious left.

So one of the questions with which this book wrestles in the aftermath of Trump's 2016 election to the presidency is an attempt to signify the identity of today's "whore of Babylon." Could it be Christians, specifically white Christians? There was a time when white Christianity had a disproportionate say in American politics. No doubt, the 1980s were the heyday of white Christian political influence. But much has happen in the past thirty-five years: the recognition of same-gender loving marriages; a decline in the white birth rate, which means that whites will represent less than 50 percent in demographics; a black president; the dismantling of a system, through affirmative action programs, that for centuries ensured that job opportunities and college admission went mainly to white males; police officers being scrutinized and held accountable for what once was the unrestrained norm of killing unarmed people of color. Since the '80s, a different, scarier world developed for those accustomed to power and privilege. They have had to adjust to a more pluralistic environment in which the birthright of white privilege has been questioned and chipped away. Faith leaders, who once upon a time had great political sway, now struggle to reclaim some of their previous power and prestige. But at what price?

The 2016 election was marked by self-proclaimed faith leaders rushing to present Trump as God's faithful servant. We were left to wonder if once again the church was being pimped to the highest political bidder? Let's be clear: no political party, especially the

Republican or the Democratic, is ordained by God. No president, emperor, prime minister, king, or queen is or ever was ordained by God. There is not, nor was there ever, any theological truth in a divine right of royalty. Trump's (or Hillary Clinton's for that matter) Christianity, or lack thereof, is unimportant in the secular voting booth, because we are not a theocracy. This does not mean people of faith should not be engaged in the political process; by their involvement they should serve as the conscience of whichever party or political candidate they support. And yet, as I review the 2016 presidential political season, I cannot help but wonder if indeed some communities of faith simply prostituted themselves in exchange for a say in who would sit on the Supreme Court.

Since the recent election, many of us from different faith communities have struggled to find a proper response. For such a time as this, we who are scholars of religion, activists, and ministers must provide the general public with critical analysis and practical praxis in which to engage. In the matrix of alternative facts, fake news, doublespeak, rants, and hand wringing, a systematic, clear, and unmistakable voice for justice is desperately needed; a voice that is unashamedly multiracial, multiethnic, multifaith; a voice rooted in the redundancy of the term "true facts." We who contributed to this book are not seeking simply to contribute a harangue about why we think Trump is the antithesis of what we claim are the core beliefs of any faith rooted in justice. What we wrestled with is the why of Trump, specifically our own complicity with the election results; and a practical response to the consequences of Trump, specifically what becomes the call to our faith communities in resisting the next four or eight years. Each chapter has attempted to (1) define the problem, (2) ground the perceived problem in actual data, (3) analyze the problem, and (4) propose action.

To a certain extent, this book is written to the couple with whom I had a chance encounter at a hotel bar. While employing a critical analytical focus, we have nonetheless strived to write in an accessible manner. Democracy flourishes only when the electorate is well informed, a difficult goal in an age in which misinformation has become the norm. For some readers, this book is simply one contribution to the overall discourse. Whether you agree or disagree with different perspectives is of lesser importance than that you wrestle with the book's contents. For others, this book is an attempt to outline how to engage in faith and resistance in an age of Trump. We who penned the following pages came together to say, in one voice: *¡Basta!*—Enough! We dare not only to dream of a different future based on our different faiths, but to outline how to make such dreams a reality. We invite you to join us in this radical call for justice. We do not make a call to take back our country, for the fact is this country never belonged to the disenfranchised. Nor do we make a call to make America great again, because America is "great" only when it rests on the backs of those never meant to belong—be they Native Americans, blacks, women, Latinx, etc. Our call is to create a new America that moves beyond its oppressive racist, imperialist, and misogynist past toward a new possibility, a possibility that takes seriously the rhetoric of "liberty and justice for all." This is a vision for a new America that has yet to exist, an America that cannot be achieved under a Trump administration. For this reason, we have no choice, if we care to be faithful, but to resist.

CHAPTER 1

Make America Truly Great Again

STEVEN GREENBERG

"Make America Great Again" was registered with the U.S. Patent and Trademark Office on November 12, 2012. It was six days after President Barack Obama won his second term when Donald Trump began considering a run for the presidency. He had toyed with a shorter slogan, "Make America Great," but he thought it too negative, implying that American hadn't ever been great. "Again" clinched the deal. "Make America Great Again" became the phrase that best telegraphed the campaign's ethos of disappointment, promising to restore a lost American greatness.[1]

This shorthand reference to an idealized past is a staple of conservative politics. The Trump campaign was able to employ it to unify a number of different calls for turning the clock back. For Steve Bannon, the chief strategist for the president, that ideal age was America of the 1930s, before Franklin D. Roosevelt's New Deal. For many of the men suffering from unemployment, for those caught in cycles of welfare, depression, and addiction, the halcyon age was the 1950s, when factory jobs were plentiful, when coal was king, and when a single man could support a family of five on his

---

1. Pamela Engel, "How Trump Came Up with His Slogan 'Make America Great Again,'" *Business Insider*, January 18, 2017.

salary. For racist white folks it was before the civil rights movement in the 1960s, before the dramatic increase of racial and ethnic diversity in America, and most certainly before Barack Obama
demonstrated how far a black man could rise in power. For disgruntled older men, it was before women's equality began to level
the playing field. For most Catholics, evangelicals, and Mormons
it was before the sexual revolution, the availability of contraception and abortion, and most recently, before the normalization of
LGBT identities. Many of these religious voters may have held their
noses at the sins of lust, gluttony, pride, and greed for the sake of
Trump's promises to turn back the clock on gay marriage and abortion rights. And for others the Trump time machine would carry
them to a time before September 11, 2001, when the violent spec-
ter of a Islamic jihadism made them constantly afraid. The slogan
worked well to unite people with an array of diverse fears, angers,
and resentments.

Remarkably, no single Trump policy promise would or could sat-
isfy all these different segments. For many of his supporters, there
were just one or two key problems they believed Trump could fix.
The spaces between the economic woes and speed of social change,
the loss of manufacturing jobs, and the excesses of political correctness, the trade deficit, and the rise of Islamic terror did not matter.
The rhetoric of an American greatness on decline, a greatness that
candidate Trump could restore, resonated powerfully for all his
supporters. His claims to enormous wealth and business acumen,
his name emblazoned on more than two dozen towers, his lack of
political grace, knowledge of history, policy, or statecraft—in short
his not being anything like a career politician—made him the right
man to restore American power, economic strength, political dominance: He who would make America great again.

The slogan, however, is not original. Whether or not he was
aware of this, Trump simply recycled a slogan from the Reagan
campaign of 1980. As the country was suffering at that time from a
flagging economy Reagan used the phrase to stir a sense of patriotism. The portrayal of America as exceptional, a country of outsized
greatness, has a very old provenance. From its very beginnings,

America conceived of itself as a shining city on a hill, destined for greatness. That language of a city upon a hill was taken from Jesus' Sermon on the Mount. In Matthew 5:14 Jesus tells his listeners, "You are the light of the world. A city that is set on a hill cannot be hidden." Jesus was himself making reference to Isaiah 42:6-7: "I the Lord in my grace have summoned you. I have grasped you by the hand. I created you and appointed you a covenant people, a light of nations—opening eyes deprived of light, rescuing prisoners from confinement, from the dungeon those who sit in darkness."

John Winthrop, while still aboard the ship *Arbella*, admonished the future Massachusetts Bay colonists that their new community would be "as a city upon a hill," watched by the world. A number of presidents have used the image to chart a destiny for America bigger than its own narrow self interests. John F. Kennedy used it in 1961 to mark how the world looks upon the American experiment: "We must always consider that the eyes of all people are upon us . . . and our governments, in every branch, at every level, national, state and local, must be as a city upon a hill—constructed and inhabited by men aware of their great trust and their great responsibilities. For we are setting out upon a voyage in 1961 no less hazardous than that undertaken by the *Arbella* in 1630."[2]

Ronald Reagan used this image in many of his speeches as a frame for uniting Americans who do not come as "white or black, red or yellow . . . not Jews or Christians; conservatives or liberals; or Democrats or Republicans, but Americans awed by a shining city on a hill."[3] The image was used most expressively in his farewell speech in 1989: "I've spoken of the shining city all my political life, but I don't know if I ever quite communicated what I saw when I said it. But in my mind it was a tall, proud city built on rocks stronger than oceans, wind-swept, God-blessed, and teeming with people of all kinds living in harmony and peace; a city with free

2. John F. Kennedy, "City upon a Hill," address delivered to the General Court of Massachusetts, January 9, 1961.

3. Ronald Reagan, "A Vision for America," election eve address, November 3, 1980.

ports that hummed with commerce and creativity. And if there had to be city walls, the walls had doors and the doors were open to anyone with the will and the heart to get here. That's how I saw it, and see it still."[4]

This idea of an American greatness, an exceptionalism that lights the world, entails a fearless embrace of cultural and religious diversity while enjoining a solidarity driven by values enshrined in a constitution. America is a country teeming with difference whose borders are both walls and doors. The sense of greatness that was bellowed forth at the Trump rallies was of a very different sort. Both historical memory and biblical sensibility must be marshaled to resist a sense of greatness that highlights power over purpose, boundaries over exchange, fear over trust, and narrow self-interest over generosity. It is indeed a good time to open President Trump's call to greatness as an open inquiry, one that is as old as John Winthrop in defining a shared American vision. What can be said about the sort of greatness to which we ought to aspire and against which we ought to measure our success and that of our leaders? Beyond the shining city on the hill, our religious traditions have a great deal to say about the longing for greatness, both for individuals and nations. The Jewish tradition is quite explicit in its portrayal of the challenge of greatness.

In the Hebrew Bible the word *gadol* in the book of Genesis means great, large, elder. Great lights, great sea creatures, a great city are all about size. The root of *gadol* can be found in the famous narrative about a tower (*migdal*) in Babylon built as resistance to dissolution, with an explicit desire of the builders to "make a name" for themselves. In response to a notion of greatness that rests on fame, monuments, and tall towers, heaven acts not quite with punishment but with a will to interrupt this singular project by means of a confusion of difference, the babel of many languages.

The Jewish sages, eager to moralize the story, added a layer of violence to the picture. They claimed that in the process of building

---

4. Ronald Reagan, "Farewell Speech," speech to the nation, January 11, 1989.

their ziggurat many fell to their deaths. When a man fell down and died, no heed was paid. But when a brick fell down, they stopped work and wept (*Pirke de-Rabbi Eliezer* 24:7). Babel epitomizes a corporation, "a group of people authorized to act as a single entity," that wields enormous power to accomplish amazing public works, but which can easily undermine the fundamental value of individuals. The overreaching of the generation of the Tower of Babel and its misperception of greatness leads the biblical storyline to Abram, to the man chosen to be the founder of a great nation.

In Genesis, chapter 12, we meet Abram, the singular man urged to leave the cradle of civilization and become an immigrant, a stranger in a new land. There he will found a *goy gadol*—"a great nation." God will bless him and make his name great and all the families of the earth shall be blessed through him. The shift in greatness is palpable, but how will this one man found a great nation that will spread blessing to the world? We are left to wonder how this will work till chapters 18 and 19, when we discover that the nation's promised greatness will not be a matter of its size but of its moral commitments. Abraham will be the father of a great nation because he will teach his progeny to do *tzedek* and *mishpat*, righteousness and justice.

Adding to the image of a city on a hill, Genesis offers a tent in the desert and a city on the plain as two models of human community. Abraham and Sarah's tent is a refuge for vagrants, migrants, immigrants, and travelers of all sorts. "And he lifted up his eyes and looked, and, lo, three men stood by him; and when he saw them, he ran to meet them from the tent door. . . . 'Pray let a little water be fetched to wash your feet and rest yourselves under the tree. Let me fetch you a morsel of bread to refresh your hearts.'" Juxtaposed to Abraham and Sarah's famous hospitality is the city of Sodom in the next chapter.

The rabbinic legends about Sodom in rabbinic lore help to draw the contrast. They describe an area of unusual natural resources, precious stones, silver and gold. Every path in Sodom, say the sages, was lined with seven rows of fruit trees. Jealous of their great wealth and suspicious of outsiders' desires to share in it, they agreed to overturn the ancient law of hospitality to wayfarers. The legislation later included the prohibition to give charity to anyone.

The rabbis speak of a Sodomite bed (*mittat sedom*), which the people of Sodom provided for weary guests. However, when the wayfarer would lie down they made sure that he fit the bed perfectly. A short man was stretched to fit it and a tall man was cut to size. The people of Sodom are not only protective of their wealth and punishing of acts of charity, but they are also desperate to force everyone to fit a single measure. They have a well-to-do gated community that makes sure no beggars disturb their luxury and peace. They have zoned out both poverty and difference. For Sodom, the needs of others are experienced as a threat; for Abraham, they are opportunities for communion. For Sodom, the response to difference is violence; for Abraham, curiosity.

This is not to claim that greatness is only a spiritual or moral quality. Greatness is ascribed to the patriarch Isaac three times in one verse, and it seems to refer to his knowledge of husbandry and his expanding wealth. "And Isaac sowed in the land and reaped in the same year a hundredfold. The Lord blessed him and the man became great and gained more and more until he became very great."

However, immediately in response to this achievement of great material wealth, the neighboring Philistines envy him; they stop up the wells his father dug and eventually force him to leave the land. It appears that physical greatness can be a boon. There is no inherent moral failure in wealth or power. However, they both invite dangers. Power and wealth can lead to greedy appropriation, but they can also tempt others to envious aggression. They are valuable resources but not independent values. Greatness itself is a matter of character, of righteousness and justice, of generosity and care.

God is part of this story as well, because God is also described as great. In Deuteronomy, Moses praises God, to whom "belongs the highest heavens, the earth and all its contents." However, this exuberant praise isn't what Moses marks as God's greatness. Instead, a triplet of divine greatness is identified as God's love of the weak and embrace of the outsider.

> Behold, unto the LORD God belongs the heavens, and the heavens beyond the heavens, the earth and all that is in it. . . . You must cut away the thickening of your hearts and no longer stiffen your necks, for the LORD your God, He is God of gods, and Lord of lords, *the great God, the mighty, and the awesome,* who is not partial and takes no bribe. He executes justice for the fatherless and widow, and loves the stranger, giving him food and clothing. So you must love the stranger; for you were strangers in the land of Egypt. (Deuteronomy 10:14-19)

God's greatness appears in the execution of justice, in the care for the vulnerable, and most remarkably, in the love of the stranger. This portrayal of divine greatness is to be imitated. The description of God's awesome greatness ends as a calling to humanity to imitate God's love of the stranger.

The imitation of divine humility and love as the epitome of greatness becomes the duty of kings. Rabbi Moses ben Maimon (Maimonides), the medieval legalist and philosopher, in his Laws of Kings articulates clearly the sorts of greatness required of human leaders.

> Just as Scripture has granted [the king] great honor and obligated all in honoring him, so has it enjoined [the king] to be humble and empty (of self-pride). . . . He should not act more proudly than necessary toward [the people of] Israel. . . . He should be gracious and merciful toward the lowly and the great. He should show concern for their property and welfare. He should show regard for the dignity of the lowliest. When he addresses the public, he should speak gently. . . . He should always behave with great modesty. . . . He should bear with their troublesomeness, burdensomeness, complaining, and irritation as a governor bears with an infant. Scripture dubs him a shepherd. . . . "As a shepherd He pastures his flock: He gathers the lambs in His arms and carries them in His bosom . . . (Isaiah 40:11)."

Great leaders require sufficient self-esteem to wield proper authority. Nonetheless, they must excel in modesty and forbearance. They should be able to give honor to others freely, behave with modesty and gentleness, take counsel graciously and nourish an open hearted, if critical, ear in order to make good decisions.

In the early rabbinic period, following the destruction of the Temple in 70 CE, Jewish sovereignty was lost to Rome, and a remnant of scribes and sages developed new forms of leadership. The *Ethics of the Fathers*, written after the destruction, addresses four qualities of leadership: wisdom, power, wealth, and honor. A famous aphorism that begins the fourth chapter of the *Ethics* offers resistance to the brutal forms of power that made Rome "great." In Rome, qualities of elite aristocrats, the very resources of domination, are transformed by these rabbis into forms of relationship and care. "Ben Zoma would say: Who is wise? One who learns from every man. . . . Who is powerful? One who controls his inclinations. . . . Who is rich? One who is satisfied with his lot. Who is honorable? One who honors his fellows" (*Pirkei Avot* 4). Greatness according to these sages is found in curiosity, self-restraint, acceptance, and respect for others.

It was in scripture that our founding fathers found the greatness toward which they honed their own characters and nourished a vision of the republic they were building. The same greatness that was celebrated by Winthrop was echoed by great American poets like Emma Lazarus and Walt Whitman. In a poem entitled "The New Colossus," Lazarus describes the Statue of Liberty as "a mighty woman with a torch . . . a Mother of Exiles." Speaking as if from the lips of the colossus, not of Rome, but of New York Harbor, she calls out to the world literally holding up a light to the nations: "Send these, the homeless, tempest-tost to me, I lift my lamp beside the golden door!"

The poetry of Walt Whitman set out to encompass all of America in order to heal the deepening of the divisions of the Civil War era. He strove to articulate an American spirit of largesse, a generosity and a vulnerable confidence that speaks volumes to our moment of fracture and our national hunger for greatness. He too marks a way to recover the shining city on the hill that is America. This excerpt is from the Preface to "Leaves of Grass":

The United States themselves are essentially the greatest poem. In the history of the earth hitherto the largest and most stirring appear tame and orderly to their ampler largeness and stir. Here at last is something in the doings of man that corresponds with the broadcast doings of the day and night. Here is not merely a nation but a teeming nation of nations. Here is action untied from strings necessarily blind to particulars and details magnificently moving in vast masses. Here is the hospitality which forever indicates heroes.[5]

Making America Great Again may actually be happening as I write these words. Mass protests, town hall gatherings, resistance from judges, patriots, and civil servants are mounting. Insistence by governors and mayors, by religious communities, civic organizations, and ordinary citizens to stand up to bad executive orders, dangerous policies, conflicts of interest and reckless governance is growing. Perhaps President Trump is serving a role, not as a prophet, but as a goad to urge us all to determine the true nature of our greatness. Mercifully, he is not in charge of this discourse, no matter how often he tweets. During this challenging time as we navigate the tensions of our diversity, our different visions of goodness and well-being, the wonderful and painful challenges of technological innovation and increasing globalization of markets the American people can still be a beacon, a light unto nations, and a city upon a hill. In the words of JFK, we are still "constructed and inhabited by people aware of their great trust and their great responsibilities." As the world looks on . . . this great American conversation, happening now from sea to shining sea, unoccasioned by violence or force, is our shared American legacy, and what truly makes us great.

---

5. Walt Whitman, "The American Sublime as 'Song of Myself,'" in *American Sublime: The Genealogy of a Poetic Gene,* ed. Rob Wilson (Madison: University of Wisconsin Press, 1991), 147.

CHAPTER 2

Donald Trump and the "Exceptionalist" Truth about America

KELLY BROWN DOUGLAS

How did it happen? How has a man whose campaign was filled with racist, xenophobic, and misogynistic vitriol and who mounted a racialized "birther" campaign against the nation's first African American president, while promising "Law and Order"/Wall Building protectionist policies—how has this man been elected president in a country that proclaims "life, liberty, and the pursuit of happiness" for all?

There are those who have argued that Trump's election had "little if anything to do with sexism, religious bigotry, or even racism."[1] They go on to claim that he won because he paid attention to the "economic anxieties" of those in the "Rust Belt" of the United States and that his election represents a revolt by white working-class voters.[2] Those who espouse this narrative further suggest that to claim racism played a factor in his victory is to "play a race-card," which is tantamount to reverse racism. On the other hand, there are those who argue that to downplay the racist, sexist, and bigoted narratives that defined much of Trump's campaign is to "follow a script first honed . . . [a]fter the Civil War, [by] 'Lost

1. Paraphrased in John Blake and Tawanda Scott Sambou, "How Trump's Victory Turns into Another 'Lost Cause,'" *CNN*, December 28, 2016.
2. The "Rust Belt" generally refers to states from the Great Lakes and Midwest also known as the industrial heartland, as its economy relied on the steel and automobile industry.

Cause' propagandists [who] argued the war wasn't fought over slavery—[but] was a constitutional clash over state's rights."[3]

Nevertheless, just as it was clear that slavery was a central precipitating factor in the Civil War, troubling chauvinistic rhetoric was a central part of the presidential campaign. To be sure, Trump's campaign resonated with the fears, anxieties, and economic woes of a particular white working-class "Rust Belt" demographic, but inasmuch as it did so, it linked their feelings to a narrative "coated with racism."[4] The point of the matter is, the deeply differing perspectives on the nature of Trump's campaign and the factors leading to his victory reveal a sinister truth about our nation—in fact a truth that the Trump campaign guilefully tapped into, and in so doing, has left our nation as racially divided as it has ever been. This begs the question: What does this divide—indeed Trump's victory—tell us about our nation? This chapter attempts to address that very question.

Trump and the Truth about America

What is the truth about America that Trump's campaign not only tapped into but brought into clear relief? Simply put, the Trump campaign tapped into America's defining narrative of Anglo-Saxon exceptionalism and the supremacist culture of whiteness that serves to protect it.

When America's Pilgrim and Puritan forebears fled England in search of freedom, they believed themselves descendants of an ancient Anglo-Saxon people, "free from the taint of intermarriages,"[5] who uniquely possessed high moral values and an "instinctive love for freedom."[6] Their beliefs reflected an Anglo-Saxon myth initiated by the first-century Roman philosopher Tacitus, who in his book

---

3. Quoted in Blake and Sambou, "Lost Cause," *CNN*. The preceding characterization is also informed by this article.

4. Ibid.

5. Tacitus, *Germania*, Medieval Sourcebook, https://sourcebooks.fordham.edu/source/tacitus1.html.

6. Reginald Horsman, *Race and Manifest Destiny: The Origins of American Racial Anglo-Saxonism* (Cambridge, MA: Harvard University Press, 1981), 26.

Germania touted the unique superiority of these Anglo-Saxon people from the ancient woods of Germany. Fueled by this myth and considering themselves the heirs of these mythic Anglo-Saxon people, the early Americans crossed the Atlantic with a vision to build a nation that was politically and culturally—if not also demographically—true to their "exceptional" Anglo-Saxon heritage. Moreover, this was for them a divine vision as they traced their Anglo-Saxon heritage through the ancient woods of Germany back to the Bible. Consequently, they considered themselves not just an Anglo-Saxon people but also the "new" Israelites carrying forth a divine mission. Central to their vision, therefore, was not simply to build an Anglo-Saxon nation but to build a religious nation—one that reflected the morals and virtues of God. If these coincided with the virtues and morals of their freedom-loving Anglo-Saxon ancestors, that reflected the assumption that God was essentially Anglo-Saxon. This divine Anglo-Saxon vision was soon to be shared by the nation's founding fathers, including Thomas Jefferson and Benjamin Franklin.

Jefferson was a thoroughgoing and unabashed Anglo-Saxonist. He was resolute in his thinking that Americans were obligated to establish a form of government commensurate with their Anglo-Saxon past. He, like his Puritan and Pilgrim forebears, also considered Anglo-Saxon Americans the New Israelites, and in this he was not alone; Benjamin Franklin believed the same.[7]

Through political architects such as Jefferson and Franklin, as well as its Pilgrim and Puritan founders, America's democracy was conceived as an "Anglo-centric" divine calling. These founders gave sacred legitimation to their Anglo-Saxon mission at the same time as they gave sacred validity to the Anglo-Saxon myth that undergirded it. As such, America was envisioned as a testament to the sacredness of Anglo-Saxon character and values, if not people.

In order to safeguard this vision a pervasive culture of whiteness

---

7. See, for instance, the seal that Franklin proposed, as described by John Adams in "Letter from John Adams to Abigail Adams, August 14, 1776," Massachusetts Historical Society, http:// www.masshist.org. For more on Jefferson's and Franklin's Anglo-Saxon chauvinism, see Kelly Brown Douglas, *Stand Your Ground; Black Bodies and the Justice of God* (Maryknoll, NY: Orbis Books, 2015).

was born. Why? For the simple reason that not everyone who looks like an Anglo-Saxon in the United States is actually Anglo-Saxon. The perpetually vexing problem for the nation is that from its very beginnings it has been an immigrant nation with migrants—even European migrants—who were not Anglo-Saxon. Yet there was a mitigating factor, at least for those who came from Europe; they were after all white, and this whiteness made all the difference. Not only did whiteness allow a person to pass as an Anglo-Saxon, but it also signified that an individual was capable of assimilating to Anglo-Saxon ways and values. In fact, President Theodore Roosevelt argued non-Anglo-Saxon whites could be properly assimilated to Anglo-Saxon ways "within the space of two generations."[8] Such beliefs provided the foundation for the emergence of a white supremacist culture. Within this culture, to be white was to be considered Anglo-Saxon enough. Hence, to be white was to be privileged to enter certain spaces and to claim certain rights, even as this culture conferred upon whiteness a presumption of moral virtue and moral innocence. As others have pointed out, the idea of whiteness as a sign of superiority if not supremacy became a "religion of sorts."[9] Deep faith was placed in it, as it served as a signal of America's exceptionalism.

Essentially, whiteness became the passport into the exceptional space that was American identity as defined by the Anglo-Saxon myth. From its very origins, therefore, America's social-political and cultural identity was inextricably linked to the myth of Anglo-Saxon superiority. Thus, America's sense of exceptionalism was Anglo-Saxon exceptionalism.

In his book *The Racial Contract,* Charles Mills argues that America's democracy is qualified by an unspoken subaltern contract that is defined by race.[10] He essentially argues that the liberty

---

8. See David B. Roediger, *Working toward Whiteness: How America's Immigrants Became White* (New York: Basic Books, 2005), 64.

9. See, for instance, Michelle Alexander, *The New Jim Crow: Mass Incarceration in the Age of Colorblindness,* rev. ed. (New York: New Press, 2012), 26.

10. Charles Mills, *The Racial Contract* (Ithaca, NY: Cornell University Press, 1997).

America promises to its citizens is intended only for its white citizens. Mills's observations are apt, except that the racial limitations of America's democracy are not actually the result of a "subaltern" contract. Rather, they result from the very explicit Anglo-Saxon chauvinism that defined America's beginnings. In the words of John Wilkes Booth, the assassin of Abraham Lincoln, "This country was formed for the *white*, not for the black man."[11] And so, the "city on the hill" that the early Americans were building was nothing less than a testament to Anglo-Saxon chauvinism. Novelist Toni Morrison captures it best: "Deep within the word 'American' is its association with race."[12]

There is simply no getting around it; the myth of Anglo-Saxon exceptionalism has shaped and continues to shape America's sense of self. It is in the very DNA of this country. To reiterate, America's exceptionalism is Anglo-Saxon exceptionalism, and, as such, it is ingrained in the collective consciousness of America. This brings us to the Trump campaign.

This very defining narrative of Anglo Saxon exceptionalism is what Donald Trump tapped into with his call to "Make America Great Again" (and why many African American, Latinx, and other persons of color had a visceral reaction to this slogan the minute they heard it). Even if unspoken, America's "greatness" has been defined by a myth of Anglo-Saxon exceptionalism that determines who is a "real" American and who is not—that is, who is entitled to the rights of "life, liberty, and the pursuit of happiness," and who, therefore, has a right to occupy spaces and cross borders, much less the right to be considered a "true" citizen and therefore to preside over the Oval Office. These are rights of whiteness, or what W. E. B. Du Bois called the "wages" of whiteness.[13]

---

11. Quoted in Ta-Nehisi Coates, "The Case for Reparations," *The Atlantic*, June 2014.

12. Toni Morrison, *Playing in the Dark: Whiteness and the Literary Imagination* (Cambridge, MA: Harvard University Press, 1992), 47.

13. See W. E. B. Du Bois, *Black Reconstruction in America: An Essay toward a History of the Part Which Black Folk Played in the Attempt to Reconstruct Democracy in America, 1860–1880* (New York: Free Press, 1935).

These wages, as Du Bois says, are not about income. In fact, they even supersede the instances when the white worker might not be compensated as much as the black worker. This was essentially evinced during the 2016 election season by the reality that many of Donald Trump's supporters who felt economically dispossessed did not find common cause with black people, who are disproportionately economically dispossessed. That they did not relate to the black dispossessed was revealed in the racially defined displays of vitriol and racist symbols that accompanied some of Trump's campaign rallies along with the dearth of "color" at his rallies. The fact of the matter is, the wages/privileges of whiteness are far more valuable than economic compensation, for they concretize the distinction between white people and all others. They are, as Du Bois points out, "a sort of public and psychological wage."[14] They are the added bonuses not only for being Anglo-Saxon enough, but for protecting the Anglo-Saxon space. They are the privileges that make whiteness an impregnable wall between America's myth of Anglo-Saxon exceptionalism and those persons on the other side of whiteness.

The privileges of whiteness essentially make it possible for whiteness to "stand its ground" against those who are non-white and who are thus seen as a threat to all that whiteness protects—the Anglo-Saxon space, which for all practical purposes is the American/white space. It is in this way that white culture is nothing less than a "stand-your-ground culture," as it stands its ground, by any means necessary, against all that is non-white. To appreciate this fact is to understand why, in the era of a black president, whiteness stood its ground with fierce intensity, thereby putting young black lives in a heightened sense of deadly danger (the Trayvons, Renishas, Jordans, Tamirs, Michaels, Sandras). A black man had entered a space that was never intended for black bodies—the white space that is the White House—so whiteness stood its ground in every way it could from birther campaigns to fatal police brutality.

That which white culture could not do to the black man in the White House, it would do to his black political base.[15] In this regard,

---

14. Ibid., 700.

15. Though arrived at independently, Ta-Nehisi Coates makes a similar claim in "My President Was Black," *The Atlantic*, January/February 2017.

understanding the insidious reality of the culture of whiteness should help one to appreciate the absolute need, if not inevitability, for the Black Lives Matter movement. For inasmuch as black lives are seen as a threat to the privileges of whiteness they don't matter; they are literally expendable, unless they can be maintained and controlled in such a way that they do not interfere with this nation's myth of Anglo-Saxon exceptionalism. In other words, as long as black bodies are trapped in crippling conditions that circumscribe their life options, and are thereby stuck in inhumane conditions of living that will insure their failure, if not death, while white bodies are granted the privileges that foster their achievement and success—as long as these opposing black and white realities exist, then the myth of "Anglo-Saxon" exceptionalism is maintained. The condition of cruel and brutal deprivation that the social, economic, and political systems and structures to which white culture relegates black lives is essentially a vile Faustian pact that America has made with its mythic self: if black people are kept in their place, then let them live. If they manage to escape their place, then destroy them by any means necessary. It is for this reason that Frederick Douglass's words some 170 years ago continue to ring true: "Killing a slave, or any colored person, . . . is not treated as a crime, either by the courts or the community."[16] This brings us to the sobering inevitability of Trump's campaign and election.

What happened on election night November 9, 2016, while it may be alarming to some should not come as a real surprise. In fact, to appreciate America's sense of exceptionalism and the culture that protects it is to come to the disconcerting realization that Trump's campaign and even election was as American as apple pie. It is not an American anomaly. It happened following the Emancipation/Reconstruction era with Black Codes, Jim Crow, the Ku Klux Klan, and lynchings. It happened after the civil rights movement with Richard Nixon's "Law and Order"/"War on Drugs" agenda, taken up later by Ronald Reagan. And so, it was predictable that it would happen again, now following eight years of a black man as president. The

---

16. Frederick Douglass, *Narrative of the Life of Frederick Douglass* (Mineola, NY: Dover Publications, 1995), 14.

ascendency of Trump to the presidency is about nothing less than whiteness standing its ground to protect America's Anglo-Saxon mythic self with a law-and-order agenda and wall-building promises. It is a reflection of a historical pattern of "white backlash" to any movement toward black people's success or freedom.

The ironic twist is that it was the fact of President Obama that made Trump possible. Starkly put, *President* Trump is nothing less, in a country defined by an Anglo-Saxon narrative, than the proportional response to a black man in the White House. Lest anyone be confused by his motivation for running—that is, to make America white again—Trump did all he could to mitigate the confusion with a campaign that, as Ta- Nehesi Coates says, "freely and liberally trafficked in misogyny, Islamophobia, and xenophobia," notwithstanding the fact that he rose to "political prominence by peddling the racist myth that [President Obama] was not American." As Coates rightly points out, "It was birtherism—not trade, not jobs, not isolationism—that launched Trump's foray into electoral politics."[17] Joseph Ellis, a Pulitzer Prize–winning historian, thus rightly says, "Anybody who says that the recent election is not, at least in part, [I suggest in large part] a racial event is functioning as an apologist, whether they know it or not, for white prejudice."[18]

Returning to the opening question of this essay: How did Donald Trump become president? By unearthing and revitalizing a "truth" about America that resonated with far too many of its citizens, including, according to Pew polls, 58 percent of white Protestants, 60 percent of white Catholics, and 81 percent of white evangelicals.[19] Essentially, Trump dared to do openly what those who previously ran for office refused, at least explicitly, to do in their bids for the presidency, even when the opportunity arose: to play into the Anglo-Saxon culture of whiteness that is the odious underside of America's identity.

Who could forget when Senator John McCain quieted the

---

17. Coates, "My President Was Black."
18. Quoted in Blake and Sambou, "Lost Cause."
19. See Gregory A. Smith and Jessica Martínez, "How the Faithful Voted: A Preliminary 2016 Analysis," *Pew Research Center*, November 9, 2016.

bigoted shouts during one of his campaign rallies by proclaiming then-candidate Obama "a decent family man [and citizen]," whom he admired and respected, although they disagreed on various policies.[20] Instead of rejecting notions of white supremacy, as did Senator McCain, Donald Trump fostered them with his "Make America Great Again" campaign. This leads to another troubling aspect of Trump's campaign, if not presidency: that America's narrative of Anglo-Saxon exceptionalism and concomitant white culture includes the makings of American fascism.

Is Donald Trump a fascist? Many have raised this question. Of course he and his followers would loudly reject such a label, just as loudly as they have protested the labels of bigot, misogynist, anti-Semite, and racist. The fact of the matter, however, is that Trump's campaign resonated with a fascist narrative as much as it bore the marks of these other labels. The more disturbing truth is this, however: inasmuch as America itself is defined by a narrative of Anglo-Saxon exceptionalism, then it has provided the perfect soil for a fascist regime to emerge. Fascism takes root, as historian Isaac Chotiner has pointed out, through the "use of ethnic stereotypes and exploitation of fear of foreigners" at the same time that it creates a narrative—even if it is a false narrative—about national decline.[21] This appears to be taken straight out of Trump's "Make America Great Again" playbook. Such a playbook is made far too easily because America's sense of exceptionalism sets up a natural enemy—those who are non-white and hence considered not American enough, if American at all.

Once again, Trump's campaign simply exploited something that lies in America's very DNA by fostering a notion of non-white foreigners and then associating them with national decline. In so doing he brought two things together: the anger of those feeling economically and politically disenfranchised and a fear exploited by the Trump campaign of America's actual changing demographic

---

20. Jonathan Martin and Amie Parnes, "McCain: Obama Not an Arab, Crowd Boos," *Politico*, October 10, 2008.

21. See Isaac Chotiner, "Is Donald Trump a Fascist? An Expert on Fascism Weighs In," *Slate*, February 10, 2016.

identity. For, according to most projections, by the year 2055, if not sooner, the United States will not have a single ethnic/racial majority group, meaning that white Americans will no longer constitute the majority; in fact, whites will make up significantly less than 50 percent of the country's demographic. In this regard, instead of whiteness standing its ground it will have actually lost ground, and that can only spell a decline for a nation whose "greatness" revolves around its mythic Anglo-Saxon identity.

Moreover, Trump bolstered bigoted fears by linking this demographic shift with crime. He did this in two ways. First, he did this most directly (not, as one analyst pointed out, with "dog whistles" but with "a bullhorn") when he called Mexican immigrants "rapists."[22] Second, he consistently described black communities as virtual enclaves of overwhelming danger and violence, pronouncing that African American communities are absolutely "in the worst shape they've ever been before."[23] In fact, his birther campaign actually served as a precursor to this narrative, as another analyst pointed out, by playing upon some Americans' fears "that their physical and psychological space was being invaded by the demographic changes embodied by Obama."[24] In short, by connecting crime with a growing non-white demographic, Trump carried forth the kind of racial/ethnic/religious "scapegoating" that bears the markings of fascism.

Whether or not one might agree that Trump's campaign reflected an incipient fascism, what is clear is that it reflected America's root identity—and this is nothing less than an oppositional identity—with whiteness functioning as the dividing line between those who reflect America's Anglo-Saxon "greatness" and those who do not. In fact, Trump's election answered another question: To what lengths will America go to protect its mythic identity of Anglo-Saxon greatness? Answer: The election of Donald Trump as president. This is the truth about America.

---

22. Blake and Sambou, "Lost Cause."

23. Jose A. DelReal, "African Americans Are 'in the Worst Shape They've Ever Been,' Trump Says in North Carolina," *Washington Post*, September 20, 2016.

24. Blake and Sambou, "Lost Cause."

CHAPTER 3

No *Middle Ground between Collaboration and Resistance*

JOHN FIFE

Guadalupe Garcia de Rayos began her day on February 8, 2017, by going to Mass with her husband and two children. Her prayer was simply that her check-in with the ICE immigration office in Phoenix would be exactly like the previous seven visits. Immigration agents would verify she had not committed any crimes, that her address and phone contacts were up-to-date, and that she was complying with their directives. Guadalupe had come under immigration court-ordered ICE supervision after she was arrested in a workplace raid at the water park where she worked in 2008. She was convicted of the crime of felony criminal impersonation. In plain English, her "felony crime" was that she used another person's Social Security number when she applied for work. At fourteen, she had come with her parents to the United States, where she was educated, married, and had two U.S. citizen children.

This visit to ICE would shatter her family—possibly forever. Guadalupe Garcia de Rayos was arrested, detained, and deported to Mexico within twenty-four hours. She may well be the first person deported under the terms of President Trump's executive orders on immigration. "The truth is I was there [in the United States] for my children, for a better future, to work for them. I don't regret it, because I did it for love." Phoenix Mayor Greg Stanton called her deportation a travesty. "Rather than tracking down violent criminals and drug dealers, ICE is spending its energy deporting a woman with two American children who has lived here for more than two decades and poses a threat to nobody."[1]

At the same time, the week of February 6–10, 2017, ICE agents conducted widespread raids on workplaces and homes nationwide in multiple states. Raids in New York, Georgia, Illinois, California, North Carolina, South Carolina, Texas, Florida, Kansas, and Virginia were reported. While ICE officials described the actions as "routine" and "targeted enforcement actions," local municipal and congressional officials described door-to-door stops in a Latino neighborhood asking for residents' papers. President Trump seemed to directly contradict the ICE characterization on February 12 when he tweeted, "The crackdown on illegal criminals is merely the keeping of my campaign promise. Gang members, drug dealers, and others are being removed."[2]

We should have known! Donald Trump inaugurated his campaign on June 16, 2015, with this description of Mexican immigrants: "When Mexico sends its people, they're not sending their best. . . . They're sending people that have lots of problems, and they're bringing those problems with us. They're bringing drugs. They're bringing crime. They're rapists. And some, I assume, are good people." A few days later, he told CNN, "You have people come in and I'm just not saying Mexicans, I'm talking about people that are from all over, that are killers and rapists and they're coming to this country." He even claimed in August 2015, "The Mexican government is much smarter, much sharper, much more cunning. They send the bad ones over because they don't want to pay for them."

Along with that blanket description of the threat of immigrants, Trump promised his solution. "I will build a wall—and nobody builds walls better than me, believe me—and I'll build them very inexpensively. I will build a great, great wall on our southern border, and I will make Mexico pay for that wall. Mark my words." Then to broaden the sweep of Trump's determination to protect America from immigrants and refugees, on December 7, 2015, he

---

1. *CNN*, February 10, 2017.
2. Claire Galofaro and Juliet Linderman, "Immigrants Wait in Fear after Raids," *Washington Post*, February 12, 2017.

declared, "Donald J. Trump is calling for a total and complete shutdown of Muslims entering the United States until our country's representatives can figure out what is going on."

It should have been no surprise or shock to anyone when, shortly after his inauguration, on January 25, 2017, Trump issued his executive order titled, "Protecting the Nation from Foreign Terrorist Entry into the United States." This immediately become known as the "Muslim Ban." As this chapter is being written, a federal judge has issued a Temporary Restraining Order on the Muslim Ban and a three-judge panel of the Ninth Circuit Court of Appeals has unanimously upheld the restraining order. It is likely that the matter will be tied up in the federal courts for some time or be rewritten to be more amenable to the Constitution and U.S. law.

Because the "Muslim Ban" executive order resulted in immediate chaos at airports around the world and ports-of-entry across the United States, too little public and media attention has focused on the January 25, 2017, executive orders. They must be closely examined for the purposes of this chapter on immigration and border security. The first order is titled "Enhancing Public Safety in the Interior of the United States." It begins by stating the fundamental need for the Executive Order and dramatic change in policy.

> Section 1. Purpose . . . Many aliens who illegally enter the United States and those who overstay or otherwise violate the terms of their visas present a significant threat to national security and public safety.

This is simply unsupported by any studies of crime rates comparing the rates of criminal convictions by undocumented immigrants with citizen populations of the same ethnicity and age.[3]

> Section 5. Enforcement Priorities . . . the Secretary of Homeland Security shall prioritize for removal those aliens described by the Congress ... as well as removable aliens who:

---

3. Philip Bump, "Surprise! Donald Trump Is Wrong about Immigrants and Crime," *Washington Post*, July 2, 2015.

a.) Have been convicted of any criminal offense;

b.) Have been charged with any criminal offense;

c.) Have committed acts that constitute a chargeable criminal offense;

d.) Have engaged in fraud or willful misrepresentation in connection with any official matter;

e.) Have abused any program related to the receipt of public benefits;

f.) In the judgment of an immigration officer, otherwise pose a risk to public safety or national security.

In that list of priorities with no ranking, everything and everyone is a priority for deportation. If you were issued a traffic citation for a faulty tail light, if you wrote a bad check, if your child benefited from a school lunch program, or if in the judgment of a low-level immigration official you pose a risk to public safety, you are a priority for deportation. Note: If you crossed the border without documents at any time, you have committed a chargeable felony and the executive order has already determined that aliens are a threat to public safety. The low-level immigration officer now has sole discretion as prosecutor and judge to place the person in expedited removal. In addition, the executive order directs the secretary of Homeland Security to:

Section 7. Hire and train 10,000 additional ICE agents.

Section 8. Revive the program 287(g) which authorizes local and state law enforcement officers to perform the functions of federal immigration officers in the apprehension and detention of aliens.

Section 9. Ensure that local and state jurisdictions which refuse to comply with local law enforcement's full cooperation with ICE detainers (sanctuary jurisdictions) lose their eligibility for federal grants.

While the term "sanctuary jurisdictions" is not defined, the secretary of DHS is given the authority to designate any city, county, or state to be such. The Attorney General is authorized to take enforcement action against any entity that has a policy or practice that hinders the enforcement of federal immigration law.

The second executive order, of January 25, 2017, is titled, "Border Security and Immigration Enforcement Improvements." While it is primarily concerned with the building of a wall across the southern border of the United States, there are other sections that change border enforcement and immigration policy dramatically.

Section 3. Declares that "operational control" of the southern border shall mean the prevention of all unlawful entries into the U.S. and all narcotics and other contraband.

"All," I assume, is what the dictionary defines as the total amount. Operational control will never be achieved.

Section 5. The Secretary of DHS is directed to immediately construct and operate detention facilities or contract with private prison corporations to construct and operate immigration detention facilities along the southern border.

Section 8. Hires and trains 5,000 additional Border Patrol agents.

Section 10. Reiterates the mandates to restore the 287(g) program to empower local and state law enforcement officers to enforce federal immigration law.

This mandate is repeated because many law enforcement agencies have refused to comply with ICE detainers or have limited their cooperation because multiple federal courts have found that ICE detainers have violated the Fourth Amendment to the Constitution.

Section 11 states that parole and asylum laws have been abused by refugees seeking asylum and instructs the secretary of DHS to take action ("in his sole unreviewable discretion") to limit reasonable fear determinations to "the plain language of those determinations."

In plain language, asylum pleas and reasonable fear for refugees are about to plummet under the Trump administration.

As a result of Trump's campaign rhetoric and promises on immigration, the concept of major institutions throughout the United States becoming "sanctuaries" for the undocumented is being widely considered. Major cities such as New York, Chicago, Los Angeles, and San Francisco have been cities of sanctuary for decades. Colleges and universities by the hundreds have been petitioned by faculty and students to become a sanctuary to protect undocumented students and employees. When the studies were done, over 430 local police and sheriff's departments had policies of noncooperation with federal immigration officials. Churches had for the past decade been declaring sanctuary for undocumented mothers and fathers threatened with deportation orders to protect those families from being destroyed.

Most importantly, in the 1980s the Sanctuary Movement to protect refugees fleeing the repression of death squads, massacres of villages, torture, and civil wars of Central America had succeeded in stopping the deportation of refugees and gaining temporary protected status for undocumented Salvadorans and Guatemalans. That movement had been based in hundreds of churches and synagogues that declared the faith community to be a sanctuary. Seventeen cities, countless universities, and even the state of New Mexico became sanctuaries.

The question under the Trump administration became, Can the ancient tradition of "sanctuary" become a viable strategy to resist the massive deportations now ordered by Trump? The defining text of the faith and ethical mandates of that question was contained in a letter sent by a cofounder of the Sanctuary Movement, Jim Corbett. The letter was sent in 1981 to the congregation of Southside Presbyterian Church, Tucson, Arizona, along with Jim's request that the church provide hospitality and protection for refugees from Central America. Jim wrote:

> Because the U.S. government takes the position that aiding undocumented Salvadoran and Guatemalan refugees in this country is a felony, we have no middle ground between collaboration and resistance. A maze of strategic dead ends can be averted if we face the imperative nature of this choice without attempting to delude ourselves or others. For those of us who would be faithful in our allegiance to the Kingdom, there is also no way to avoid recognizing that in this case collaboration with the government is a betrayal to our faith, even if it is a passive or even loudly protesting collaboration that merely shuts out the undocumented refugee that is at our door. We can take our stand with the oppressed, or we can take our

stand with organized oppression. We can serve the Kingdom, or we can serve the kingdoms of this world—but we cannot do both. Maybe, as the gospel suggests, this choice is perennial and basic, but the presence of undocumented refugees here among us makes the definitive nature of our choice particularly clear and concrete. When the government itself sponsors the crucifixion of entire peoples and then makes it a felony to shelter those seeking refuge, law-abiding protest merely trains us to live with atrocity.[4]

In 1981, there was clearly no middle ground. We had exhausted every possibility: meetings with congressional representatives, demonstrations and marches, prayer vigils, grants written, legal defense organizations formed, and even civil suits filed in federal courts. Corbett's conclusion led directly to the beginning of the Sanctuary Movement in 1982. With no middle ground, faith communities chose resistance in their ancient traditions.

Is that the circumstance in which we find ourselves in 2017? Under the Obama administration, there appeared to be a broad expanse of middle ground called Comprehensive Immigration Reform. Even though Obama set records for deportations and built hundreds of miles of walls, the possibility of immigration reform by Congress became the dominant hope and organizing ground. Now in the Age of Trump, sanctuary has become the predominant resistance strategy being considered and implemented in major institutions (public and private) across the nation. Cities of sanctuary, counties of sanctuary, universities of sanctuary and, of course, hundreds of faith communities have already committed to the Sanctuary Movement. They include Protestants, evangelicals, Roman Catholics, Jews, and Muslims. Just last week an appeal was launched on social media to organize Sanctuary Restaurants to protect kitchen employees. The tradition of sanctuary is as ancient as recorded history and encompasses diverse religions and cul-

---

4. Jim Corbett, "The Covenant as Sanctuary," in *Sanctuary: A Resource Guide for Understanding and Participating in the Central American Refugee Struggle,* ed. Gary MacEoin (New York: Harper & Row, 1985), 19.

tures across the globe. Linda Rabben, in her book *Sanctuary and Asylum,* has extensively documented the tradition of sanctuary, as well as the recent advent of asylum law as secular nation-states assumed that responsibility from the church and sacred sites. Her thesis documents the failure of nation-states to fulfill their responsibility because of anti-immigrant political movements.

> Everywhere capital encounters no obstacles, but the movement of human beings is blocked. Even if they manage to cross deserts, oceans, and fortified borders, people fleeing persecution, poverty, and conflict can find no sure welcome or refuge. The structures of humanitarian protection have corroded and failed over time. The legal framework of asylum perversely seems to exclude, imprison, and segregate the stranger. . . . Their promise of shelter and safety has been broken, especially for the weak and vulnerable. . . . As government support for asylum has degenerated into lip service, public opinion has turned against the institution. In response, sanctuary movements have become the self- appointed instrument striving to close the gap between the needs for a safe haven and the official grants of political asylum. . . . In our time the pendulum has swung: asylum has become corrupted and discredited while sanctuary has regained its moral authority.[5]

From the perspective of the sweep of history then, the Sanctuary Movement is rising again. In the Age of Trump, the Sanctuary Movement is rising because there is no middle ground between collaboration and resistance.

---

5. Linda Rabben, *Sanctuary and Asylum: A Social and Political History* (Seattle, WA: University of Washington Press, 2016), 266–67.

CHAPTER 4

National Capitalism
Religious Resonances and Alternatives

JOERG RIEGER

For almost four decades, neoliberal capitalism has been the ruling school of thought in the United States and many other places. From its beginnings in the late 1970s and early 1980s under the administrations of Prime Minister Margaret Thatcher in Britain and President Ronald Reagan in the United States, neoliberal capitalism got a major boost with the fall of the Berlin Wall and Soviet-style Communism. Since the Reagan administration, both Republican and Democratic administrations have supported neoliberal capitalism in their own ways.

The main tenets of neoliberal capitalism are well known: deregulation of market and trade, privatization, lower taxes, reductions in government spending, and structural adjustment policies. The underlying logic holds that if the elites are doing better (and have their way) everyone is doing better, expressed in commonly held ideas of a rising tide lifting all boats and the assumption that wealth invariably trickles down. Furthermore, it is assumed that privately owned enterprises are more efficient and productive than public ones.

The actual results of neoliberal capitalism, meanwhile, are heavily contested. It is hard to deny that in almost four decades rising tides did not lift all boats as the rich got richer and the poor poorer. As income levels of top managers continue to rise, income levels of large parts of the population are stagnating or shrinking. In addition, the wealth of the superrich is growing at astronomical rates. In 2001, 225 individuals owned as much as the bottom half of the world's population. In 2015, 62 individuals and in 2016, 8 individuals own what the bottom half of the world's population owns.[1]

Growing frustration over such inequalities seems to have been one factor that led substantial numbers of voters, both working class and middle class, to vote for Donald Trump. Trump's promise to "make America great again" was heard by many as a pledge to empower them and to improve their well-being, while Senator Hillary Clinton seemed to maintain the economic status quo of (a slightly tempered) neoliberal capitalism that her husband Bill Clinton pursued while in office. Trump's promise rests on a strange mix of neoliberal capitalism on steroids and the introduction of regulations and controls that have led some economists to suspect the end of neoliberal capitalism as we know it.[2] This has raised concern even among supporters of neoliberal capitalism Republican style, like the Koch brothers and their networks. At the same time, among other conservatives and many representatives of the alt-right, this has created excitement.

This mix of deregulation and regulation, weak government and strong government, globalization and nationalism supports my claim that with Trump's administration neoliberal capitalism is giving way to what might be called "national capitalism." Considering this term as the frame for my observations on the new economy under Trump, I was taken aback by the realization that this term had already been in use by alt-right pundits for some time who make it no secret that their use of the expression is developed in relation to the notion of national socialism.[3] With

1. United Nations, *Human Development Report* (New York: Oxford University Press, 1998), 30. For more recent statistics, see Oxfam International, "Just 8 Men Own Same Wealth as Half the World," press release, January 16, 2017, https://www.oxfam.org.

2. See, for instance, the comments of economist Richard Wolff on the Thom Hartman Program, "How Trump Could Bring on the Crash of 2017," December 2016, http://www.thomhartmann.com.

3. Dota, "National Capitalism—A Third Alternative?" *Alternative Right Blogspot*, July 24, 2015, http://alternative-right.blogspot.com. In this blog entry, both communism and neoliberalism are critiqued for being internationalist, that is, for a lack of concern for the nation. At a 2014 event at the Vatican, Trump's major strategist Steve Bannon critiqued what he considered "objectifying" and "crony" forms of capitalism in favor of nationalist solu-

this mix it is hard not to suspect that there is trouble ahead, but what kind of trouble?

Although it is still too soon to pronounce definite judgments, the early days of Trump's administration have given us some clues as to what this brand of national capitalism might look like. Neoliberal efforts at deregulation and globalization rejected by Trump include the Trans-Pacific Partnership (TPP), a free-trade agreement with major economic forces modeled after President Bill Clinton's neoliberal North American Free Trade Agreement (NAFTA), and his strong stance against immigration and undocumented workers (raids began within weeks of his inauguration), especially from some Muslim countries with which his businesses have no economic relations, and efforts to pressure American corporations to keep jobs in the country. Add to that his commitment to improving the country's crumbling infrastructure, which was never a priority for neoliberals.

On the other hand, Trump is pushing further deregulations that intensify the neoliberal ethos, for instance, in environmental standards, building codes, health care, and education; and he is in favor of repealing regulations of banks and lending agencies that were introduced in the wake of the Great Recession (including the Dodd-Frank Act and the Consumer Financial Protection Bureau). In addition, one of the earliest official actions of Trump was the repeal of the construction ban of the Dakota Access Pipeline.

The early days of this national capitalism have seen economic indicators rising; after Trump's election the Dow Jones Industrial Index reached 20,000 for the first time. The question, of course, is who benefits from all of this, and can the new brand of national capitalism be sustainable within the parameters of global capitalism. Is another major economic crash avoidable, and who will get hurt the most?

Religious Themes

While the Trump administration has not justified any of these moves by providing religious arguments, there are some religious

---

tions. See J. Lester Feder, "This Is How Steve Bannon Sees the Entire World," *BuzzFeed News*, November 15, 2016.

categories that throw light on what is going on and that might explain to some degree the surprisingly strong support from certain religious groups for a candidate who does not have a strong religious pedigree. After all, according to widely publicized exit polls, 81 percent of voting evangelical Christians backed Trump.

First of all, Trump's brand of national capitalism appears to divide the world into good and evil, quasi-theological categories that are applied on the basis of "us" vs. "them." Economic agents who are either American or seen as friendly to Americans are judged as good, thus meriting deregulation and reduction of oversight. Economic agents who are seen as different from Americans or as a potential challenge to Americans are judged as evil, meriting either greater regulations or the severing of relationships altogether. Relationships with China, Mexico, and certain Muslim countries obviously fall into this latter category.

Second, power is envisioned as most appropriately held by the elites, mirroring quasi-theological categories of divine power as unilateral and top-down. More specifically, such power is seen as embodied by potent business leaders (mostly white) like Trump and the majority of his cabinet. As Trump remarked in his inauguration address, channeling strong nationalist leaders in the past, "I alone can fix it."[4] Other prominent leaders who are seen as friendly to America are endorsed as well, including Russian President Vladimir Putin. On the other hand, prominent leaders who are seen as hostile to America are blocked, as is the case with almost all of the power that emerges from the grassroots or from the people. The time-honored phrase "God bless America" now functions as an endorsement of the Trump administration, which alone decides whether, where, and when to apply the tools of neoliberal capitalism, like deregulation and privatization, or the tools of national capitalism, like regulation and strong leadership by the president and his cabinet.

Finally, faith plays an important role. At the point of this writing, Trump's election has produced considerable economic euphoria. The stock market has risen to new heights and the dollar

---

4. Peter Ross Range, "The Theory of Political Leadership That Donald Trump Shares with Adolf Hitler," *Washington Post*, July 25, 2016.

has gained strength against many other international currencies. Unlike in many other periods of economic upswing, these developments are not rooted in performance indicators but in faith that Trump's leadership will be beneficial for the economy. If anyone ever doubted the power of faith, the power of faith in Trump and his administration is proving them wrong.

What is lacking here is any consideration of alternative theological models of good and evil, of divine power and blessing, or of faith. Accordingly, this is where our engagement with Trump's model of national capitalism must begin.

Mixing and (Mis)matching

Dichotomies between good and evil and between top and bottom are often questioned in contemporary theological discourse, based on the damage they have done in the past. While there may be some use for these dichotomies in the context of resistance struggles,[5] they can indeed be detrimental and harmful when applied in blind faith and by the wrong forces. This can be demonstrated in the case of the Trump administration.

Applying the dichotomies of good and evil along the lines of nation and race, for instance, creates not only the fairly obvious problems of national chauvinism and racism that are widely noticed and critiqued. After all, Trump's approval ratings are a historically low 40 percent.[6] However, another problem with nationalism and racism, less commonly discussed, is it leads to misidentifications that harm many of the nationalists and racists themselves. If workers of one nation allow themselves to be pitted against workers of another nation, for instance, or if white workers allow themselves to be pitted against nonwhite workers, they forget that they may have less in common with their bosses and the wealthy of the same nationality or race than with their fellow workers of other nationalities and other races. In the long run, the blind faith of national-

---

5. See Joerg Rieger, *Globalization and Theology* (Nashville, TN: Abingdon Press, 2010), chapter 3.

6. Rebecca Savransky, "Trump's Job Approval Rating Hits a New Low," *The Hill*, February 12, 2017.

ists and racists in the benevolence of the elites of their own nation or racial identity will hardly benefit these nationalists and racists themselves. Many who voted for Trump are likely to find out that they are not part of America made great again.

Applying the dichotomies of top and bottom leads to a different set of problems. In this case, it is commonly assumed that those at the top, unlike those at the bottom, are more or less beyond reproach. This is expressed, for instance, in the remuneration of CEOs and other prominent leaders, which is now several hundred times above that of average workers. A similar dynamic can also be observed in situations of emergency and in the aftermath of catastrophes. When Hurricane Katrina destroyed much of New Orleans, for instance, there was great reluctance to support displaced residents and widespread suspicion that what little support was given to them ($2,000 debit cards[7]) would be misspent. At the same time, there was much less objection to handing significantly larger sums of money to corporations charged with cleaning up and rebuilding. Politicians and large sectors of the public seemed to be in agreement that top actors were trustworthy and people on the bottom were not.

Faith in top leaders is still strong and undergirds and resonates with the actions of the Trump administration at various levels. Whether it will actually produce results, however, is another question. In the case of New Orleans, studies have shown that much of the support was funneled to the top, where it was misappropriated and wasted.[8] In the case of the remuneration of CEOs, even supporters of capitalist economic principles have questioned whether the great income inequalities between ordinary workers and CEOs are justified and produce results.[9]

---

7. Jordan Weissmann, "Did Katrina Victims Really Spend Their Relief Money on Gucci Bags and Massage Parlors?," *The Atlantic*, October 31, 2012.

8. See, for instance, Vincanne Adams, "Corporate Recovery: The Dark Side of Hurricane Katrina Aid Efforts, *Utne Reader*, September/October 2013, http://www.utne.com, describing the disaster of "philanthrocapitalism."

9. Even President Trump has criticized CEO pay, although his efforts to dismantle the Dodd-Frank Act will most likely lead to a reversal of the requirement of reporting CEO/worker pay ratios.

The Logic of Downturn

"Faith without works is dead," as the Letter of James famously stated (2:17). In our context, this could be taken to mean that faith that is disconnected from performance indicators is misguided and not sustainable in the long term. Faith and euphoria can indeed produce effects, as we are currently observing, but these effects can hardly be sustained long term. This would not be the first time that faith without attention to performance indicators has led to the creation of a bubble, both in the economic and the religious marketplaces. As one commentator put it, the current sugar high of the market will be followed by a sugar low.[10]

It is commonly accepted that one of the traits of capitalism is that it goes in cycles. Bull markets will be followed by bear markets, followed by bull markets. Economists do not know the exact timing, but few doubt that periods of downturn are part of capitalism, and many fear that the next correction of the market will be substantial, with the potential to wipe out 50 percent or more of its current value. What is less commonly acknowledged, but of existential importance to large numbers of the population, is that the upswings following recent downturns have benefited fewer and fewer people. While markets have recovered, the fortunes of increasing numbers of the population have not.

It is during the periods of downturn that the true face of national capitalism will become more obvious, just as it became obvious for neoliberal capitalism. How will national capitalism be able to protect those who are most vulnerable from the consequences of a downturn, a feat that neoliberal capitalism was never able to accomplish? Can economic protectionism work for all but a select few? What I have called "the logic of downturn" in the context of the Great Recession can once again help us shine light not only on the soundness of Trump's economic policies but also on its religious underpinnings.[11] Hopefully, we will be able to anticipate some of its lessons before it is too late.

---

10. Ben White, "Economy Could Soar and Then Crash under Trump," *Politico*, November 14, 2016.

11. See Joerg Rieger, *No Rising Tide: Theology, Economics, and the Future* (Minneapolis: Fortress Press, 2009).

A crucial question for all economic reflection is: Who is benefiting from economic developments? As the Great Recession has shown, the brunt of the economic downturn was born by the working and middle classes, compounded by the factors of ethnicity and race. Many of the thirty-year gains of the black middle class, for instance, have been wiped out.[12] When the economy recovered, with the support of government bailouts for banks and financial institutions, those who were hit the hardest were the ones who gained the least. Most of the jobs that came back were of lower quality than the jobs that were lost. And more faith was put in the big banks to recover than in the thousands of homeowners who were foreclosed on.

While national capitalism, unlike neoliberal capitalism, rejects the idea that capitalism must benefit the whole world, it will have a hard time to live up to its promises to provide sustainable wealth for a whole nation. Keep in mind that even in the shift from neoliberal capitalism to national capitalism the production of profit for the elites remains the basic principle. While the faith generated by Trump has produced results in the short term, it is questionable whether these results can last and whether they will ultimately benefit more than just a small elite. The contradictions are enormous: While nationalism promises that benefits will be distributed along the lines of nationality, privatization means that benefits will accrue primarily to those who own and control property (and in particular the means of production). The fact that in the United States the top 1 percent controls more than 40 percent of all wealth makes living up to the ideals of nationalism even more difficult if not impossible.

Alternative Religion, Alternative Economy

Yet faith does not necessarily have to be tied to the production of unsustainable bubbles, and faith does not have to be blind. Jesus, when challenged, did not promote blind faith but evidence: "Go and tell John what you hear and see: the blind receive their sight,

---

12. Dawn Turner, "Black Middle Class Economically Vulnerable," *Chicago Tribune*, October 7, 2012.

the lame walk, the lepers are cleansed, the deaf hear, the dead are raised, and the poor have good news brought to them" (Matthew 11:4-5). Faith, in this example, is tied to evidence, and good news to the poor is tied to tangible experiences of lives being improved. Good news to the poor is not pie in the sky but the reality that they will no longer be poor and that the conditions that create poverty have been overcome.

This leads to a criterion by which to measure the promises of national capitalism: Will it work for the benefit of the "least of these" or not? Some of this depends on Trump's resolve to make a difference, but there are two problems that I predict will prove to be unsurmountable for national capitalism. One is that it is still capitalism, and as such it cannot do away with the structures of exploitation that have historically benefited the top more than the bottom. The other is the fate of those who are not part of this particular nation and who will not stand by idly when tariffs are leveraged, borders closed, and unilateral aggression is the name of the game.

Finally, the question of power will have to be reconsidered as well. If the "least of these" are merely the recipients of the benevolence of the elites, what guarantee is there that things will ever change? Only if power and agency change hands can we hope for a fundamental change of the current situation, which is marked by inequality. What is needed here are not efforts to temper capitalism or to return to some forms of globalizing neoliberalism, however well intentioned they may be. What is needed are forms of power that move from the bottom up, starting with the people. Such forms of power already exist in many places, be it in people's movements that have picked up further strength since the election of Trump, cooperative workplaces where profits are distributed in democratic ways, and even in expressions of religion that follow a God who is found in solidarity with the people rather than at the top of some self-proclaimed economic hierarchy.

CHAPTER 5

Low-Wage Workers and the Struggle for Justice

SIMONE CAMPBELL, SSS

We are almost two decades into the twenty-first century, and we continue to believe in our nation's motto: "If you work hard and play by the rules you will get ahead." Our image of those who are living in poverty is stuck in a twentieth-century stereotype that "those people" are poor because they are lazy. Many think if "they" would just get a job and stop relying on government handouts, they would not be poor and the country would be better off. This is a lie. Until we engage the twenty-first-century reality we will not be able to address the crying need of our time. Stated starkly, the vast majority of people living in poverty today are working families where the adults often have two or three jobs. The primary issue is wages!

The Twenty-First-Century Truth about Poverty

Between 1949 and 1979 all income levels in our U.S. population shared in our growing economy. During that period, the bottom 20% income grew 116% and the top 20% grew 86%. This is the source of one of our myths: If you work hard and play by the rules, you will do better than your parents did. But this is not true now and our people are suffering. Beginning in 1980 this changed. Between 1980 and 2014 the bottom 20% of households *lost* almost

9% of their income while the middle class has seen their income grow only 16%. However, the top 20% went up 61%. Even more chilling is that the top 5% of income households went up 106%, and the top 1% went up 168%.[1] This unequal income growth has left whole swaths of our population still believing the myth but not living it. In my experience, it is the "gap" between the myth and the reality that is generating much of the anger and distress in our nation that has fueled the "Trump reality."

The power of the myth is manifested in the cherished stereotype (at least among Republicans in Congress and elsewhere in our nation) that "the poor" are lazy and have to be "incentivized" to work. This is not accurate. Of those who are living in poverty 35% are unable to work (children, the retired, and the disabled). Of the 65% remaining, 63% are working full or part time and only 37% are not working.

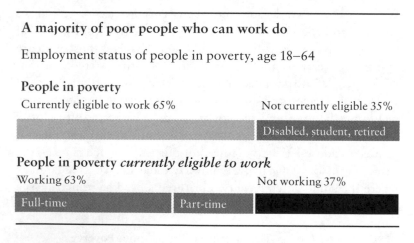

A majority of poor people who can work do

Employment status of people in poverty, age 18–64

People in poverty

Currently eligible to work 65%   Not currently eligible 35%

Disabled, student, retired

People in poverty *currently eligible to work*

Working 63%   Not working 37%

Full-time   Part-time

This chart indicates that work is not paying enough to bring families out of poverty. Thirty-five years of stagnant and declining wages have kept workers and their families in poverty. How did we get here when it was not the situation from 1949 to 1979? Quite

1. My organization has studied this reality in depth and has aggregated material on our website at https://networkadvocates.org/advocacytoolbox/educate/mindthegap.

simply: President Reagan's support of "trickle down" economics is at the heart of our twenty-first-century poverty. This policy states: If you give the top income household substantial tax breaks they will create more jobs, pay higher wages, and everyone will benefit. He advocated for and got a cut in the top income tax bracket from 80 percent to 33 percent. This began to create the divide between salaries for top management and ordinary workers.

Another Reagan policy undermined wages by eroding workers' bargaining power through unions. Additionally, his extension of credit through personal credit cards masked the impact of stagnant wages. Finally, the fact that more women went into the outside labor market masked the reality of flat wages on a household by bringing in added revenue. The result is the tremendous income gap in our nation.

How Does the Working Poor Survive Today?

How does a family of four make ends meet when their annual salary is below $24,600?[2] One way for families with custody of minor children is for parents to claim the Earned Income Tax Credit, which significantly augments income by giving this mythical family an additional $3,100 in income each year. In addition, the Child Tax Credit can add additional income of $1,000 per eligible child. But while this cash is critical for survival, it still is not enough to get by on. Some of these families and others get by by using what is left of the "social safety net." The most important support for people living in poverty is Medicaid, which is the government health care program for low income families; 61 percent of the enrollees are working poor families.[3]

The second most important program is the Supplemental Nutrition Assistance Program (SNAP), formerly called "food stamps." These electronic benefits (like a controlled debit card administered

---

2. This is the national poverty level for a family of four. See https://aspe.hhs.gov/poverty-guidelines.

3. This percentage would be even higher if all of the states had expanded Medicaid in the implementation of the Affordable Care Act, but this is another issue that cannot be explored here.

by the states) get much needed money for food into 36 percent of working poor households.[4] The average SNAP benefit to a family of four is $465 per month.

Remember, these are working families who are using the safety net to survive. These programs were designed for families who had fallen on hard times. But with stagnant wages and fluctuating hours and no benefits, these programs save working families' lives. The top three occupations for high use of safety net programs for survival are front-line fast-food workers, child-care providers, and home-care workers. Each of these occupations has at or near 50 percent of its workforce in families with at least one family member relying on a public assistance program.[5] So the American myth of "working hard and playing by the rules" has resulted in the reality that working families live in multigenerational poverty. But it has also resulted in businesses forcing their workers to rely on the social safety net to survive. This has moved these programs from being just for those who have fallen on hard times to being actual business subsidies.

One Web of Relationships Keeping People Poor

A couple of years ago I met Jason, an entrepreneur who had built a large business. He told me he was getting angry because he realized his taxes were going to fund his competitors. I asked him what he meant. He explained that he paid all of his workers a living wage because he thought it was the right thing to do. His competitors, however, did not do the same. These competitors paid their lower skilled workers low wages and expected them to use Medicaid, SNAP, and other safety net benefits to get by as a family. Therefore, Jason's competitors had lower personnel costs and could underbid Jason for contracts. This was making him angry. Jason believed

---

4. "The High Public Cost of Low Wages," http://laborcenter.berkeley.edu.

5. But it is not just low-skill workers in the service sector who rely on the safety net for survival. Fully one quarter of part-time college faculty and their families are enrolled in at least one of the public assistance programs available.

that these competing businesses were using a government subsidy (welfare) and not charging the actual costs in their contracts.

Over the following year, our organization, NETWORK, hosted various business roundtables around the country. At one conversation in Denver, I raised Jason's concern. A businessman was puzzled by Jason's complaint and boldly stated, "If you can get an advantage, why wouldn't you take it?" I realized it is the plight of low-wage workers that he saw as being an "advantage" to be taken. Without any bargaining power, low-wage workers have not been able to fight for increased salaries. That is why the "Fight for $15" campaign is so important.[6]

At another business roundtable in Chicago, I raised the fact that the average salary of a CEO of a publicly traded company was $10 million dollars a year, and they were seeking $11 million. I had done a quick calculation and discovered such a CEO earned in three hours what a federal minimum wage worker earned in a whole year. I knew CEOs were as dependent on the minimum-wage worker as the minimum-wage worker was on the CEO. So I asked the gathered businessmen: Are you seeking $11 million because you are not getting by on $10 million a year? One entrepreneur said it was not really about the money. I asked what it was about. The response was that business leaders are very competitive and want to win. It just happens that the measure of winning is money!

When we did our business roundtable in Manhattan, we had a number of venture capitalists in the group who invest in startup companies and in the growth of existing businesses. They said the pressure to get a "quick return on investment" caused all of the businesses they invested in to turn every penny into profit. This pressure from the investors meant there was a disincentive to invest in the employees by paying a living wage. These investors said the pressure on them for profit came from the retirement-fund investors who have clients counting on the return on investment to live on during their retirement years.

It was during the last of the business roundtables that the circle

---

6. Fight for $15 is a nationwide campaign to get a minimum of $15 per hour for fast-food workers.

of the problem was completed for me. When raising the issue of wages, a business owner in Richmond, Virginia, said there was extreme pressure from the customers for lower prices. He told me he thought only boutique stores who catered to the high-end customers could charge prices that would support living wages. So I as a consumer am part of the cycle keeping wages low. I want or need a bargain, and I had not considered the ripple effect.

The Economic Web and Politics

In this cycle of conversations throughout the country I came to know that low-wage workers are caught in a tight web of relationships that includes owners, investors, and customers. Being caught means people are not living up to the "American promise." In 2016, as I talked with people around the country, I met several supporters of Donald Trump. They were often middle-aged white men who felt betrayed by the economic system. Talking with one man in Indiana, I realized he felt that he had not lived up to his parents' expectation for him, and his children were having an even more difficult time. I'm not sure what tipped me off, but I asked him if he felt ashamed. He got surprisingly teary eyes and nodded. But this moment of vulnerability morphed quickly into anger at the "system" and "politicians." This sense of disappointment and sometimes shame leads to anger and blame. There is anger that people have "played by the rules" and lost out. Rather than owning the fact that many of the middle class and working poor supported policies that made their lives worse, their anger and blame gets channeled into a Trump-style iconoclastic presidency.

The Way Forward

In *Evangelii gaudium* Pope Francis does not mince words when he writes about this failed economic policy. In paragraph 53 he states: "Just as the commandment 'Thou shalt not kill' sets a clear limit in order to safeguard the value of human life, today we also have to say 'thou shalt not' to an economy of exclusion and inequality. Such an economy kills." Those whose spirits are being killed in our nation include the man I met in Indiana who is ashamed he did not measure up to his parents' expectations and is worried about his children. Those being excluded from our economy include all of the people working hard and living in poverty. Those excluded include the elderly, the disabled, and those challenged by our economic system. Those excluded include many supporters of President Trump. Many of the excluded have unwittingly supported "trickle down" economic policies that have perpetuated their exclusion. Our people are suffering, and it is up to all of us to work for change.

Policies for Change

There are three key federal economic policies that can change this economy that is killing our people. They are:

- Tax policy: Creating a tax policy that has everyone who benefits from our nation (including corporations) paying their fair share of the costs would be a major step forward. Policies such as raising the actual tax rate for the top income earners, which would reduce the incentive for money being the measure of winning; ending the mortgage interest deduction for second homes or yachts, which would help level the playing field; and funding our government by ending tax loopholes that corporations use to hide profits "offshore"—a move that would increase income for needed federal programs. Tax policy can also be used to put money into the hands of working people through enhancing the Earned Income Tax Credit for adults without custody of minor children.
- Enacting living wages: Too often we fight over the minimum wage, yet we know minimum wages keep workers in poverty. We need to shift to a federal law that sets up the criteria for establishing regional living wages[7] and gives a preference to businesses that commit to fair wages. Additionally, we need to strengthen workers' organizing in order to give them the ability to negotiate for what they actually need in today's market.

---

7. Living wages are calculated to include actual costs of housing, food, childcare, transportation, health care and all of the general costs of living in an area. See: http://livingwage.mit.edu/.

- Family friendly work places: Finally, we need policies that create affordable child care and support families with needed benefits including paid time off to care for themselves or relatives.

Policies such as these would change our economy in the direction of being more inclusive and less divisive. These policies would take the heart out of the Trump phenomenon by actually focusing on what is wrong in our economy and fixing it.

Shared Responsibility for Action

As Pope Francis notes in *Laudato si'* (paragraph 232), "Not everyone is called to engage directly in political life. Society is also enriched by a countless array of organizations which work to promote the common good." So, while my current contribution is in the political realm, I urge everyone to engage in some fashion. We can all do something to make a difference. We can be interested in others' stories and exercise "holy curiosity." We can share the truth about poverty in our nation in the twenty-first century. Perhaps, most important of all, we each need to be grounded in our communal reality and not be afraid of people who think differently. The anger responsible in creating our current political reality is based on isolation and fear. If we embrace the truth of our time and anchor ourselves in the Spirit of the all-inclusive gospel, then we can be reweavers of our society. We must accept the challenging truth that we have been created and called for this time. Those being killed by our economy are crying out for our engagement. We must respond. Let us join together in the struggle for the common good.

CHAPTER 6

Water and Racialized Infrastructures in the Era of Trump

CHRISTIANA ZENNER

President Donald Trump noted in his inaugural speech that the nation's infrastructure "has fallen into disrepair and decay." On the campaign trail and from the inaugural podium, he promised to reconstruct decrepit roads, highways, and more.[1] Amid the generally nationalist, narcissistic bravado that currently parades as executive leadership, the attention to infrastructure may perhaps have glimmered with the distant possibility that water watchers had long advocated: namely, that intersections of environmental and social disenfranchisement could be attenuated by ameliorating the ongoing disrepair of U.S. cities' water and sanitation infrastructure, or substantively engaging concerns about gas and oil pipelines crossing water sources in historically marginalized regions. Alas, systemic environmental racisms and colonial disenfranchisements stand every chance of remaining fully intact during a Trump presidency. Moreover, historical amnesia is a constant way for the powers that be to ignore fundamental intersections between environmental and social equity. Yet in 2017 and beyond, the ascending visibility of intersectional activisms surrounding water access can provide both a source of hope and a necessary caution that progress is neither neutral nor assured in a country where the burdens of natural resources infrastructures are borne most dramatically by racialized and historically silenced bodies.

---

1. Aaron Blake, "Trump's Full Inauguration Speech Transcript, Annotated," *Washington Post*, January 20, 2017.

Scholars and activists have long used the term "intersectional" to refer to oppressions that evidence multiple and overlapping forms of social bias, such as at the intersection of gender and race.[2] Environmental justice movements proceed with a similar recognition that environmental degradation most dramatically affects already-marginalized populations in predictable ways and that these problems are systemic in nature. In the United States, much of the offloading of toxic wastes and environmental degradation has consistently occurred in communities that are historically poor and often predominantly racial or ethnic minorities.[3] These problems and patterns predate President Trump. What the Trumpian moment represents, then, is not necessarily a new form of oppression but rather an opportunity for dominant white America—with all of its internal diversities but so often swathed in a cocoon of ignorant privilege—to awaken to the reality of its own complicity. What is happening now is a broad-scale conscientization regarding the systemic textures of these kinds of problems. Because of the visibility of racism and exclusion in the rhetoric and reality of President Trump, the next four years may be an opportunity for privileged populations to act ethically and collectively.

Donald Trump's rise to power reveals—in stark, mainstream ways—the collective, racist, and colonialist *id* upon which so much of "American" excellence and self-righteousness has been carefully built.[4] This essay describes what is at stake through the lens of two water-based intersectional activisms that have surfaced into public consciousness since 2014. Identifying key problems and patterns in Flint and Standing Rock, this essay concludes that Trump's rise to power is—among many other things—an opportunity to fore-

2. See, for example, Kimberlé Crenshaw, "Mapping the Margins: Intersectionality, Identity Politics, and Violence against Women of Color," *Stanford Law Review* 43, no. 6 (1991): 1241–99.

3. See, for example, United Church of Christ, *Toxic Wastes and Race and Toxic Wastes and Race at Twenty,* http://www.ucc.org.

4. The Trumpian adjective of "American" has rhetorical efficacy with a certain political base, even as residents of the Americas more broadly—and the discipline of American Studies, in academe—have moved beyond a simplistic equation of "America" with the "United States."

ground long-simmering questions of racialized histories, colonial legacies, and the ongoing struggle for resource equity.

Water and Race: From Detroit To Flint

During the summer of 2014, attempting to limit economic losses as part of the city's bankruptcy management, Detroit Water and Sewerage District (DWSD) began shutting off the water supply to account holders in arrears, ranging from corporate clients to individual homeowners. But implementation was dramatic and uneven. Stories trickled out of people—some elderly, some homebound, many living below the poverty line—whose water had been cut off without an apparent appeals process, and who were disproportionately African American. National outcry by local water justice advocates attracted international attention, leading to a public condemnation by the U.N. special rapporteur on water and sanitation. Discrimination charges were filed by legal aid organizations on the grounds that the shutoffs disproportionately and unfairly affect African American residents. Preachers preached and activists protested that water is "a gift from God" and a "human right"—and its withholding was unfair, racist, unjust, and illegal, given the 2010 U.N. designation of access to clean, fresh water as a fundamental human right.

Nearby, in Flint, Michigan, another story was unfolding, underwritten in related ways by decades of structural and spatial racism. The lead-poisoning epidemic in Flint crested into public consciousness in 2014 and became a federal emergency by January 2016, with the National Guard involved in distributing replacement water supplies. The events and causes of lead poisoning and water contamination in Flint have forced a genuine reckoning among some government officials about how sustained environmental (in)justice has led to a massive public health crisis in the backyard of middle America. A city, state, and federal state of emergency were ultimately affirmed. In February 2017, the Michigan Civil Rights Commission (MCRC) published the result of their findings.

The very first pages of the report claim that "We must come to terms with the ongoing effects of 'systemic racism' that repeatedly led to disparate racial outcomes as exemplified by the Flint Water Crisis.

This can no longer be ignored."[5] Importantly, this report sought not to assign blame for discrete actions (other investigations took on those important tasks) but—addressing itself directly to residents of Flint, Michigan—acknowledged that "your voices were ignored by state, state-appointed, and local officials. . . . The people of Flint have been subjected to unprecedented harm and hardship, much of it caused by structural and systemic discrimination and racism that have corroded your city, your institutions, and your water pipes, for generations."[6] As Malini Ranganathan had observed in 2016, certain forms of racial liberalism (which the MCRC might call "racialized structures")—"particularly as it was translated into urban renewal and property making in mid-20th century urban America—drove dispossession," and has been a major factor "underlying the city's financial duress, abandonment, and poisoned infrastructure."[7]

While some of the recommendations are directed at institutional reform, others are distinctly and deeply moral in quality. The report calls for the state to "acknowledge the role race and racism have played in our history, and how it continues to impact our present . . . [and to r]ebuild trust and credibility through the creation of a 'Truth and Reconciliation Commission' and the integration of a racial equity framework within state government."[8] To invoke the language of post-apartheid reconciliation mechanisms is a profound statement about the depth of moral violation that has occurred historically and into the present day. The suggestion is especially potent given this administration's amnesia toward historical disenfranchisements, as well as the incessant nationalist rhetoric of American superiority in the perpetuation of liberal-superior forms of life—rhetoric, it hardly needs to be said, that glosses over the very real and endemic oppression upon which U.S. prosperity continues to be built.

---

5. Report of the Michigan Civil Rights Commission, "The Flint Water Crisis: Systemic Racism through the Lens of Flint," (February 17, 2017), iii.

6. Ibid., iv.

7. Malini Ranganathan, "Thinking with Flint: Racial Liberalism and the Roots of an American Water Tragedy," *Nature Capitalism Socialism* 27, no. 3 (2016): 17–33.

8. "Flint Water Crisis," 5.

In this era of the consolidation of xenophobic sentiments into ill-conceived executive orders, it is also important to note that such queries are not substantially distinct from concerns about immigration and legal status. As the MCRC notes, some people in Flint were under the impression that one had to be a citizen of the United States in order to receive bottled water relief; in fact, the MCRC sought to provide "information in multiple languages" to ensure that residents understood both the problem and the relief efforts, and to clarify "that proof of citizenship was not required to receive bottled water for those exposed to lead contamination."[9] When perception of access to water is contingent on one's racial, ethnic, or legal status, this is more than a hint that real and structural issues between liberalism and equity are at play. The MCRC authors rightly pose a trenchant question: "If, without [explicit] racist intent, a systemic problem repeatedly produces different results based on people's skin color, how long does it take before leaving the system in place is itself racism?"[10]

Standing Rock[11]

Circum-Atlantic chattel slavery was rightly and often named as America's "original sin" during the 2016 presidential election. But evils are not mutually exclusive; it is crucial to remember that the marginalization and genocide of Native populations are also worthy of that accurate and egregious moniker. Moreover, just as racialized structures of access and privilege led to morally unacceptable outcomes in Flint, so too have racial and ethnic legacies of marginalization and cultural decimation of Native communities in the United States led to patterns of disenfranchisement and suffering in ways that are visible, once more, through the mediating substance of water

---

9. Ibid., 8.

10. Ibid., 6.

11. Parts of this section were adapted from Christiana Zenner, "*Laudato Si'* and Standing Rock: Water Justice and Indigenous Ecological Knowledge," in *Theology and Ecology across the Disciplines: On Care for Our Common Home*, ed. Celia Deane-Drummond and Rebecca Artinian-Kaiser (London: Bloomsbury, forthcoming 2018), ch. 12.

under conditions of capitalist pursuits of resource extraction and the expedition of permits for transportation infrastructures.

In 2016 the Army Corps of Engineers fast-tracked the Dakota Access Pipeline (DAPL) through the Standing Rock reservation in the Dakotas in order to transport fossil fuels from the Bakken oil shale formation, crossing and traveling under the Missouri River. Energy Transfer Partners, the operating company, asserts that it has followed due procedures in soliciting input from the Sioux. Indigenous Environmental Network elaborates on the situation rather differently:

> In North Dakota, Indigenous leaders from the Standing Rock Nation are fighting the Dakota Access Pipeline (DAPL). This pipeline will carry over a half a million barrels of oil per day from the Bakken Oil Shale Fields. The route the pipeline will take, if approved, will be laid under multiple bodies of water, to include the Missouri River located a half mile upstream from the Standing Rock reservation. This river not only supplies drinking water to the tribe but is a major tributary to the Mississippi River where more than 10 million people depend on it for both human consumption and irrigation for the nation's "bread basket." This pipeline when it fails—and it will fail—will destroy land and water with little, if any, chance of remediation / cleanup. . . . Protesters have continued to resist construction peacefully, despite surveillance and intimidation from the state.[12]

Massive collaborative protests emerged in Standing Rock throughout 2015 and 2016. As a result of focused social media activisms and tangible examples of disproportionate uses of force (spraying peaceful protesters with hot water from hoses during a winter freeze, for example), the efforts at Standing Rock have gained national and even international attention. As the American Civil Liberties Union summarized:

> The protesters are defending the land and water using little more than the right to assemble and speak freely—a protec-

---

12. See Indigenous Environmental Network, www.ienearth.org/stand-with-standing-rock-no-dapl.

tion afforded by the U.S. Constitution. In response to the protests, North Dakota's government suppressed free speech and militarized its policing by declaring a state of emergency, setting up a highway roadblock, and calling out the National Guard.[13]

So there was some cautious optimism when in December 2016 President Obama refused to grant a "last remaining easement" to "drill under the Missouri River at Lake Oahe and complete construction of the pipeline," requiring instead an environmental impact statement that would evaluate the possible negative outcomes of passing the river at that site and examining alternate routes.[14] Such momentary reprieve, however, must be understood in the context of a political climate characterized maximally by what Ranganathan calls "racial liberalism," and minimally by an administration that is unlikely to honor the wisdom of indigenous environmental activists on this pipeline or other projects or to take a careful stance toward environmental impact statements.

Indeed, on February 8, 2017, the Trump administration granted an easement (in contradiction of the Obama administration's stay). On February 14, the Standing Rock Sioux tribe filed a lawsuit alleging that the environmental impact statement was wrongfully terminated. The mechanisms of legal review and countersuit will take their course. The point here is broader: Lest we blame a particularly egregious individual for these inequities, let it be known that these actions have occurred not just under President Trump, but under the Obama administration as well, revealing the prevalence of systemic tendencies within cherished forms of liberalism despite the radical personality differences in those two presidents.

The conflict at Standing Rock embodies a tangle of disenfranchisements over water, land, sovereignty, and economic benefit that obviously exhibit unique features in the case of DAPL. Roxanne

---

13. ACLU of North Dakota, "Stop Government Suppression of the Right to Protest in North Dakota," https://action.aclu.org.

14. Sacred Stone Camp, "DAPL Easement Suspended but the Fight's Not Over," December 5, 2016, http://sacredstonecamp.org; and Doug Hayes, "What's Next for Standing Rock and the Dakota Access Pipeline Fight?," *Sierra Club*, December 13, 2016.

Dunbar-Ortiz, in the award-winning book *An Indigenous People's History of the United States,* notes:

> Through economic penetration of Indigenous societies, the European and Euro-American colonial powers created economic dependency and imbalance of trade, then incorporated the Indigenous nations into spheres of influence and controlled them indirectly or as protectorates. . . . In the case of US settler colonialism, land was the primary commodity.[15]

Bill McKibben also situates the conflict within this larger history of disenfranchisement:

> Native Americans live confined to bleak reservations in vast stretches of the country that no one thought were good for much of anything else. But those areas—ironically enough—now turn out to be essential for the production or transportation of the last great stocks of hydrocarbons, the ones whose combustion scientists tell us will take us over the edge of global warming. And if former generations of the U.S. Army made it possible to grab land from Native people, then this largely civilian era of the Army Corps is making it easy to pollute and spoil what little we left them. . . . A spill from this pipeline would pollute the Missouri River, just as spills in recent years have done irreparable damage to the Kalamazoo and Yellowstone rivers. And that river is both the spiritual and economic lifeblood of the Standing Rock Reservation, one of the poorest census tracts in the entire country.[16]

Thus, even while DAPL has unique features, it is also inextricably interwoven with legacies of racism, economic exploitation, and geographic marginalizations that make this particular case a familiar kind of story in ways that resonate with the water crisis in Flint, Michigan.

---

15. Roxanne Dunbar-Ortiz, *An Indigenous People's History of the United States* (Boston: Beacon Press, 2014), 7.

16. Bill McKibben, "After 525 Years, It's Time to Actually Listen to Native Americans," *Grist*, August 22, 2016. http://grist.org.

Finally, into the shared space of racialized liberal environments, some uncomfortable questions need to be raised about the habits of the dominant society's attention. Does media attention fawn on Standing Rock but pass over Flint in uneven ways? Just as there has been intersectional activism for Standing Rock, are there similar intersectional forms of advocacy for Flint—and if not, why not? Only by investigating this nation's founding myths, legacies of racialized geographic privilege and oppression, and selective reification of the exotic other can real answers be found and real ways forward identified.

Conclusion: When the Invisible Becomes Visible

We stand at the birth of a new millennium, ready to unlock the mysteries of space, to free the earth from the miseries of disease, and to harness the energies, industries, and technologies of tomorrow. A new national pride will stir our souls, lift our sights and heal our divisions. . . . And whether a child is born in the urban sprawl of Detroit or the wind-swept plains of Nebraska, they look up at the same night sky, they fill their heart with the same dreams, and they are infused with the breath of life by the same almighty creator.[17]

Sweeping though the presidential rhetoric may be, children in the United States do not, in fact, have the same dreams or live supported by the same lifelines. Water is currently among the most visible sites of differential, systemic privilege. It is through the substance of water that race, class, and geography in Flint and Standing Rock are revealed to be intimately and dangerously related. What has become clear in an era of Trump is how deeply entrenched such phenomena are. This chapter has endeavored to show, in a very practical way, that ecology is about society, is about ethics, and is burdened by all the legacies that shape those realities in the past and present. Gus DiZerega has suggested:

Ecology is based upon the view that all things are intrinsically interconnected in such a way that boundaries are ultimately

---

17. Blake, "Trump's Full Inauguration Speech."

conventional, partial, and porous. *Where we draw boundaries depends upon the particular relationships that we are interested in defining.* In other words, an individual being cannot be fully understood separately from its relationships with everything else. In fact, to a large degree, it is defined by them.[18]

The cases of Flint and Standing Rock demonstrate how water bears the boundaries of race and class, geography and history, systemic and liberal forms of life in ways that differently burden bodies in the contemporary United States.

The production of ethics is a socially mediated phenomenon, with all the selectivities and vagaries attendant therein. Currently, much attention is directed at alarming presidential patterns: selective, obsessive attention to certain issues; the propagation of "alternative facts," truly believed and vehemently asserted; aggressive and demeaning comments on social media that belie desperate appeals for affirmation and attention; nepotism and cronyism, including the placement of family members and fossil fuel executives in positions of considerable power; ill-conceived executive orders that circumvent democratic processes; and an apparent vampiric desire to dismantle government agencies and perhaps even legislation that formed the scaffold of environmental protections in the twentieth-century United States.

But even as it continues to be clear that a power-hungry narcissist holds the Oval Office, it is also crucial to remember that the egregious antics of the present administration also cast a light on our collective "American" id. Whether speaking of Trump or of Flint or of Standing Rock, it is a moral imperative to look squarely at what has become visible in the liberalized, racialized structures of environmental and social burdens. As the Michigan Civil Rights Commission suggested, "this crisis offers a painful lesson, one that will be repeated if we do not learn from it."[19]

---

18. Gus DiZerega, "Individuality, Human and Natural Communities, and the Foundations of Ethics," *Environmental Ethics* 17 (Spring 1995), 23 (italics in original).

19. "Flint Water Crisis," 11.

CHAPTER 7

Truth, Environment, Trump

ROGER S. GOTTLIEB

I

Wilhelm Reich, writing about the joint socialist and communist failure to effectively resist the rise of German fascism, observed: "While we presented the masses with superb historical analysis and economic treatises, Hitler stirred the deepest roots of their emotional being."[1] Ring any bells about the rise of Trump? Here's one aspect of people's "deep emotional being" he understood that "we" (the left, liberals, moderate Republicans, etc.) did not get—or at least, not get enough: that truth is evaporating from public discourse. Trump's ability to dispense with truth is the end of a long historical process, including the lies that accompany various forms of oppression (racism, sexism, anti-Semitism, etc.); extreme forms of mass propaganda by fascism, communism, and liberal capitalism; and television's neurological colonization of the psyche through advertising.

These practices have created a discursive context in which public language is *first* shot through with lies, distortions, concealments, and emotional manipulation via affecting phrases, images, and music, and *then* progressively ceases to have a significant connection to truth at all. I doubt that people "believe" advertising. Rather, what the words *would* mean is simply an emotional stimulus to fear, greed, lust, and escapist fantasy. The words and images make us feel something because *if* they were true (if x were

---

1. Wilhelm Reich, *Sex-Pol* (New York: Vintage, 1972), 283–84.

a danger to our health, if y would make our families happy) then an emotional response of, say, fear or attraction would make sense. However, we simultaneously know that the ads are not true and also have an emotional reaction as if they were. They constitute, as it were, a pornography of desire. As a result, statements parading as fact are now experienced as having the same relation to truth as the dragons in *Game of Thrones*: they excite us, frighten us, and perhaps lead us to cheer them on—even as we know they are not real.

Do Trump supporters really believe his obvious lies and phony promises? For example, "I'll sue the *Times*," "Nobody respects women more than I," "I had record breaking numbers at my inauguration." I suspect not. However, there is a kind of visceral excitement in seeing a public figure brag without shame, threaten a media outlet you hate, and heap scorn on women (a pleasure both for sexist men and self-hating, male-identified women). Constrained by a stagnant economy, disoriented by cultural change and loss of privilege, threatened by social catastrophes far beyond their understanding (the 2007 economic meltdown, ISIS, global warming) there is a deep pleasure in identifying with a man who is unafraid to break conventional boundaries of assertion, who offers simple answers to vastly complex questions, and who is not hedged in by lack of money, political correctness, or respect for the established institutions that have left the typical Trump supporter awash in economic and social insecurity.

True? Who knows? But we don't ask if a warm bath is true, or a pleasing song, or an ice cream sundae. We just enjoy the way they make us feel. Believe him? Perhaps. Or maybe just relish a few moments of pleasure in watching him perform, in the feelings he arouses. And since everyone else is lying as well—all the conventional politicians, the news sources, the ads—we might as well go with the lies that are amusing, reassuring, exciting, or just plain fun to watch. Didn't do what he said he'd do? That was last week's ad; what's on today?

And the internet. Much has been made of the websites designed to spread lies for advertising revenue. We can just add here that one obvious political significance of the internet is the way it takes publishing out of the hands of the wealthy. For a pittance I can make my ideas available around the world; millions for a printing press or TV station are not required. At the same time, however, the internet also makes possible a kind of democratization of ignorance and delusion. There are no editorial boards, no peer reviews, no community discussions necessary for a posting or a website. As an isolated, atomized individual, without connection to possible correction, re-thinking, awareness of other positions, or fact-checking, the web (and thus the world) is my oyster. Like the isolated act of voting, the isolated internet voice does not reflect self-conscious, mediated, relational, communal intelligence, but far too often simply the prejudices and slanted ignorance of an individual or a parochial, narrow-minded, intellectually insular community.

Years ago the German philosopher Jürgen Habermas warned of a future society divided into two groups: the social engineers and the inmates of closed institutions.[2] The more truth is removed from ordinary political discourse and ethical interaction, the more we are closed into institutions of fantasy, emotional manipulation, and domination by corporate and political elites. Or as Leonard Cohen put it: "I have seen the future . . . it is murder."

II

What does this mean for environmental issues? It means an EPA head who denies both climate change and the well-known negative health effects of fracking. A Republican Congress that proposes allowing fossil fuel extraction in forty National Parks, while denying that this is a threat to everything the parks are. Countless other examples have arisen and will continue to arise. But, it might be argued, because it tells us about reality we avoid the truth at our peril. And while the reality of some things might be indeterminate ("That man is handsome," "Coke is it"), in other contexts it is not ("That bridge will support the morning commute," "The water doesn't have lead in it"). Even the Bad Guys need the truth, because they live in the real world, and if they commit to distortions, denials, delusions, and Big Lies, it will negatively affect their ability to function. And these consequences will ultimately lead to their defeat.

---

2. Jürgen Habermas, *Theory and Practice* (Boston: Beacon Press, 1971), 282.

However, the scope of modern technology removes the truth from immediate accessibility. I can see with my own eyes that plants that usually bloom at the end of March are coming up in my neighbor's front yard in February. I know that I've been wearing a fall jacket in much of this year's January. But I have no immediate access to climate change as a *global* crisis: melting glaciers, droughts in Africa, oceanic acidification. I can know such realities only through reports from media, experts, local observers, environmental reporters, and so forth.

Why should I trust any of these? If all the media are biased; if fake news abounds; if everyone has "an agenda"; if anything beyond my immediate experience is filtered by one side's experts or the other's, then the question is not, "Which expert or unbiased news source can tell me what's going on?" but "Which source of distortions, omissions, and slants makes me feel better?"

Even further: suppose that the dreadful happens and we have some kind of environmental catastrophe. A few years ago a West Virginia town was flooded with oil because of a rupture in a pipeline not unlike the one planned for Keystone XL. So the good citizens of West Virginia saw the truth up close, saw that pipelines are dangerous, and that promises that "our safety measures are so sophisticated you don't have to worry" are empty. Similarly, and ironically, while the resistors at Standing Rock were being reassured of the safety of the pipeline they were fighting, a similar accident happened just some 150 or so miles away.

But outside of the people immediately affected by these spills, how many people cared? How many other residents of West Virginia or North Dakota were given the full information? How many wrote it off as regrettable, but surely not worth lessening their own access to fossil fuels in the slightest degree? For, after all, it is well known that environmentalists seek to destroy our nation's economy and that they exaggerate environmental threats to increase their funding and attack consumers' freedoms. Further, while such accidents are surely regrettable, how often do they happen? Whose fault was it? And won't what we learn from the incident make us even safer in the future? Anyway, life is full of risk, right?

West Virginia and North Dakota voted overwhelmingly not for

the environmentally at least somewhat cautious Clinton, but for the reckless servant of fossil fuel and pipeline lover, Donald J. Trump.

III

These reflections suggest, as American philosopher W. V. O. Quine argued,[3] that beliefs do not connect to the world in a one-to-one fashion. Rather, we have a *system* of beliefs that are more like a grid or a web than a series of individual bricks tied to particular facts. When something unexpected happens, when something contradicts what we thought was true, there are countless different ways in which the system can accommodate the new reality.

If you are committed to fossil fuels, you can deny the severity of the accidents or climate change disasters, attribute them to other causes, blame someone else (immigrants, liberals, coastal elites) for climate-caused economic problems. A government can refuse to keep accurate records of droughts and floods, or refuse to make the records public. People who tell the country what is going on can be fired. The population can be distracted by yet another spectacle. How many news reports of "Hottest year on record!" have we had, and yet the White House can, with little response, remove climate change from its website, while the media dither on about the latest ridiculous, and soon to be forgotten, presidential tweet.

In the long run, I suspect that the room for epistemological maneuvering will get smaller and smaller. After a while the Catholic Church did have to believe that Galileo was right; male supremacists (at least in much of the world) have had to stop claiming that women are incapable of politics, technology, or corporate authority. And in the long run, at least with regard to climate change and some other of the more gross forms of pollution (e.g., the Pacific Garbage Patch) excuses, denials, avoidances, and blame shifting will get harder and harder. Yet in the long run, as John Maynard Keynes observed, we will all be dead. By the time the long run comes around, it is likely to be too late not to have a changed climate that will take the lives and livelihood of millions, perhaps

---

3. W. V. O. Quine, "Two Dogmas of Empiricism," *The Philosophical Review* 60 (1951): 20–43.

tens or hundreds of millions, of human lives; and the lives of untold numbers of other living beings as well.

IV

Do people learn from experience? Sometimes yes. After three brutal wars in seventy years, it is doubtful that France and Germany will ever experience another one. But keep in mind how much suffering was necessary before the lesson could be learned. Choking smog in Los Angeles, rivers catching on fire in Ohio, a warning cry from internationally famous writer Rachel Carson—these were some of the "experiences" that led to the initial environmental activism and governmental action of the 1970s. Yet if the rise of Trumpism makes anything clear, it is that we cannot count on past political accomplishments that stemmed from earlier learning. The Republican agenda threatens things most of us felt settled: the New Deal, the social safety net, at least verbal public commitment to equal treatment for women, abortion rights, voting rights for racial minorities.

In particular, the idea of scientific expertise—hostilely affected during the George W. Bush administration[4]—will almost certainly come under attack. Trump's chief strategist and advisor, Steve Bannon, advocates the moral superiority of the "Judeo-Christian West" and "humane" capitalism, an advocacy that so denies the crimes and follies of both it is not clear if he would like to roll back the Enlightenment along with gender equality and environmental regulations. How long will it be until government reports on issues besides climate change get limited, slanted, denied, and colored? Government employees will probably be forbidden, as they were by Florida's governor, from addressing climate issues.[5] Critiques of fracking will probably be off limits—even though Trump's pick for EPA head

---

4. Chris Mooney, *The Republican War on Science* (New York: Basic Books, 2005); and Chris Clarke, "Bush's Bizarre Science," *Earth Island Journal* 18, no. 2 (Summer 2003), 36–40.

5. Tristram Korten, "Florida's State Employees are Preparing for Climate Change, Even as Their Governor Bans the Phrase," *New Republic*, March 22, 2015.

comes from a state (Oklahoma) in which wastewater from fossil fuel extraction has increased the incidence of earthquakes from three to nine hundred in six years.[6] Already all information related to the Animal Welfare Act has been removed from the Department of Agriculture's website.[7] Of course the attack on science will be selective. Weapons, computers, the people who service Trump's personal plane—all these will be rigorously technical, nonpolitical, on the up and up. And there will be resistance to the denigration of science by America's technological elite.[8] But will it be enough?

V

Are there political, intellectual, or spiritual implications to the dire straits we are in? I believe there are, but while I think they make sense, these are merely guidelines, not solutions, for I do not think there is any solving Trump. There is, at best, surviving him.

First, solidarity on the "left"—with that term interpreted absolutely as broadly as possible. As Hitler solidified power in Germany, the socialist and communist parties—long established, large, institutionally fortified—wasted huge energies fighting each other. Right now every anti-Trump supporter needs every other one. Any carping over details, drawing of political lines in the sand, or demands that fellow fighters follow our particular ideological shibboleths is at this point an exercise in the most profound denial of just how bad things are. We do not have the choice to restrict cooperation with those who see the world just as we do, to belabor macroaggressions and intersectionality, and argue over who is most oppressed; for radicals to knock sell-out liberals or liberals to be contemptuous of pie-in-the-sky radicals. Limit Trump's power.

---

6. Bill Whitaker, "Oklahoma's Rise in Quakes Linked to Man Made Causes," *CBS News*, May 8, 2016.

7. Sarah V. Schweig, "U.S. Government Removes All Animal Welfare Info from Its Site," *The Dodo*, February 3, 2017, www.thedodo.com.

8. A resistance made complicated by the fact that scientific expertise is fallible, often shaped by political and corporate power, and too often reflects forms of social domination like racism and sexism. Yet there is a profound difference between these inevitable limitations and the self-conscious manufacture of facts and the threats to punish those who raise inconvenient truths.

Reject his horrible policies. Discredit his revolting appointees. Support his victims. That's it.

Second, we need to phrase our environmental concerns in as broad and inclusive terms as possible. If we advocate for the end of coal (as we should), the very next sentence should offer policies of job training and support for the workers whose lives and communities depend on coal. Our talk of "pollution" is often an abstraction. "Your neighbors with cancer and lung disease" is not.

Third, tell each other, coworkers, church group members, family, and friends about whatever victories there are. This is not about whistling in the dark, though that's not necessarily a bad thing. Rather, it's about not distorting reality by *only* repeating the facts that make us feel powerless.

Fourth, our own attention to reality must be scrupulous. We must lead by example in telling the truth as we see it, even if that includes noting something Trump does that's a good thing. The environmental consequences of NAFTA and the World Trade Organization have been awful. I saw no evidence that the TPP would have been much better. The globalization agenda is in part about destroying local environmental protections. For whatever reasons he holds it, Trump's position here has some merit.

Why should Trump supporters—not the rabid ones, but those who still retain a modicum of sanity—pay attention to us if we can't say the truth no matter how it runs against our general position? The point is to maintain our connection with reality. That is far more important than any short-term strategic goal of saying how *everything* Trump does is wrong. What he does is not wrong because he does it. It's wrong for other reasons. And we can say exactly what those reasons are.

Fifth, accept how much we don't know. We should not assert a hope, fear, or possibility as knowledge, nor pretend that we can be sure what will happen from this or that political action, proposal, or plan. It has never been easy to combine activist commitment with level-headed skepticism of our own beliefs and actions. Yet it has never been more important. We can recognize the truth and act on it only to the extent that we are able to face the truth of how often the truth evades even those of us who treasure it.

CHAPTER 8

Sexual Justice in an Age of Trump

MARIE ALFORD-HARKEY

... the political institutions of any nation are always menaced and are ultimately controlled by the spiritual state of that nation.
—James Baldwin, *The Fire Next Time*

In the summer of 2016, the Religious Institute board and staff planned a board meeting for November 10. As the head of this organization that promotes sexual health, education, and justice in faith communities and society, I thought November 10 would be the perfect day to celebrate and look to the future under a sympathetic presidential administration. Instead, we gathered to begin planning our religious resistance to a hostile administration.

This election did not reflect the moral vision put forth by our organization and the people of faith in our network. Indeed, the election of Donald Trump as president of the United States will be the beginning of a complete assault on sexual, gender, and reproductive justice. We elected a president who bragged about sexually assaulting women. We elected a president who stalked another candidate—a woman—on the debate stage on national television. We elected a president who promised to bar certain religious groups from entering the country. We elected a president who promised to split up families and deport immigrants, even children, who have been in this country for more than a decade. We elected a president who proudly blew the dog whistle of "law and order," thereby promising to continue to subject black and brown people to state violence in the United States. We elected a president who promised to take away health insurance from millions of people and strip reproductive health care from millions more.

President Trump's campaign and election revealed to all of us what many people in this country experience every day: sexism, heterosexism, misogyny, transmisogyny, racism, and Islamophobia. The campaign and election heightened fear and anxiety for lesbian, gay, bisexual, transgender, gender nonconforming, and queer people, women, immigrants, refugees, black and brown people, people with disabilities, people who have experienced sexual assault, and so many others.

After the election, President-Elect Trump's supporters and others downplayed the danger of his administration. We were urged to "give him a chance." But this is not a typical administration, nor was this a typical election. We who ground our justice work in our religious faith must remind ourselves and the country of this fact, lest we slip into complacency. We must not normalize this administration. We cannot be complacent while people are denied health care and human rights. Specific threats to sexual, gender, and reproductive justice have already emerged, barely three weeks into this new administration. There is every reason to believe that these threats will continue.

Threats to Reproductive Health, Rights, and Justice

Threats to health care abound in the Trump administration, and they target people who are the most vulnerable. President Trump promised to repeal the Affordable Care Act (ACA) and to strip federal funds from Planned Parenthood Federation of America (PPFA). Tom Price, President Trump's secretary of Health and Human Services (HHS), has opposed the Affordable Care Act (ACA) since its inception and has promised to repeal it. Similarly, he supports stripping federal funds from PPFA. Secretary Price seeks to make abortion illegal and does not support access to contraceptives without a copay for those who have health insurance. Congress is laying the groundwork for both actions.

Repealing the ACA would be catastrophic for millions of people, disproportionately affecting poor people, people of color, and LGBTQ people. One report estimates that 24 million people will lose healthcare coverage in the next four years if the ACA is repealed.[1] Of those 24 million, 63.3 percent have incomes below $23,600. Under the ACA, insurance companies cannot discriminate against women or transgender people by charging higher premiums or blocking certain kinds of health care. Given the administration's actions against transgender people, there is little doubt that they would lose this protection if the ACA is repealed.[2] The Kaiser Family Foundation reports that people of color face more barriers to accessing health care than white people, and that they are more likely to be uninsured. Because of this disparity, people of color have had larger gains in coverage under the ACA.[3] Repealing it would be a huge step backward for these communities. It is profoundly immoral to deny health-care coverage based on income, sexual orientation, gender identity, or race. Yet that is exactly the effect of repealing the ACA. People who have always had access to health care will continue to have it. People who just gained access to health care will be denied it again. This is antithetical to religious values of caring for our neighbors as ourselves and caring equally for all people, not just certain groups of people.

Defunding Planned Parenthood also targets those who can least afford to lose health care: poor people, people of color, and people

1. Matthew Buettgens, Linda J. Blumberg, John Holahan, and Siyabonga Ndwandwe, *The Cost of ACA Repeal*, Robert Wood Johnson Foundation Urban Institute, June 2016.

2. Jennifer Kates, Usha Ranji, Adara Beamesderfer, Alina Salganicoff, and Lindsey Dawson, *Health and Access to Care and Coverage for Lesbian, Gay, Bisexual, and Transgender (LGBT) Individuals in the U.S.*, Kaiser Family Foundation, November 11, 2016.

3. Samantha Artiga, Petry Ubri, Julia Foutz, and Anthony Damico, *Health Coverage by Race and Ethnicity: Examining Changes under the ACA and the Remaining Uninsured*, Kaiser Family Foundation, November 4, 2016.

in rural communities. Such a move would deny health care to 2.8 million people, 79 percent of whom have incomes below $17,700 per year.[4] In addition, Planned Parenthood reports that more than half of its clinics are in rural and underserved communities, which means that the closure of a Planned Parenthood clinic would deprive an entire community of health care.[5] The rationale for targeting Planned Parenthood is that some PPFA health centers provide abortions, and many who want to defund Planned Parenthood claim a religious rationale. However, religious values teach that we are to be concerned about the lives of living, breathing human beings who will no longer have access to cancer screenings, treatment for sexually transmitted infections, contraception (which helps prevent the need for abortions), pregnancy tests, prenatal care, and the other services Planned Parenthood health centers provide. Religious values also support the moral agency of people who, informed by their own values, choose to have an abortion.

Consequences reach beyond the United States. On January 23, 2017, President Trump signed an executive order reinstating and expanding the Reagan-era "Mexico City Policy," which prohibits State Department family-planning funding (and now any U.S. government health assistance) from any organization that performs or provides information about abortion, even if U.S. money is not being used for those purposes. Marie Stopes International, which provides contraception and safe abortion services worldwide, estimates that "without alternative funding, the loss of our services during Trump's first term, between 2017 and 2020, could result in 6.5 million unintended pregnancies, 2.2 million abortions, 2.1 million unsafe abortions, and 21,700 maternal deaths."[6] Suzanne Ehlers of Population Action International says that this expansion

---

4. Government Accountability Office, *Health Care Funding: Federal Obligations to and Expenditures by Selected Entities Involved in Health-Related Activities, 2010–2012*, GAO-15-270R, March 20, 2015.

5. Planned Parenthood, *The Urgent Need for Planned Parenthood Health Centers*, 2016.

6. Marie Stopes International, *Re-enactment of the Mexico City Policy*, January 23, 2017.

brings the amount of aid that will be cut from $575 million to $9 billion. She points out that most of the burden will be borne by the "poorest women in the world."[7] The injustice of stripping health care from the poorest women in the world based on ideological religious claims is striking. This action will result in the deaths of women and increases in the number of abortions.

Religious traditions affirm that our humanity is all that is required to render us worthy of love and dignity. People who can't afford health care are no less valuable than people who can. People who need reproductive health care are no less valuable than those who don't. People who live in the developing world are no less valuable than people who live in the United States. It is immoral to deny reproductive health care to people who need it. Our connection through our common humanity calls us to responsibility to and for one another.

Legalizing Discrimination

President Trump has promised to sign the "First Amendment Defense Act" (FADA), and Senator Ted Cruz has promised to reintroduce it. This piece of legislation, first introduced in 2015, allows anyone (including a business) who "believes or acts in accordance with a religious belief or moral conviction that: (1) marriage is or should be recognized as the union of one man and one woman, or (2) sexual relations are properly reserved to such a marriage" to "act in accordance" with that belief or conviction without consequence.[8] This would legalize discrimination against LGBTQ people and anyone who has sex outside of marriage. A company could fire an unmarried pregnant person. An emergency medical technician could refuse to treat a transgender person. A landlord could refuse to rent an apartment to a legally married, same-sex couple. These are only a few examples of allowing personal convictions to impact civil rights.

---

7. CBS, "Trump Expands Anti-abortion Ban to All U.S. Global Health Aid," January 24, 2017.

8. First Amendment Defense Act, H.R. 2802, 114th Congress, 2015.

Attorney General Jeff Sessions has said that the Department of Justice will not be defending the Obama administration's guidance on interpreting Title IX (the federal law that prohibits sex discrimination in schools).[9] This guidance from the U.S. Departments of Justice and Health and Human Services clarified that transgender students are protected under Title IX. Refusing to enforce this guidance puts transgender students at further risk of bullying, violence, and discrimination in their schools.

Rhetoric about "religious freedom" is being used to advocate for discrimination and denial of basic human rights. Yet religious texts teach that we are our siblings' keepers insofar as we must value their lives as our own. Religious values teach us to work for liberation of all people because our own liberation is bound up with everyone else's.[10] As we confront attacks on sexual, gender, and reproductive justice throughout the term of this administration, we must maintain our connection to one another and resist the urge to look out only for the interests of our own communities. Our resistance must not leave anyone behind.

Religious Resistance

The sum of these actions is riskier than any one specific policy, executive order, or cabinet appointee. This administration has and will continue to launch an all-out assault on sexual, gender, and reproductive justice. Lives are at stake, and resistance is a moral imperative. To engage in a religious resistance, we must break the stigma and silence around sexuality in our religious spaces and speak out for sexual, gender, and reproductive justice in the public arena. What does religion offer to those who ground their resistance in their faith? It offers spiritual practices, story, prophetic speech, and holy imagination. Of course, none of these are the exclusive purview of religion, but religion is uniquely positioned to offer these gifts, especially in times of crisis.

---

9. Andrew V. Pestano, *Trump's DOJ Withdraws Obama Effort over Transgender Bathroom Case*, United Press International, February 13, 2017.

10. An idea often attributed to Lilla Watson, an aboriginal Australian social worker.

Practices

Community practices like prayer, singing, setting intentions, meditating, sharing a sacred meal, or reciting holy texts unite community members across lines of difference. Because such practices require a degree of vulnerability, religious communities can foster deep connections and a sense of shared values among their members. When our practices connect us to our bodies through movement or by engaging our senses, they help break down artificial barriers between body and soul. When we engage in religious practices on our own, we connect to our deepest values, restoring our relationship to the divine and replenishing our resources.[11] As we continue to resist injustice, taking time for spiritual practices that nourish and connect us becomes a necessity and no longer a luxury.

Story

Stories are the most effective way to learn about other people. In religious communities where we are already connected to others, we have a frame and a place for sharing stories with one another. Hearing stories helps us understand experiences that we have not had and gain perspectives that are different from our own. Telling our own stories allows us to share ourselves and speak of our most important values. Our holy texts use stories to illustrate values and timeless truths. In my religious communities, I've heard a transgender woman connect the biblical story of the transfiguration to her story (Matthew 17:1-8), and I've heard a black father describe the conversations he had with his teenage son about how to behave in public so that he wouldn't be viewed as a threat. Hearing these stories has changed me. They helped me to connect justice work to real lives and real bodies. These stories and many others fuel my own passion for justice and compel me to look beyond my own identities and self-interest in that work.

---

11. I am indebted to Teo Drake for his teaching on using spiritual practices to renew resources for the fight for justice at a workshop at Creating Change in January, 2017.

Prophetic Speech

Prophetic speech in my Christian tradition dates to those figures who called God's people back from their selfish ways. Prophets chastise and challenge, reminding us that our responsibility is to people at risk of being forgotten—poor people, people without societal power or status, and people who are strangers in our land. As we resist the divisiveness of the Trump administration, we can engage the prophetic tradition within our communities of faith and in public forums, speaking for justice from our faith and values. Our religious communities and leaders must overcome the silence and stigma around sexuality and religion. We must speak out about the dignity and worth of transgender people when they are targeted by bogus "bathroom bills" and the rollback of protections in schools. We must speak out about the injustice of stripping away options for reproductive health care in poor, rural, and black and brown communities. We must engage our holy anger at the injustice of state violence against black people, and the fear of black parents that their children will not come home. At every turn, we must remind the public and our own communities that the religious narrative of hate and divisiveness and control is a false one. We must use our prophetic traditions to proclaim the value of justice and dignity for all human beings.

Holy Imagination

Finally, religion engages holy imagination in offering a different view of the world. At the heart of my faith, and of many other religious traditions, is the belief that the world can change, that human beings and societies can be better than we are. As people of faith, we are charged with creating a better world. Our faith traditions require us to confront the misery of injustice and still commit to imagining and working toward another kind of world. As we engage in resistance, it will be difficult to raise our heads above the struggles of the moment to re-engage our imaginations, but it will be critical that we do.

Conclusion

While many people have urged a wait-and-see approach to the Trump administration, such an approach ignores very real threats to sexual, gender, and reproductive justice. Access to health care, especially reproductive health care and abortion, is already being curtailed. Civil rights for transgender people are being rolled back. Religious rhetoric is being misused to promote discrimination against LGBTQ people and people who seek reproductive health care. Immigrants and refugees are being scapegoated for fictitious terrorist attacks. In every case, those who stand to lose the most are those who already are at increased risk in U.S. society.

In this climate of legitimate fear and anxiety, those of us who ground our work for justice in our religious beliefs have a unique role to play. Not only can we take back the narrative about religion and sexuality from the religious right, we can and must use our religious resources to fuel the resistance.

CHAPTER 9

The System Is Rigged

MIGUEL A. DE LA TORRE

The vote is a trust more delicate than any other, greater than life, honor, and future for it involves the interests of the voters. Those who do wrong and use against them the office they owe the voters is a thief.

—*José Martí*

It begins with a lie. A lie so outrageous, so preposterous it titillates simple minds and seduces those who should know better because they want to believe the lie. The lie is crucial because it serves an important purpose—to delegitimize. The lie can subvert and undermine legal authorities, as in "The president was born in Kenya." Regardless of birth certificates provided, the lie plays to the racist fears of whites who have a black man as their president, insinuating that Barack Obama cannot be a "real" American. The lie keeps embers of hatred simmering while keeping the father of the lie—the self-professed crusader for truth—in the spotlight.

Shortly after the 2016 election, the instigator of the birther movement, then President-Elect Donald Trump, gave us a new lie to ponder, one whose purpose was to delegitimize the democratic process and explain away how even after winning the Electoral College (306 to 232), he still lost the popular election by almost 2.9 million votes.[1] According to his tweet, Trump actually won the popular

---

1. "Presidential Results," *CNN Politics*, http://www.cnn.com.

vote in the general election, but fell short because "over three million illegals [*sic*] voted in California."[2] No evidence was given; no verification was needed, for the burden of proof rested not with the accuser, but with those who were reproached. In the era of Trump, any claim, unless proven false, remains true.

People who ought to know better look away, out of political expedience, and thus allow the democratic political process to be destabilized with falsehoods. When Senate Majority Leader Mitch McConnell was asked to comment on Trump's allegations about voter fraud, he deflected: "It does occur, there are always arguments on both sides about how frequent and all the rest."[3] Speaker of the House Paul Ryan responded with a dismissal: "I don't know. I'm not really focused on these things." When pressed he snapped: "I have no way of backing that up. I have no knowledge of such things."[4] But they do! In an election where over 137.7 million votes were cast,[5] investigative reports based on scholarly evidence show that voter fraud was a minuscule problem. Twenty-six states plus the District of Columbia reported no case of fraud; eight states reported just one alleged case of fraud (eight total). Tennessee investigated forty cases, while Georgia reported twenty-five possible cases. Thus, the 2016 election was "plagued" with possibly sixty-three credible cases of suspected fraud or 0.00000046 percent of all votes casts.[6] These numbers are in line with an earlier three-year study conducted by the U.S. Justice Department, under then-President George W. Bush, which discovered that out of all the votes cast during the 2000, 2002, and 2004 federal elections, only

---

2. Michael S. Shear and Maggie Haberman, "Trump Claims, with No Evidence, That 'Millions of People' Voted Illegally," *New York Times*, November 27, 2016.

3. Nicholas Fandos, "The Truth behind a Lie on Voting Fraud," *New York Times*, January 25. 2017.

4. Scott Pelley (correspondent), "Speaker Ryan's 'Strange Bedfellows' Partnership with Trump," *60 Minutes*, CBS, December 4, 2016.

5. Michael McDonald, "2016 November General Election Turnout Rates," *United States Election Projects*, http://www.electproject.org.

6. Michael Wines, "All This Talk of Voter Fraud? Across U.S., Officials Found Next to None," *New York Times*, December 18, 2016.

twenty-six individuals fraudulently registered to vote, or voted, representing 0.00000132 percent of all votes cast.[7]

A couple of dozen cases in 2016—of which few if any were based on a malicious intent to commit fraud—remains a far cry from the three million Trump says voted, or about which McConnell and Ryan claimed ignorance. But the lie is perpetuated nonetheless, because if the electoral process is questioned, laws might be passed privileging those who might not otherwise be able to win. Justifying the passage of laws to undermine the democratic process and the will of the people is a hard sell; easier to push for laws protecting the integrity of the voting booth with the myth of voter fraud.

For months prior to the November election, then-candidate Trump kept insisting the electoral system was rigged,[8] probably one of his few comments with which I wholeheartedly agree. Rigging elections is not a new phenomenon. Throughout most of U.S. history legal strategies have been employed to disenfranchise a sizable portion of the electorate via literacy tests, competency tests, or poll taxes. Until the 1960s, policies were established—especially in Southern states—to ruthlessly disenfranchise nonwhites in every facet of daily life. While such Jim and Jane Crow tactics may seem to belong to some bygone era, suppression of votes continues against blacks and poor whites (and Latinxs along with other marginalized communities), though now by more sophisticated methodologies. How does a political party, supported by a minority of the population, stay in power? By blaming the disenfranchised for fraud. The system is indeed rigged through (1) an electoral college that disproportionately favors small, rural states; (2) gerrymandering; and (3) voter suppression laws. While these strategies are as old as the Republic, the 2016 election introduced a new strategy in the form of foreign interference. Is it any wonder the Electoral Integrity Project, which monitors the quality of hundreds of elections

---

7. Lorraine C. Minnite, *The Myth of Voter Fraud* (Ithaca, NY: Cornell University Press, 2010), 13.

8. Jenna Johnson, "Donald Trump Says the Election is 'Rigged.' Here's What His Supporters Think That Means," *Washington Post*, October 18, 2016.

throughout the world, ranked the United States 52nd out of 153 countries, behind all developed Western democracies?[9]

Electoral College

The electoral college is a system conceived in racism; creating a representative as opposed to direct democracy, where voters do not vote for a candidate but instead elect delegates whose allegiance is to the party, even though it is the candidate's name on the ballot. Whoever wins the state's popular vote receives all the electoral votes of that state regardless of the margin of the win (with the exception of two states, Maine and Nebraska). Even though the popular vote in Florida was split 50%–50% in 2000, Bush won all twenty-seven electoral votes and thus the presidency, regardless that Gore won the U.S. popular election by over half-a-million votes. This phenomenon repeated itself in 2016 as Clinton nationally received almost three million more votes than Trump. The undemocratic nature of the Electoral College disenfranchises more liberal states like New York or California. For example, one electoral vote in a more diverse California represents 508,000 voters while one electoral vote in a more homogeneous white conservative state like Wyoming represents 143,000 voters. Hence in the presidential election, a Wyoming voter is worth 3.5 California voters, giving more power to white America. Both Bush and Trump may have lost the popular vote, but more clout given to white voters carried the day for both candidates.[10]

The myth is that delegates to the 1787 Constitutional Convention wished to protect smaller states from too much power resting with large states via a direct democracy. The reality was not small

---

9. Pippa Norris, Ferran Martínez Coma, Alessandro Nai, and Max Grömping, *Why Elections Fail and What We Can Do About It: The Year in Elections, Mid-2016 Update* (Sydney, Australia: The Electoral Integrity Project, Department of Government and International Relations, 2016), 5.

10. Each state is allotted an elector for each member of its congressional delegation, a number providing a numerical advantage to smaller states because they have two senators. This number changes every ten years based on the new census.

vs. large states, but the problem with "the blacks." Slave states with large populations had fewer eligible voters (slaves couldn't vote); thus the Electoral College was designed as a compromise giving more clout to slave states in choosing a president. Not surprisingly, five of the first seven presidents were slave-owning Southerners. If not for the Electoral College, which, according to the U.S. Constitution, counted slave men (even at a 2/5 discount), the North, which outnumbered Southern voters, would probably have had a greater say in choosing presidents.

Gerrymandering

Gerrymandering consists of redrawing political boundaries for the sole purpose of providing a numerical advantage to one party over and against another. The best way to grasp this concept is to imagine a state with five districts and a hundred people, where sixty are registered Democrats and forty are Republicans. Political lines can be drawn to evenly split them (districts comprised of only Democrats or Republicans), sending three Democrats and two Republicans to Congress. Unfortunately, drawing districts is a bit more complex and thus susceptible to manipulation. Let's say Democrats control the state legislature after the census was conducted (every ten years); they can draw the lines so each district is comprised of twelve Democrats and eight Republicans, thus securing all five congressional districts. But let's say the Republicans end up controlling the state government. With creative boundary drawing, they can divide the Democrats into two districts comprised only of Democrats and thus secure three congressional seats for themselves (by dividing the remaining twenty Democrats among the remaining districts). Hence the minority secures a majority of congressional seats.

This latter strategy has become the norm, creating safe districts in which politicians pick their voters, eliminate competition, and ignore shifting demographic realities. Due to Republican successes in 2010 in state legislatures, they were able to draw 55 percent of congressional districts to favor Republicans. In the 2012 congressional election most voters cast their votes for Democrats, which means that the 113th Congress, if the majority ruled, should have been controlled by Democrats instead of by Republicans. But the system was rigged, as illustrated by the swing state of North Carolina, which is almost evenly divided between Republicans (suburban and rural voters) and Democrats (big cities). Even though Democrats won more votes in 2012, ten Republicans and three Democrats were elected. Before we make this solely a misuse of power by Republicans, it should be noted that Democrats are as likely to participate in this brazen grab for power, as was the case with Maryland. This is a form of electoral abuse that existed before there was a Congress. In 1788, as Virginia voted to ratify the Constitution and join the Union, Patrick Henry lobbied to draw the 5th Congressional District to force his political enemy James Madison to run against the then-powerhouse James Monroe.

Why discuss a rigged congressional electoral system when focusing on Trump? Because of a proposition being considered since 2012 in some Republican-controlled legislatures (Michigan, Ohio, Pennsylvania, Virginia, and Wisconsin) to replace the Electoral College winner-take-all system with a proportional allocation based on congressional districts. If this were the case in 2012, Obama, who won the popular vote in these states, would have lost the vast majority of the Electoral College vote. And if such a system had been in place nationwide, Mitt Romney would have been the 45th president of the United States. The Electoral College already prevents direct democracy; tying the presidential votes to gerrymandering would rig the system yet more in favor of the minority.

Voter Suppression

Voter suppression has become the singular domestic policy of the Republican Party since 2000. During the 2016 election, there were not statistically enough (white) votes to elect Trump. Thus, Republican either had to win over nonwhite voters or suppress their participation. States controlled by Republicans chose the latter, using the mythical threat of voter fraud as an excuse, even though not one of these states had documented any voter irregularities. Nevertheless, they insisted on instituting voting identification requirements, scrubbing voter rolls, and restricting voter registration procedures.

The requirement for voters to show some form of identification at the polls has increased from fourteen states in 2000 to thirty-two today. The blue state of Wisconsin, which Trump won by 27,000 votes, experienced the lowest voter turnout in the first election in which ID was required. Election officials reported the difficulty that residents of poorer, more diverse areas had in casting a vote, with many turned away for not having a proper ID. The City of Milwaukee, which counted 41,000 fewer votes than in the previous election, and where 70 percent of the state's African American population resides, is a case in point. Even states that do not have voter ID laws, like Michigan and Pennsylvania, which Trump won, turned away voters for not having proper identification.[11] And even if one attempted to get a state-issued ID to vote, as is required in Alabama, the state closed thirty-one driver's license offices in mostly low-income neighborhoods.[12]

Purging voting rolls is another strategy employed. In the battleground state of Ohio, some two million registered voters were purged, with Democrats at twice the rate as Republicans.[13] We should also consider the more than six million citizens unable to vote because of a felony conviction. One out of thirteen African Americans has lost the right to vote, even though they have paid their debt to society. In four states—Florida, Tennessee, Virginia, and Kentucky—about a quarter to a fifth of the African American community is thus disenfranchised.[14] In Florida, shortly after the Civil War, white legislatures denied voting rights to felons to dilute the voting power of blacks, a remnant of the infamous "Black Codes," which are still effective today when we consider that Trump won Florida by 119,770 votes while about 1.5 million Floridians were denied the vote because of past convictions.

---

11. Justin Elliot, "What We Don't Know: The Full Effect of Voter Suppression and Voter ID Laws," *ProPublica*, November 8, 2016.

12. Associated Press, "New Rules in These States Are Frustrating Voters," *Fortune*, November 7, 2016.

13. Andy Sullivan and Grant Smith, "Use It or Lose It: Occasional Ohio Voters May Be Shut Out in November," *Reuters*, June 2, 2016.

14. Liz Kennedy, *Voter Suppression Laws Cost Americans Their Voices at the Polls* (Washington, DC: Center for American Progress, 2016).

The 2016 election was the first in fifty years without full voter protection since the Supreme Court's 2013 decision to gut the 1965 Voting Rights Act. Chief Justice Roberts's pronouncement that "racism is over" seems naïve when we consider the results: early voting was reduced in Ohio and totally eliminated in North Carolina, negatively impacting African Americans. Also, according to the Leadership Conference Education Fund, there were 868 fewer places to cast a vote in 2016 than in past elections, contributing to hours-long lines, a time luxury the working poor cannot afford.[15] Not surprisingly, all 868 closures occurred in states once protected by the 1965 Voting Rights Act. In Arizona many voting precincts were closed in Latinx communities, as was the case in Maricopa County, which witnessed a 70-percent reduction in voting sites since the last election. Success in voter suppression was celebrated by some Republican officials, as shown in the press release on November 7 by the North Carolina Republican Party. The press release rejoiced over fewer African Americans casting early ballots than in 2012: "African American Early Voting is down 8.5% from this time in 2012. . . . As a share of Early Voters, African Americans are down 6.0%." The statement also cheered the rise of "Caucasian" voters when compared with 2012.[16]

Foreign Interference

Foreign interference is a new phenomenon witnessed during the 2016 election, which runs the risk, ironically, of making the United State the newest "banana republic." The twentieth century was defined by the rise of the U.S. Empire via "gun boat diplomacy." The full force of the U.S. military was at the disposal of U.S. corporations, specifically the United Fruit Company, to protect business interests. Any nation in "our" hemisphere attempting to claim its sovereignty to the detriment of U.S. business interests could expect

---

15. Scott Simpson et al., *The Great Poll Closure* (Washington, DC: The Leadership Conference Education Fund, 2016), 4.

16. Kami Mueller, Press Release: "NCGOP Sees Encouraging Early Voting, Obama/Clinton Coalition Tired, Fail to Resonate in North Carolina," November 7, 2016, http://us2.campaign-archive2.com.

the U.S. to send in the Marines to set up a new government. Hence the term "banana republic"—coined in 1935 to describe servile dictatorships.

Throughout the twentieth century, eleven Caribbean-basin countries experienced twenty-one U.S. military invasions and twenty-six covert CIA operations. No country was allowed to determine its leaders without the express permission of the U.S. ambassador. For banana republics to function, the foreign entity required a charismatic strongman, a *caudillo* who cooperated with their hegemonic northern neighbor in return for wealth, power, and privilege. With a veneer of patriotic nationalism sustained through fear of the Others, intellectuals, social workers, labor leaders, and anyone else who questioned authority, these strongmen appointed cronies to governmental posts and skewed the wealth of the nation toward a handful of powerful families.

The art of the con convinced the majority of people that only the *caudillo* had the answers to their poverty and problems; only he could make their country great again. All too often, the church became a willing accomplice, establishing a space within the regime in which it too could profit. True, some clergy—Catholic and Protestant—resisted, facing martyrdom for making a preferential option for the oppressed. As the century worn on, invading other countries for the purpose of "regime change" and/or poorly masked CIA interventions led to more sophisticated methodologies for the creation of banana republics. Rather than participating in military ventures, influencing elections became a preferable strategy, as was the case in Chile, where the CIA channeled $5 million to help Eduardo Frei beat socialist Salvador Allende in the 1964 presidential election.[17] Of course, when the same strategy failed and Allende won the 1970 election, he was eventually overthrown in a CIA-supported military coup.

With the dawn of the twenty-first century, we must wonder if a new banana republic is emerging in the Western Hemisphere. Trump's plea to a foreign power to hack his opponent's emails ("I

---

17. "Religion: Cope-and-Dagger Stories," *Time Magazine*, August 11, 1975.

was being sarcastic," he later claimed) and the intelligence community's belief (as of this writing) that Russian interference skewed the results of the election leave us speculating if we are becoming the newest banana republic? Is the end of an empire, any empire, signified when other foreign powers have a hand—regardless as to how miniscule—in determining its own national sovereignty?

Conclusion

The lie serves a crucial function. It maintains focus on imaginary fraudulent election rigging rather than on the actual forms. Such lies, referred to as "alternative facts," justify further rigging of the system to safeguard it from imaginary rigging. Putting America First means Putting Whites First, at least when it comes to our electoral laws and procedures. No doubt, strenuous efforts to safeguard democracy are required, not just during an election or immediately afterward, when abuses are most obvious. Election reform to fix a rigged system is required between elections. If Trump and the Republicans who now control Congress had won in fair and open elections, I would no doubt still be disappointed, while nonetheless respecting the will of the people. My call in that case would be to mobilize the "loyal opposition," rather than my current call for total and outright resistance against an illegitimate presidency. If we want to be the global paragon for the democratic process, and not fifty-second on the list as per the Electoral Integrity Project, then election probity must be a focal point in our advocacy for justice. But even if these tactics to suppress voters played a minimal role in influencing the 2016 election, nonetheless, the fact that one party passes legislation to disenfranchise people of color, the working poor, and young people (who normally vote for the opposing party) remains the textbook definition of a "rigged election."

Democracy requires election reform, which will not be initiated either by the Trump administration or the current Congress, both of whom owe their station to the current rigged system. While many options exist to combat this current threat to democracy, the sad fact is that many never even bothered to vote, probably convinced that because the system is rigged their vote would not count.

Such an opinion is partially responsible for Trump's election. But here is the good news. The 2018 mid-term election is just around the corner, and hopefully we all learned our lessons on the importance of voting.

What if you don't like the choices? Then run yourself. Those who have no desire whatsoever to engage in the electoral process must nevertheless do so as a civic duty. Scientists must run for office because we need their expertise in a legislative process that casts doubt on the reality of climate change. Latinx must have a seat in Congress as we debate and vote on immigration issues. Lesbians, gays, bisexuals, and transgender people must be in the room as their civil rights are stripped away. African Americans must participate in enacting laws to assure that black lives matter. Millennials must have a hand in creating the future of their country. True, these groups are already represented in Congress, but a critical mass is obviously missing. If indeed we are serious about resistance, then we must do more than simply sign Facebook petitions. Now, more than ever, requires those with a worldview for social justice to engage in the political process. Every office from dog catcher to U.S. senator—regardless of political party—which is not currently occupied by someone resisting the injustices of the Trump administration must have one of us challenge them. The system is rigged because most of us choose to do nothing but complain. Maybe, thanks to Trump, that might change.

CHAPTER 10

Trump and Changing Geopolitics in Asia-Pacific

KWOK PUI-LAN

Donald Trump wanted to take American foreign policy in a radically new direction in his presidential campaign. He wanted to "Make America Great Again" by bombing the Islamic State, strengthening the military, controlling the borders, building a wall between the United States and Mexico, deporting undocumented persons, banning Muslim immigration, limiting refugees, renegotiating trade agreements, and imposing stiff tariffs on Chinese and Mexican goods. Although his new administration got off to a rocky start, Trump and his strategists made plans to fulfill his campaign promises.

During his campaign, candidate Trump had repeatedly said that other countries are taking advantage of the United States and that the country is in serious trouble. "We have lost the respect of the entire world," he said. This is rather disingenuous, considering that the United States is the most powerful nation on earth. The U.S. economy is the world's largest in terms of nominal GDP, coming in at $18.5 trillion in 2017, and is approximately 24.5 percent of the gross world product. The United States spends more on its military than the next seven nations combined. In 2014, U.S. military spending was $614 billion, making it 34 percent of the world total.

Trump's campaign slogan, "Make America Great Again," can be compared to the slogan "Chinese Dream" popularized by President Xi Jinping after he became the leader of China in late 2012. The Chinese Dream signals the great rejuvenation of the Chinese nation, modernization and economic prosperity, and national glory. In the next four years, will Xi's "Chinese Dream" be realized or will Trump's "Make America Great Again" be accomplished first? The relationship between China and the United States, the two largest economies of the world, will determine the future geopolitics of Asia-Pacific, with far-reaching impact for the world.

While Trump has become a strident critic of globalization, President Xi positioned himself as a defender of globalization and free trade at the World Economic Forum in Davos, Switzerland, in January 2017. Xi said no one will emerge as a winner in a trade war, and even though some problems are linked to globalization, there is no justification to write it off altogether. Trump has chastised globalization for making the financial elite wealthy, while leaving millions of workers nothing but poverty. Soon after Trump assumed the presidency, he withdrew the United States from the Trans-Pacific Partnership (TTP) with the Pacific Rim nations and wanted to renegotiate the North American Free Trade Agreement (NAFTA). In contrast, China exerts great influences in the Regional Comprehensive Economic Partnership, a rival of TTP, which includes many of the same countries but excludes China. The rise of China in the past three decades depended to a large extent on economic globalization and free trade. China has overtaken the United States as the world's largest trading nation, and the Chinese Dream could not be realized without continued economic development.

There are sharp disagreements between the United States and China. Trump has vowed to label China a currency manipulator, to bring the allegation before the World Trade Organization, and to close the trade deficit between the United States and China by imposing punitive tariffs on Chinese imports. But these measures will mean that American consumers will have to pay more for Chinese goods. Chinese officials have warned that Beijing is ready to retaliate, and a destructive trade war will ensue. Despite Trump's rhetoric to bring back jobs to the United States, low-skilled manufacturing jobs are not coming back from China and other parts of Asia, since U.S. businesses want to keep labor costs as low as possible.

Trump caused alarm internationally when he dangled the idea of using relations with Taiwan as a bargaining chip against China on trade and other issues. Despite recognizing the People's Republic of China, the United States has kept close ties with Taiwan since 1979, including providing it with defensive weapons. The Beijing government has staunchly insisted that Taiwan is part of Chinese territory and there is only one China. The United States has pressured Taiwanese leaders not to move toward independence and upset the fragile status quo. Relations between Washington and Beijing soured after President-Elect Trump took a congratulatory phone call from Taiwan's president, Tsai Ing-wen. Commentators in Taiwan debated whether it is a curse or a blessing when Taiwan is used as a bargaining chip between two big countries. Then in February 2017, Trump reversed course and endorsed the one-China principle that has defined relations with China for four decades. Trump changed his tone because of the advice of seasoned diplomats and of mounting pressure from business people, among whom are his close advisers, who have big stakes in China.

During the Cold War era, the United States adopted a containment policy against China. Trump and his new administration have to devise new strategies to deal with the present China. Trump's relationship with President Vladimir Putin has been a thorny issue during the campaign. The Russian government was accused of cyber-hacking in an attempt to influence the election in favor of Trump. Trump wants to maintain a close relationship with Russia because he needs Russia's help in containing China and in dealing with North Korea. The Obama administration had begun negotiations with South Korea over the possible deployment of an American missile-defense system in Korea. China has objected to it because this would allow American military radar to penetrate deeper into China, compromising China's security. The future of this missile-defense system has yet to be decided because of the impeachment of South Korea's president, Park Geun-hye.

Trump caused anxiety in Japan when he said during the presidential campaign that he would pull back from the mutual defense treaty with Japan unless Tokyo agreed to pay more to reimburse the United States for defending Japanese territory. Trump was oblivious to the many demonstrations in Japan over the years against having American military bases on Japanese soil. During Prime Minister Shinzo Abe's visit to Washington in February 2017, Trump reaffirmed America's commitment to Japanese security. Japan has suffered from recession in the past decades, and it has ongoing territorial disputes with China and Russia. A close alliance with the United States is strategically important for its balance of power with China and Russia.

Commentators have offered different predictions about the changing geopolitics of Asia-Pacific in light of the rapid rise of China. The first position warns that China and the United States might fall into the Thucydides Trap and go into war. The ancient Greek historian predicted that conflicts would arise between ruling powers and the rising ones that threatened to replace them. Both President Xi and President Obama referred to the Thucydides Trap during their summit in 2015 and were quick to disavow the inevitability of war between the two countries. However, Trump's unconventional foreign-policy positions and his "Twitter diplomacy" have brought global instability and threatened China-U.S. relations. He is also surrounded by conservative advisors, such as Steve Bannon, who sat at one time on the National Security Council. Bannon is an ultraconservative ideologue who believes in the clash of civilizations between the Christian and Muslim worlds, and, while associated with the alt-right website Breitbart, also predicted that the United States would go to war with China in the South China Sea in five to ten years.

The second position suggests that the world is moving from the United States as the sole superpower to multipolar centers, and this change will be better for world peace and stability. In *The Post-American World*, Fareed Zakaria argues that what we are seeing is not the United States in decline but rather the rise of everyone else.[1] But is the United States willing to adjust to this new global reality and what will be the relationship among the multipolar centers? Will the rest of the world be ruled under the hegemony of the

---

1. Fareed Zakaria, *The Post-American World: Release 2.0* (New York: Norton, 2012).

United States, Russia, and China? It is clear from Trump's nationalist and populist rhetoric that he wants to put "America first" and does not want to share power. He is a demagogue who appeals to white males who think that the United States has lost its global command and must regain control. According to election exit polls, more than two-thirds of noncollege educated white men and 53 percent of college educated white men voted for Donald Trump. Contrary to expectation, Trump has not shown that he would pivot to the center after the election to widen his support. Instead, his early executive orders and policies showed his intention to appease his base, which supports his agenda of putting "American first."

The third position argues that a stable and prosperous China will be beneficial to the global economy. As the economies of the United States and China are so much interconnected, direct confrontations between the two countries will hurt both. Even though China and the United States have different positions over trade, security, and the South China Sea, they will find ways to resolve differences to avoid a collision. This has been the public position of Chinese leaders. In the United States, the conservative think tanks want to see a stronger American military presence in Asia to balance the rise of China, but do not advocate for war or military conflict. It remains to be seen whether China and the United States can find ways to cooperate with each other, given that both countries face tremendous challenges. China's economy has become stagnant, and Chinese labor is no longer cheap, compared to other Southeast Asian countries. The U.S. national debt has climbed to nearly $20 trillion, and it will further increase if Trump wants to lower taxes but increase expenditures on infrastructure. Both countries will need to compete for resources and markets in order to sustain economic growth. The gap between the rich and the poor has widened enormously in both countries, causing unrest and periodic eruptions of protests.

Resistance in the Trump era must take into consideration changing geopolitics in Asia-Pacific and in the rest of the world. The rise of Trump is part of a strong populist and anti-establishment movement sweeping across the United Kingdom, France, Italy, and other European countries. From a postcolonial perspective, the current political ethos can be seen as a form of colonial nostalgia, as many want to return to past glory and national pride. Many people in Europe and the United States still desire to uphold white hegemony and domination. They are against Islam and against refugees and immigrants, whom they regard as threats to their ways of life. They cannot see their complicity in creating and maintaining a globally unjust system that forces so many people to leave their homelands. There are also strong nationalistic sentiments and conservative voices in China and Japan. The slogan "Chinese Dream" has enormous appeal because China has suffered humiliation under Western powers and Japan in the past. Many want to see the sleeping giant rise again and return to glory. Although Chinese leaders have said that the rise of China is a peaceful one and China does not want to exert hegemony, many fear that China is on the road to compete with the United States as the world's superpower.

In order to create a global resistance movement, we cannot simply denounce those who support populist movements without trying to understand their fear, anger, and feeling of loss. Many of them have not benefited from globalization and feel left behind in the neoliberal economy. They can be swayed by politicians like Trump who claim to represent their interests. We have to conscientize people about the macrosocial and political forces that are shaping the world in order to become global citizens. We must offer an alternative way to imagine the future of the world that is not defined by narrow national interests and remind people of the dangers of imperial impulses, past and present.

After Trump's election, Mark Lilla of Columbia University warned that we must move beyond identity politics and diversity issues and engage in conversations about class, war, political economy, and the common good.[2] It is time that we focus not only on race, gender, class, and sexuality issues in the United States, but also the ways these issues have morphed and are being reconfigured by changing global politics. There needs to be more dialogue between American and Chinese people, especially among people in the grassroots movements, in order to strengthen the

---

2. Mark Lilla, "The End of Identity Liberalism," *New York Times*, November 18, 2016.

international civil society and foster peace and solidarity across the Pacific.

Resistance movements in our time must be organized locally and globally. The workers who lose their jobs in the U.S. Midwest and the Chinese workers who provide cheap labor for American companies are both exploited by the transnational capitalist class. Instead of pitting themselves against each other, they have to organize and unite to demand a more responsible and accountable global economic system. While the transnational capitalist class can easily move capital, labor, and resources across national borders, workers have yet to find ways to organize transnationally to protect their interests. New forms of creative resistance must be sought in our interconnected world. Global networks of grassroots movements can exchange information, support one another, and share strategies and tactics in the struggles. One recent example is the Women's March after Trump's inauguration, an idea first shared in social media and spread to different cities in the United States and around the world.

Churches and faith communities have important roles to play in the resistance movements. Many churches belong to global organizations and networks that can facilitate the sharing of information and resources. Through education and prophetic witness, they can help nurture a democratic culture that respects human dignity, encourages participation, and brings different voices into dialogue. Inspired by Jesus' teaching to care for the least among us, churches can provide support for the vulnerable in society. Many churches in the United States have already declared that they would provide sanctuary to undocumented persons who may be deported under orders from Trump's administration.

Churches and faith communities need to develop a spirituality of resistance for the long haul. Trump and his strategists will implement conservative policies that will have an impact on the United States and the world for a long time to come. As inspiration for our resistance, we have to recover Jesus' revolutionary teaching and ministry. As a colonized Jewish person living in the Roman Empire, he dared to rise up against the most powerful empire the world had seen in his time. When we feel discouraged and even despair, we can draw courage from those faithful witnesses who have gone before us. Chinese Christians, who have survived the suppression of the Cultural Revolution and who will remember how the churches were all closed down, can teach us much about faithfulness and perseverance during turbulent times.

A spirituality of resistance for our time is not based on self or national interest, but on God's self-giving love for creation. It is expressed by countless individuals who fight the good fight and dare to hope. The Letter to the Hebrews says, "Faith is the assurance of things hoped for, the conviction of things not seen" (11:1). In a time of political uncertainty and global anxiety, we need to cultivate faithfulness and hopefulness for the long road ahead, knowing that the Spirit is with us and among us, guiding us to truth, justice, and reconciliation.

CHAPTER 11

Who Is My Neighbor?
Catholics and the Trump Administration

MIGUEL DÍAZ

Introduction

In his first trip outside of Rome, Pope Francis chose the island of Lampedusa to preside at a Mass for immigrants. His homily focused on what has become the central theme of his papacy, namely, the rejection of human indifference. Similar to our Ellis Island, the island of Lampedusa in southern Italy is where African immigrants first enter the European Union after fleeing from various sociopolitical, economic, and environmental hardships. Commenting on the book of Genesis, the pope's homily offers a theological reading of the human condition after the fall of Adam and Eve and attributes to this postlapsarian condition the proclivity of human beings to turn away from their neighbors in love.[1] But love, as the pope's homily clearly suggests, is not just a private and individual human act. Because God created human beings as communal beings, the love of one's neighbor must necessarily embrace social and political actions.[2] Indeed, as a consequence of being political creatures

---

1. See Pope Francis, "Visit to Lampedusa: Homily of Holy Father Francis," July 8, 2013, http://w2.vatican.va.

2. On the sociopolitical implications of love of neighbor, see Miguel H. Díaz, "On Loving Strangers: Encountering the Mystery of God in the Face

(as Aristotle in his *Politics* defined humans), Christian love must be expressed through political agendas, policies, and actions that make a difference for persons and the earth they inhabit, especially the poor and the marginalized.

Three questions frame Pope Francis's homily: (1) Where are you, Adam? (2) Where is your brother? and (3) Who among us has wept for these things and things like this (referring to the tragedy of migrants)? These questions focus on one's place in the world, the place of one's neighbor in creation, and the preferential option for those who suffer. The pope argues that Adam's disorientation or "loss of place in creation" prevents him from understanding and living in right relationship with self and with others.

Providing a timely interpretation of original sin, Pope Francis associates dislocation and disorientation with the experience that comes with failure to live in right relationship with God and neighbor. As a consequence of sin, persons fail to recognize their God-given orientation toward their neighbors. More significantly, in this state of disorientation humans put themselves first and above others, creating a false sense of human greatness and power. "The dream of being powerful, of being as great as God," the pope warns, "even of being God, leads to a chain of errors that is a chain of death, leads to shedding the blood of the brother!"

Drawing from Spanish literature, Pope Francis then turns in his homily to one of Lope de Vega's (1562–1635) famous plays, *Fuente Ovejuna*. This play, which is based on a historical incident, tells the story of the inhabitants of the city of Fuente Ovejuna who killed the governor because he was a tyrant. The challenge presented by the citizens of this city is that they committed this crime in such a way that no one knew who did it, nor did anyone claim responsibility for the action. Pope Francis decries such actions and offers what has become his signature teaching, namely, the globalization of human

---

of Migrants," *Word & World* 29, no. 3 (2009): 234–42; and Díaz, *On Being Human: U.S. Hispanic and Rahnerian Perspectives* (Maryknoll, NY: Orbis Books, 2001), 101–5 and 130–40. On the social nature of human persons, see Pontifical Council for Justice and Peace, *Compendium of the Social Teaching of the Church* (Rome: Libreria Editrice Vaticana, 204), 82–84.

indifference: "In this world of globalization we have fallen into a globalization of indifference. We are accustomed to the suffering of others, it doesn't concern us, it's none of our business." Yet this human indifference—the failure to make a difference in the lives of the most vulnerable—speaks to the blood that globally covers human hands.

My thesis in this chapter is as follows: President Donald Trump's political vision threatens life in various forms and stages (with respect to particular human communities and with respect to care of our planet). While his excessive capitalistic focus on economic competition and profit promotes a false and reductionist understanding of what it means to be human (*homo economicus*), his vision to put "America First" is politically dangerous because it undermines global interdependence and the kind of national and international relationships needed to sustain various forms of creaturely and communal life in our planet. As an alternative to Mr. Trump's economic reductionism and national isolationism, Christian tradition offers an "economic" order that mirrors God's triune self-sharing in salvation history.[3] At the heart of this economic order is God's desire for human persons (and by extension the communities and nations they cocreate) to exist *for* and *from* each other. Denouncing human indifference and loving's one's neighbor, especially the marginalized neighbor, are essential to human participation in, sharing, and reflection of divine life.

This chapter begins by first taking up the question of greatness. Contrasting perspectives from the tweeting pope and the tweeting president will ground my discussion. Second, the chapter discusses the faith-filled orientation to love our marginalized neighbors as a way to advance, socially and politically, America's greatness.

---

3. The word economy (Gk. *oikonomia*) "had the purely secular meaning of administering and managing goods or a household, or overseeing an office according to some plan or design." The Christian theological tradition builds on this ancient concept but relates it to the way God orders worldly realities and history in accordance with God's communal and inclusive relational nature as Father, Son, and Spirit. See Catherine Mowry LaCugna, *God for Us: The Trinity and Christian Life* (New York: HarperCollins, 1973), 24.

Third, the chapter concludes with the question: "Who is forgotten in Mr. Trump's America?" The purpose of this chapter is to invite Catholics to engage one another around difficult issues facing our nation from the perspective of Christian faith, to seek truth at all times, and to work for just social transformation. As Catholics we have an ethical obligation to open our hearts and minds to discern a faith that does justice in the world, especially by challenging our leaders to enact inclusive and compassionate political policies.

Defining the Greatness of a Nation: Framing Our Catholic Response

How might Christian tradition challenge Catholic support for President Trump? Catholics, especially white Catholics, voted overwhelmingly for Mr. Trump's nationalism and his campaign promises "To Make America Great Again" and "To Put America First."[4] To explore this challenge, I want to turn to the words of the tweetable pope.[5] The president is not the only world leader to take up tweeting as a way to impact public opinion. Pope Francis has long used tweets to communicate deeply held Christian values. Contrary to many of the president's tweets, which often stir controversy, fail to communicate truth, and undermine communal relationships, the pope's tweets offer community-building insights rooted in gospel truths. Consider a tweet Pope Francis sent on July 25, 2013. In this tweet @Pontifex echoes the words of Mahatma Gandhi: "The measure of the greatness of a society is found in the way it treats those most in need, those who have nothing apart from their poverty." As the tweet succinctly summarizes, for Pope Francis, what defines the greatness of any society or nation

---

4. According to Pew research "White Catholics supported Trump over Clinton by a wide, 23-point margin (60% to 37%), rivaling Romney's 19-point victory among those in this group. Trump's strong support among white Catholics propelled him to a 7-point edge among Catholics overall (52% to 45%) despite the fact that Hispanic Catholics backed Clinton over Trump by a 41-point margin (67% to 26%)." See http://www.pewresearch.org.

5. Michael J. O'Loughlin, *The Tweetable Pope: A Spiritual Revolution in 140 Characters* (New York: HarperCollins, 2015).

does not depend on economic or military successes but rather on whether nations embrace the preferential option for the marginalized (Matthew 25:31-46).

Speaking truth matters. Words do matter, even when uttered in 140-character tweets. Catholics may want to consider the tweets of a pope over those of a president on matters related to what kind of persons, communities, and policies to prioritize in efforts to deepen the greatness of our nation. The tweets of Pope Francis synthesize gospel truths. And the gospel is about life, especially the life of the poor and marginalized. The gospel does not present this truth as an "alternative fact." The gospel is not, as some would have us think, a gospel of prosperity where the wealthy, powerful, and privileged find preferential favor with God. The gospel relates God's greatness to God's compassion for the marginalized. The God of Jesus Christ is the God who stands in solidarity with the lowly, raises them in fulfillment of ancient covenantal promises and brings down the mighty from their thrones (Luke 1:46-55).

Faith-Filled Orientation: Loving Our Neighbors

Keeping true to his campaign promises to protect our border and rid the country of undocumented immigrants, Mr. Trump has set in place several policies that put millions of families at risk within and outside our national borders. Through executive orders and immigration raids, his administration seeks to significantly regulate and limit immigration and increase deportations to Latin America. His ban on Muslim refugees from seven countries (Iraq, Syria, Iran, Libya, Somalia, Sudan, and Yemen) was met with sharp criticism and lawsuits. The fact is that within a short period after his inauguration, Mr. Trump began to build "walls" of separation between neighbors within and beyond our national borders. The country is already paying a heavy human cost as a result of uncertainty and fragility in the realm of national and international relationships. Paradoxically, this isolationism and exaggerated nationalism resembles the kind of politics that has triggered for many nations in history social unrest and the migration from their homelands. As *Erga migrantes caritas Christi*, the 2004 Pontifical Council's document on the pastoral care of migrant and itinerant people, argues: "The roots of the phenomenon [of migration] can also be traced back to exaggerated nationalism and, in many countries, even to hatred and systematic or violent exclusion of ethnic or religious minorities from society."[6]

The protection of our borders and the deportation of the undocumented will remain one of the most important issues our country faces under this administration. Catholics must critically engage this issue at schools, parishes, and universities. Addressing this issue presents an opportunity not only for political action in defense of the voiceless, but also offers an invitation to concretely enact Christian faith. As Catholic social teaching underscores, "In migrants the Church has always contemplated the image of Christ who said, "I was a stranger and you made me welcome" (Matthew 25:35). Their condition is, therefore, a challenge to the faith and love of believers, who are called on to heal the evils caused by migration and discover the plan God pursues through it even when caused by obvious injustices."[7]

The strangers, or to be more precise, those that have been estranged in our country, are not only Muslim refugees or undocumented immigrants. These strangers are also African Americans, Asian Americans, Jews, and members of the LGBTQI community who have been profiled or have become victims of increasing hate crimes.[8] A fear of others and their distinct humanity perpetuates these unjust actions. Fear of human difference begets human indifference. And indifference, as Pope Francis rightly suggests, can be understood theologically and not just sociologically. Understood from a Christian theological perspective, human rejection and indifference toward our neighbors reflect the postlapsarian state of humanity that prevents persons from living in right and just relationships with one another (communion in the image of God). As contemporary Orthodox theologian John Zizioulas argues, the

---

6. *Erga migrantes caritas Christi*, 1.

7. Ibid., 12.

8. See "Post-Election Spate of Hate Crimes Worse Than Post-9/11, Experts Say," *USA Today*, http://www.usatoday.com, November 12, 2016.

pathological rejection of others "is in fact nothing but the fear of the different; we all want somehow to project into the other the model of own selves, which shows how deeply rooted in our existence the fear of the other is."[9] "Communion with the other is not spontaneous; it is built upon fences which protect us from the dangers implicit in the other's presence."[10]

Who Is Forgotten in Mr. Trump's America?

In his inaugural speech, President Trump underscored the need to return power to the people and vowed that "The forgotten men and women will be forgotten no more." Surely, when it comes to all working families in rural or urban America that have experienced economic hardships as a result of what Pope Francis has characterized as trickle-down, exclusionary, and unequal economies that kill,[11] Catholics must challenge, repeal, and replace such economic policies. The question, however, is whether Mr. Trump's political actions will justly include the already forgotten or in effect unjustly add other communities to the list of the forgotten (e.g., dropping health insurance for thousands). Moreover, Catholics across the political spectrum have plenty of reasons to be alarmed now that climate change denial has come to be part of the Washington establishment because environmental exploitation and degradation threaten all forms of life, and not just life in the womb.[12] Simply put, insuring the health of our neighbors (conceived of as more than just medical insurance) and insuring the health of our planet go hand in hand. As Catholics we must embrace political actions that advance this integral ecology of life.

Some of the words of President Trump and officials connected with his administration have at times perpetuated an atmosphere of fear and rejection of human differences with respect to race, ethnicity, religious affiliation, physical ability, gender, sexual orienta-

---

9. John Zizioulas, *Communion and Otherness* (London: T&T Clark, 2006), 2.

10. Ibid., 1.

11. *Evangelii gaudium*, 53–54.

12. See Pope Francis, *Laudato si'*.

tion, and immigration status. Most concerning is the support he has received from members of the alt-right movement. Within this context, the promise to "Make America Great Again" has become for far too many the promise to make America white, racist, sexist, and heterosexist again. Those who have experienced much marginalization in the past may now run the risk of being forgotten. Christian hope affirms, however, that God will not forget to hear their cry (Psalm 34). The hope-filled future is already here through faith in the crucified and risen Christ. Christian hope propels men and women of faith to hear the cry of the poor and work to build God's beloved community.

The question of forgetting the "poor" in our land and neglecting to care for our impoverished earth leads me to conclude this chapter with questions of power: "Who is ostracized based on arbitrary criteria determining the norm? Who is privileged and who is excluded when a particular norm is assumed as common? Who is silenced? Who loses agency? Who are the gatekeepers controlling access?"[13] Cultivating the dangerous memory of the crucified, standing in solidarity with the marginalized, and organizing against threats to all forms of life define the faith-filled orientation that will ensure greatness in *Nuestra América*.[14] From the perspective of Christian faith, we practice the love of neighbors, especially love of our marginalized neighbors, because it enables an authentic expression of power and participation in God's life.

---

13. Carmen Nanko-Fernández, *Theologizing en Espanglish* (Maryknoll, NY: Orbis Books, 2010), 19–20.

14. I use José Martí's (1853–95) well-known concept of *Nuestra América* to invite the reader to consider a more inclusive political vision of our country. In this sense, promoting the greatness of "America" would entail compassionate and just relationships not merely among the diverse and particular peoples that comprise these United States, but also with the God-given people who live beyond our national borders.

CHAPTER 12

Why Trump, and What Next?
An (Ex-)Evangelical Response

DAVID P. GUSHEE

Prelude: What White Evangelicals Just Did, in Violation of Their Own Proclaimed Values

No group of American voters bears more responsibility for the election of Donald J. Trump as the forty-fifth president of the United States than do white evangelicals. Their 81 percent vote on his behalf far exceeded his share of support in any other religious community. Given our political divisions, an 81 percent vote can only be described as overwhelming, something about as close to a consensus as one ever sees in American politics. Donald Trump received a higher share of the white evangelical vote than any Republican candidate since the dawn of the Christian Right—and therefore since 1978–79, since the emergence of white evangelicals as a mobilized voting bloc in the Republican coalition. More than Ronald Reagan. More than George W. Bush. More than Mitt Romney. In terms of the Republican/evangelical strategy of moving white evangelicals decisively into the Republican camp and turning them out to vote in large numbers in presidential elections, the election of Donald Trump can only be described as the greatest success ever achieved.

Let us ponder for just a moment five propositions about the contradiction between the character and behavior of now-President Trump and what were once believed to be evangelical values:

(1) The consensus white evangelical vote was for a candidate married three times and unfaithful in marriage, only nominally Christian, and known for his vulgarity and crude public talk about sex (not to mention the later-discovered bragging about sexual assault, along with the dozen accusations from specific women)—all of which explicitly and obviously violates the proclaimed standards of Christian commitment and personal morality cherished by white evangelical Christians.

(2) The consensus white evangelical vote was for a candidate whose character has revealed obvious flaws such as lack of self-control, lack of truthfulness, and lack of the most basic verbal discipline, and whose entire business career has been embroiled in false promises, ethics questions, and lawsuits, obviously violating proclaimed evangelical standards of personal and business integrity.

(3) The consensus white evangelical vote was for a candidate who launched his campaign with an attack on the character of Mexican immigrants, who prelaunched his campaign by leading the "birther" movement against Barack Obama's legitimacy as president, who during his campaign told lies about American Muslim responses to 9/11 and at one time called for a ban on their immigration, and then once president wrote an ill-conceived executive order partially blockading Muslim refugee and immigrant entry into the United States—violating what ought to be obvious standards of Christian morality related to treating all persons with dignity, welcoming the stranger with hospitality, and attending especially to those who are most vulnerable.

(4) The consensus white evangelical vote was for a candidate who created rally environments latent with mob violence and hate speech, who declared both the polls and the vote rigged and fraudulent, and who threatened to create a constitutional crisis by refusing to accept the results of the election if he lost—raising the question of what he will do if the votes go against him in 2020, while he is the sitting president. All of which violates obvious standards of Christian morality related to civility, violence, and support for democratic norms.

(5) The consensus white evangelical vote was for a candidate who articulated the most extreme form of nationalism seen at the presidential level in memory, who insulted many U.S. allies, scoffed at international norms and institutions, and spoke favorably about the use of torture. All of which violates what ought to be obvious standards of Christian morality.

In my view, the consensus white evangelical vote for Donald Trump has shattered whatever survived of the moral witness of white evangelicals to American culture and to the world. It also has driven many white evangelicals into the ex-evangelical camp. This includes me, though admittedly I was already hanging on by a thread. The remainder of this essay seeks to discern why 81 percent of white evangelicals voted as they did, and how those of us who dissent must now respond.

Why Trump?

It must be remembered—perhaps with astonishment—that the story does not begin when the two plausible choices were Donald Trump and Hillary Clinton. It begins when Donald Trump was one of seventeen candidates on the Republican side. Republican primary voters, including a disproportionately large and committed white evangelical bloc, by their own choices consistently selected Trump over alternatives such as Mike Huckabee, Rick Santorum, Ben Carson, Carly Fiorina, Marco Rubio, Ted Cruz, John Kasich, Rand Paul, and Jeb Bush. Every one of the other sixteen GOP candidates would have offered policy prescriptions that people like me and most readers of this book would have disliked. But not one of them could be described in the five propositions outlined above. Donald Trump stood in uniquely flagrant violation of what had once been core evangelical commitments related to the faith, character, and values of their preferred presidential candidates. This demands at least an attempt at an explanation.

Specialists in political science and voting behavior will eventually be able to put numbers to what this essay can only offer as surmises based on almost forty years of living and working among white evangelicals. But what follows are my top ten surmises as to what attracted white evangelical Christians to Donald Trump. I will arrange these claims from the least to the most controversial.

(1) White evangelicals were attracted to the security promises of Donald Trump.

Donald Trump promised to protect U.S. borders from unlawful immigrants and to protect U.S. citizens from terrorist attacks. The latter was probably more salient for more voters, but a minority had become convinced of the [Fox News] narrative that "illegals" were running rampant and committing all kinds of heinous crimes. And even though the United States has been hit by fewer mass terror attacks than have been seen in Europe in the last few years, we have seen the news coverage, and it has indeed been frightening. Voting their security fears, many white evangelicals found Donald Trump a more persuasive defender of their lives and their families than his competitors either during the primaries or in the general election.

(2) White evangelicals were attracted to the economic promises of Donald Trump.

Here I speak especially of working-class and downwardly mobile white evangelicals, and notably small-town, rural, and exurban evangelicals. (It must also be noted that the difference between white evangelicals and fundamentalists fades to invisibility in many parts of the United States, but especially in these areas.) Donald Trump's promises to restore American jobs, to negotiate tougher trade deals, and to shame American companies taking jobs to other countries were very appealing to many who have faced tough economic times.

(3) White evangelicals were attracted to the nationalism of Donald Trump.

Many American evangelicals (and fundamentalists) have been schooled in a very deep "God and country" conflation. Long after many Americans had either abandoned patriotism, abandoned religion, or both, millions of evangelicals are both deeply patriotic and deeply religious, and have not been taught any real differentiation between the two. I think of the thousands of Christian schools in which children each morning say the Pledge of Allegiance to the

American flag and the Pledge of Allegiance to the Christian flag almost in one breath. Donald Trump strikes nationalist rather than globalist notes, promises to put "America First," and conflates God and country. This was preferable to the alternative, for many evangelicals.

(4) White evangelicals were attracted to the Christian tribalism of Donald Trump.

Donald Trump often sent signals that the polite multifaith inclusivity that had prevailed under Barack Obama and would undoubtedly have continued under Hillary Clinton would be supplanted by a privileging of Christianity—America's historically dominant religion and still the stated religious belief of the strong majority of Americans. Those shopkeepers on Fifth Avenue would once again display signs saying "Merry Christmas" rather than Happy Holidays, if Donald Trump had anything to do with it. In various ways, Mr. Trump communicated that Christianity would be restored to its privileged place in the American public square. One specific aspect of this would be that Christian moral sensibilities and religious liberty concerns would be protected. An ironic aspect of these promises, of course, is that President Trump has only practiced the most nominal Christianity himself.

(5) White evangelicals were attracted to the promises of Donald Trump related to the Supreme Court.

One of the most enduring aspects of the Christian Right/GOP alliance since the late 1970s has been the GOP promise that its elected presidents would only nominate Supreme Court candidates who could be counted upon to overturn *Roe v. Wade*—and in other ways give conservative Christians what they seek from the Supreme Court. Donald Trump made perfectly clear that he would maintain this bargain. Evangelicals voted accordingly.

(6) White evangelicals were attracted to the exaggerated masculinity of Donald Trump.

Millions of fundamentalists and evangelicals, and not only white versions of the same, believe that God's will, as taught in the

Bible, is that men should lead in homes, churches, and society. The advances of feminism have softened this patriarchalism to a profound extent, but male leadership remains doctrine in many thousands of churches. It's not just maleness, it's also masculinity that matters. One aspect of modern feminism has been to challenge historic gender roles and behavioral expectations. This has only intensified with current theories suggesting that gender itself is entirely socially constructed and has no real biological, natural, or certainly not divinely established, basis. Donald Trump won among Republican candidates because he exuded a certain hyper-masculine toughness, which included belittling other candidates who couldn't quite measure up. Pun intended. And then, in the general election, when it was Donald Trump vs. Hillary Clinton, the potential first woman president, the game was up.

*(7) White evangelicals were attracted to the authoritarianism of
Donald Trump.*

Many evangelicals run their families and their churches in an authoritarian rather than democratic way. I think of the thousands of churches founded by one man and controlled by that one man with little oversight. I think of the continued popularity of Reformed church models, in which an all-male elder board functions as a kind of spiritual oligarchy. Then, of course, there are the millions of families run by the husband/father/patriarch according to the will of the Heavenly Father. While there are also millions of Christian families and churches that are governed as democracies, it is fair to say that the majority of churches in America (Catholic, Protestant, and Eastern Orthodox) are not democracies. It is my surmise that Donald Trump's tendency toward authoritarianism resonates deeply with many.

*(8) White evangelicals were attracted to the wealth, glitz, and
celebrity of Donald Trump.*

I speak here not just of those churches that have explicitly embraced the "prosperity" or "health and wealth" gospel, in which preachers teach that God rewards the faithful with worldly success. I want to broaden out to the idea that especially the massive megachurch movement within evangelicalism and fundamentalism bears a striking resemblance in many ways to the business and political model offered by Donald Trump. Everything revolves around an attractive central (male) figure, who exudes power, wealth, and success, and is usually accompanied by an equally beautiful wife and children. Donald Trump fit that paradigm.

(9) White evangelicals were attracted to the attacks on "political correctness" by Donald Trump.

White evangelicals often feel embattled and belittled by the dominant powers of American culture—Hollywood, New York, Boston; CNN, *New York Times*, and Professor So-and-So at State U. Hollywood tells us who we are supposed to want to be, the *Times* tells us what we are supposed to count as news, and Professor So-and-So tells us what counts as truth. The fact that most of the time these authorities offer views that totally contradict those of white evangelicals is not lost on the latter. Donald Trump is not a white evangelical, but his bristling attack on "political correctness" spoke profoundly to shared resentments.

(10) White evangelicals were attracted to the thinly veiled white racism of Donald Trump.

This claim will of course be the most disputed. The vast majority of white evangelicals do not believe that they hold racially prejudiced beliefs or act in racist ways. Evangelical individualism also makes it difficult for white evangelicals to accept the reality of structural or systemic racism.

The space for this essay is too short to litigate these complex issues, so let me make a quite circumscribed claim. Many American voters, including millions of Christians, believed that the total body of statements made by Donald Trump during his public career and especially the campaign, related to, for example, Mexicans, blacks, and Muslims, itself morally disqualified him from the office of president. Those who voted for Mr. Trump obviously did not agree. This at least makes them complicit with what he said and will now do in relation to race.

What Do We Now Do?

Some of us have begun to face the fact that white evangelicalism is no longer our religious community, even if it is our religious heritage. Perhaps the first step is to acknowledge the conquest of our former tribe of white Christians first by the Republican Party itself and then by this particularly noxious version of Republicanism. We must grieve, deeply. Perhaps we are now to be called postevangelicals, or ex-evangelicals, or something else. Whatever we call ourselves, it is time to move on.

We postevangelicals must then find one another and find others of like mind for shared articulations of dissent and actions of resistance. The early days of the Trump administration certainly provide a target-rich environment for dissent. Different ones of us will "feel called," in evangelical parlance, to different struggles. For some, it might be immigration/refugee issues. For others, it might be peacemaking and international relations issues. For a different group, it might be climate issues. For still others, it might be protecting advances in health-care coverage under the Affordable Care Act. Each individual has limited bandwidth, but everyone can do their part. Ultimately, we must move into a posture of radical solidarity with those who are most threatened by the new political context in which we find ourselves. We ourselves feel disempowered and afraid, but our disempowerment and fear pales in comparison to that of many, many others. Whatever privilege and power we might have, we must invest for others. We leave our morally bankrupt religious tribe. Find new community. State our clear dissent and give good reasons for it. Practice resistance where we can. Stand in solidarity with the oppressed. This is what we do now. At least, it is a start.

CHAPTER 13

American Political Theology in a Post Age
A Perpetual Foreigner and Pentecostal Stance

AMOS YONG

On November 9, 2016, Americans woke up to the realization that we were living in the twilight of the post-age.[1] By the latter designation I am referring to our sense that in the last generation or so we have been inhabiting a postmodern, postcolonial, and even post-Christian time in history. This is a world after the hegemony of the Enlightenment, one in which confidence in the European mode of rationality had been exposed by the world wars of the twentieth century; it is a time following the dismantling of the colonial enterprise, one in which Western authority has been displaced by majority-world voices and powers; it has featured the dissolution of Christendom, one accompanied by the emergence of world religious rivals to the Christian faith and the marginalization of Chris-

---

1. My use of "twilight" here is inspired by Christopher M. Driscoll, *White Lies: Race and Uncertainty in the Twilight of American Religion* (New York: Routledge, 2015), although as will become clear, what he named as the twilight of white American religion when his book was published has been followed by the dawning one year later of a new Bannon-Trump white nationalist "religiosity" and fervor.

tian control of the public square.[2] Our post discourse was indicative of what was waning, even if we were not quite sure what was coming. Yet amid these postmodern, postcolonial, and post-Christian waves, European and American whites were nostalgic about the bygone days and wondering if the former glory might be regained.

The election of Donald Trump, not to mention the Brexit vote earlier last year, indicated that developments during these last few decades had galvanized those who had been beneficiaries of the prior status quo. If white Americans have seen their dominance erode through migration (particularly after 1965), their prerogatives challenged by the emergence of civil rights for nonwhites, and their values contested by the increasingly pervasive multicultural and multireligious public square, the Bannon-Trump ideology and rhetoric sparked the possibility of ushering forward the past. The election of Barack Obama in 2008 may have been the culmination of these convergences during the previous period, but what is now clear is that two terms of his presidency witnessed instead the intensification of racial strife rather than the passage of Americans into a post-racist era.[3] However Obama's legacy is assessed in the longer run, the rise of Trump suggests that white Americans had been incited to respond to these trends that they perceived were embodied in the nation's first black president and extended in his policies. If the Obama administration deepened the anxiety of white America, Trump detonated its explosion (or, implosion,

---

2. Amos Yong, "The Missiology of Jamestown: 1607–2007 and Beyond—Toward a Postcolonial Theology of Mission in North America," in *Remembering Jamestown: Hard Questions about Christian Mission*, ed. Amos Yong and Barbara Brown Zikmund (Eugene, OR: Pickwick Publications, 2010), 157–67, and Amos Yong, "The Church and Mission Theology in a Post-Constantinian Era: Soundings from the Anglo-American Frontier," in *A New Day: Essays on World Christianity in Honor of Lamin Sanneh*, ed. Akintunde E. Akinade (New York: Peter Lang, 2010), 49–61.

3. See Amos Yong, "Race and Racialization in a Post-Racist Evangelicalism: A View from Asian America," in *Aliens in the Promised Land: Why Minority Leadership Is Overlooked in White Christian Churches and Institutions*, ed. Anthony B. Bradley (Phillipsburg, NJ: P&R Publishing Company, 2013), 45–58 and 216–20.

depending on how one might understand what is happening in the country today).

What about Asian Americans in the wake of Trump? At first glance, it would seem that the prognosis is rather bleak. I am referring not only to the fact of their relatively miniscule demographic but more so to their stereotypical model minority status. To be sure, the model minority attribution is both inaccurate and unfair for many reasons, but let's follow the analysis for a moment in order to better appreciate the uphill battle ahead. What is undeniable about what *model minority* names is that Asian success, relatively speaking, has come exactly in and through Asian assimilation into the dominant culture. Asian academics like myself, for instance, have attained the desired promotions indeed through performance according to the expectations and standards of white academia.

This issue of model minority "success" is evident especially in the evangelical world. Asian Americans, particularly those from East Asia of the Pacific Rim, have gravitated to evangelical forms of Christianity on the American frontier. Many have formed conservative Protestant communities, partly following the rationale that North American evangelical conservatism is consistent with Confucian and related traditionalisms that they brought as immigrants. Hence Asian Americans have attended evangelical seminaries by the droves, and their alumni have established congregations and churches in that mold. My point is that Asian Americans have been "good" evangelicals, perhaps even better evangelicals than whites. In that respect, Asian Americans have been accepted within the evangelical scene surely because they have modeled conservative theological beliefs and practices even as "colored" minorities.[4] They have played by the rules of the evangelical establishment and effectively integrated their Confucian conservatism into the dominant white American culture.

If this is correct, then, it would seem that there is little hope that Asian Americans can be a source of gospel prophetism in the age of Trump. If 80 percent of white evangelicals who voted sup-

---

4. I expand on this in my essay, "Asian American Historicity: The Problem and Promise of Evangelical Theology," *SANACS Journal* [*Society of Asian North American Christian Studies Journal*] 4 (2012–2013): 29–48.

ported the sitting president, then Asian American model minority sensibilities will generate a strong gravitational pull to adapt to that milieu and its concomitant values, like it or not. That would mean that even if Asian Americans might be anxious about anti-migration sentiments of white nationalists (to name just one of many objectionable elements of Trump's platform when considered from a biblical perspective), their survival and get-ahead-in-life instincts nevertheless will prompt conformity to white evangelicalism. Asian American minorities will hence be motivated, perhaps subconsciously, to mimic white evangelical thinking and practices: these model minorities will thereby continue to emulate the majority white evangelical subculture.

Is there any other way forward for the Asian American evangelical community? Part of the problem is that their deferential character is hesitant about developing their own voice that might be distinctive from, much less contrastive against, the white evangelical church. Here perhaps Asian American evangelical believers might take some cues from their African American and Hispanic American counterparts. I suggest that these other voices have been more vigorous and less likely to parrot the white evangelical mantras precisely because they have found biblical resources that embolden their witness. Hispanic American evangelicals, for instance, have drawn some energy from their compatriots in the Southern Hemisphere, in particular from Latin American liberation theology's biblical motif of God's preferential option for the poor.[5] Relatedly but yet along a discrete course, African Americans have found the exodus narrative to be significant for their own history.[6] It is not that these scriptural notions belong uniquely to Hispanic and African American evangelicals, but there is a sense in which their cries for justice have been drawn to and rooted deeply in the biblical traditions so that what might otherwise be heard as

---

5. E.g., João B. Chaves, *Evangelicals and Liberation Revisited: An Inquiry into the Possibility of an Evangelical-Liberationist Theology* (Eugene, OR: Wipf & Stock, 2013).

6. E.g., Herbert Robinson Marbury, *Pillars of Cloud and Fire: The Politics of Exodus in African American Biblical Interpretation* (New York: New York University Press, 2015).

just another case of identity politics is instead religiously and theologically resonated. In short, these "colored" voices speak not only from out of the particularities of their racialized existences but also are echoed through the scriptural register.

Asian American evangelicals ought to consider also how their own historicity might be empowered biblically. For this purpose, I urge that we turn from the model minority complex to another conventional label often applied to Asian Americans that is not without its liabilities: perpetual foreigner. The notion of perpetual foreignness stems from the sense that Asian Americans—perhaps not only but yet in distinctive ways—do not feel at home either in Asia or in America. Especially second generational Asian Americans, or sometimes even so-called 1.5 generation members—those like myself who were born in Asia but grew up largely in America to first generation immigrant parents—are often citizens of the United States and generally know of nowhere else to call home; yet their phenotypical distinctiveness often leads to the question, "Where are you from?" (meaning, where outside America did you and your family originate?). On the other hand, Asians who have been Americanized can visit the land of their parents or ancestors and also feel like strangers. There is a certain sense of kinship, to be sure, but one that is far from any feeling of belonging. As I cannot speak Chinese, for instance, I am embarrassed when on China Airlines, long before I land in Hong Kong, Taipei, or Beijing, I am asked if I want the chicken or pork dinner and I have to ask for an English explanation. In short, I remain a foreigner on both shores (and in between too!): to those in America because of my looks, but to those in East Asia because of my language and accent.

I suggest, however, that the Asian American feeling of perpetual foreignness opens up a pathway into the scriptural traditions. Here I am thinking about the sense that much of the Bible was written from out of the experience of migration and exile.[7] In the Hebrew

---

7. See also Amos Yong, "The Im/Migrant Spirit: De/Constructing a Pentecostal Theology of Migration," in *Theology of Migration in the Abrahamic Religions, Christianities of the World*, ed. Peter C. Phan and Elaine Padilla (New York: Palgrave Macmillan, 2014), 133–53.

canon, for example, Abraham is called out of Ur of the Chaldeans and invited to a journey with El. Then the ancient Hebrews were delivered from the land of Egypt to journey in the wilderness and migrate into Canaan. Even if much of the monarchic period unfolds in Canaan, some of the prophetic narratives derive from desert or rural experiences (e.g., Elijah's or Amos's), and many psalms come from (allegedly) David's shepherding period or when he was on the run from Saul, or large swaths of the wisdom literature are generated from socially marginalized situations (like the book of Job), or the historical narratives were probably not written much before the exile to Babylon and even if scripted, they were not collected except through the exilic dislocation. And so far as the exile is concerned, the majority of the prophetic literature and the demands for justice prevalent therein cannot be comprehended except as related in some or other respect to that incredibly traumatic national disruption. The point is that much if not almost all of the First Testament was produced either in or through the fires of migration or exile.

Similarly, the Christian New Testament reflects the thinking and perspectives of a messianic group that went forth from a Galilean center to the edges of the known world and the journey of Hellenized Jews from around the Mediterranean world who went to and fro from Jerusalem in their efforts to understand their newfound identity as Jesus followers and were yet in relationship to Gentiles. It is no wonder that the New Testament includes explicit references to messianists as diasporic "exiles" or "sojourners" (e.g., James 1:1; 1 Peter 1:1; 2:11). Part of the point of the Christian message or way of life was that believers were to be distinct from the world and surrounding culture. Yes, they were *in* the world, but no, they were not to be *of* the world. Although members of the *Pax Romana*, they realized they "were strangers and foreigners on the earth" (Hebrews 11:13b), questioned "Whether it is right in God's sight to listen to [imperial authorities] rather than to God" (Acts 4:19), and thereby confessed: "our citizenship is in heaven" (Philippians 3:20).[8]

My point is threefold: first, that the Christian Bible ought to be understood from this migrant and exilic perspective; second, that

---

8. Biblical quotations are from the New Revised Standard Version.

the Asian American perpetual foreigner experience provides hermeneutical advantages in this regard; and third, that it is from such marginal sites that Asian Americans can model evangelical faithfulness to the gospel in the age of Trump. True, to embrace and live into perpetual foreignness will exact its own costs, in particular the benefits that come from polite accommodation into the prevailing culture on the latter's terms. Yet also in truth, the "perpetual other" is not just the Asian American but also whoever does not fit the political status quo, including other people of color.[9] My point is less to commend alliance with or allegiance to the Democratic opponents of the president than it is to discern biblical justice amid the resurgence of white nationalism. More exactly, the goal is a shalom that is good news to not just reds, yellows, and blacks, but also to whites, within and outside the evangelical community. For this task a new scriptural imagination is needed, not least for the evangelical church that insists on being normed by *sola scriptura*, and my proposal is that such cannot emerge in this important juncture unless this church again inhabits the marginalized locations of migration and exile.

My own pentecostal perspective insists that the salvific redemption of the triune God comes in and through the many tongues of even Cretans (stereotyped, remember, as "liars, vicious brutes, lazy gluttons"!; Titus 1:12), Arabs (the historically estranged side of the "family"), and Romans, inclusive of those who had benefitted from oppressive imperial practices (see Acts 2:10-11).[10] Few if any ethnic groups historically are innocent of racist attitudes to and action toward others different from them, so even if in North America the current problem is at least in part the twilight of whiteness, pentecostal deliverance is for all of us. In fact, there is no redemption

---

9. See here Josef Soret, *Spirit in the Dark: A Religious History of Racial Aesthetics* (Oxford: Oxford University Press, 2016), 126.

10. For more on my pentecostal political theology, see Amos Yong, *In the Days of Caesar: Pentecostalism and Political Theology* (Grand Rapids, MI: William B. Eerdmans Publishing Company, 2010); cf. Steven M. Studebaker, *A Pentecostal Political Theology for American Renewal: Spirit of the Kingdoms, Citizens of the Cities* (New York: Palgrave Macmillan, 2016).

for whites without the salvation of others and vice versa. Hence the American church as the body of Christ is constituted by many members, and the people of God as the fellowship of the Spirit is drawn "from every tribe and language and people and nation" (Revelation 5:9b). All need to repent and be reconciled to one another and toward the justice of the coming reign of God in order to unleash the potent witness of the Spirit of Pentecost that continues to be poured out upon all flesh—male and female, young and old, the haves and the have-nots (Act 2:17-18)—and is supposed to reach to the ends of the earth (Acts 1:8). Asian Americans may be able to contribute something to this North American moment if they press from their perpetual foreignness toward this vision, but only if they also, along with their fellow evangelical sojourners, are open to being touched by a fresh Pentecost.[11] Come Holy Spirit![12]

---

11. I elaborate on what I call a pent-evangelical theology and praxis in my *The Future of Evangelical Theology: Soundings from the Asian American Diaspora* (Downers Grove, IL: IVP Academic, 2014).

12. Thanks to Mike Karim for comments on an initial draft, as well for his inviting my participation in "Following Jesus in a Trump Presidency: Asian American Dialogue," InterVarsity's Faculty Ministries Symposium, San Gabriel Presbyterian Church, San Gabriel, California, January 14, 2017, from out of which this essay emerged. I take full responsibility, however, for the ideas herein.

CHAPTER 14

American Muslims in
the Age of President Trump

AMIR HUSSAIN

Muslims, both within America and around the world, are the religious community that is most affected by the presidency of Donald J.
Trump. I write this chapter as both an American citizen—a Muslim from Los Angeles—and a scholar of Islam in North America.
Wearing either or both hats, I find that the next four years of the
Trump administration will continue to be difficult times to be an
American Muslim. These difficulties, it needs to be pointed out,
are not new or unique to the current administration. They were
anticipated in the last century, to take only one example, by John
Carpenter, in his 1996 film, *Escape from L.A.* In the film, set in
2013, Los Angeles has become a penal colony for those who do not
conform to the high moral standards of the American president.
One of the residents is a young Iranian woman named Taslima,
who tells the protagonist: "I was a Muslim. Then they made that
illegal." In the last century, I used to think that that line was very
funny. Now I'm not so sure. In the 2006 film *V for Vendetta*, set
in a future neo-Fascist Britain, one of the characters (Dietrich) is
taken away by the authorities for owning a copy of the Qur'an. As a
presidential candidate, Mr. Trump said very famously on *CNN* on
March 9, 2016, that "I think Islam hates us,"[1] and so one wonders
what will happen to American Muslims during his presidency.

---

1. Theodore Schleifer, "Donald Trump: 'I Think Islam Hates Us,'" *CNN*,
March 10, 2016.

This chapter was written in the first month of the Trump administration, and the situation is continually shifting for America's Muslims. I concluded this chapter on February 19, 2017. On that day, there was a "United for America Rally" in Los Angeles, held at the Islamic Center of Southern California. There, interfaith groups and politicians, and the Los Angeles city attorney showed their support for American Muslims.[2] The date was chosen as it was the seventy-fifth anniversary of the signing of Executive Order 9066, which allowed for the internment of Japanese Americans, and is commemorated as the "Day of Remembrance." It is instructive to remember that while both German Americans and Italian Americans were targeted by Executive Order 9066, only Japanese Americans were placed in internment camps. While the government knew at the time that Japanese Americans were not a threat to our country, it took over forty-five years for the Civil Liberties Act of 1988 to be signed into law by President Ronald Reagan, to "acknowledge the fundamental injustice of the evacuation, relocation, and internment of United States citizens and permanent resident aliens of Japanese ancestry during World War II."[3]

From the time of Mr. Trump's remark that "Islam hates us," one has seen a shift from the rise of Islamophobia to what I term "misoislamia," a neologism that captures the move from a fear (*phobia*) to a hatred (*miso*) for Islam and Muslims. The line that has been running over and over in my head comes from a local California band, Counting Crows: "All the anger and the eloquence are bleeding into fear." Like other Americans, America's Muslims fear for our country—our home—and what will become of it. We saw the open intolerance to Islam in opposition to new mosques proposed throughout the country. We saw seven states (Alabama, Arizona, Kansas, Louisiana, North Carolina, South Dakota, and Tennessee) passing anti-sharia laws, when not a single Muslim group in America had asked for the implementation of sharia laws. Oklahoma also voted for such a law, but it was struck down in 2012 and never implemented. We saw Lt. General Michael Flynn,

---

2. https://twitter.com/hashtag/unitedforAmericaLA?src=hash.
3. 100th Congress: Public Law 100-383, August 10, 1988.

who became President Trump's National Security Advisor, tweet that "fear of Muslims is RATIONAL" and heard him claim that Islam is a political ideology (and not a religion, and therefore not protected under the Constitution) that has become a "malignant cancer."[4] However, he resigned on February 13, 2017, though not for his comments about Islam and Muslims, but for misleading Vice President Mike Pence about his telephone calls with the Russian ambassador.

On January 27, 2017, a week after his inauguration, President Trump ordered that the United States ban travelers and refugees from seven Muslim-majority countries (Iraq, Syria, Iran, Libya, Somalia, Sudan, and Yemen). He did this at 4:42 P.M., almost at the end of the business week, after making comments that morning for International Holocaust Remembrance Day that made no mention either of the Jews or of anti-Semitism. Thousands of people protested the ban at airports across the country in the following days. I flew back to Los Angeles from Washington, DC, on January 29, and those protests were quite powerful to see, people standing up for Muslims not just or only as refugees or immigrants, but as Muslims. That was extraordinary. What has also been amazing to see is the response from the American Jewish community. They have been at the forefront of the protests, both because they know that the commandment that is repeated more than any other commandment in the Torah is to not oppress the stranger, and because they know with the painful history of the Holocaust of where the road of prejudice and intolerance ends. And with the rise of hate crimes against Muslims, over half of the hate crimes committed against a religious group in America were against Jews. The actions of the Trump administration have brought together Muslims and Jews in a way that I have never seen in my twenty years of living in America.

The travel ban was rejected by the United States Court of Appeals for the Ninth Circuit on February 9, 2017. President Trump has promised to introduce a new ban. One hopes that this one will

---

4. Matthew Rosenberg and Maggie Haberman, "Michael Flynn, Anti-Islamist Ex-General, Offered Security Post, Trump Aide Says," *New York Times*, November 17, 2016.

not affect permanent residents, visa holders, or refugees who were blocked in the first ban. It is harder to come to America as a refugee than it is to come here in every other way, with a waiting process that may take from two to four years of vetting and approval. Refugees are not a threat to our country. Neither, of course, are the citizens of the seven banned countries, who collectively are responsible for zero civilian deaths in the United States.

Instead of celebrating American Muslims as an American success story of an educated and wealthy community, some of whom are also conservative Republicans, the Trump administration openly discriminates against them. And that hatred has been exported to other countries, with the perpetrator of the January 29, 2017, terrorist attack that killed six at the Islamic Cultural Centre of Quebec City expressing support for President Trump.[5]

As a child growing up in Toronto, I saw very few nonwhite people on television, and almost no Muslims. The only ones I remember were African American athletes, Kareem Abdul-Jabbar, and the Greatest of All Time, Muhammad Ali. Those were my childhood Muslim heroes, and over forty years later, they remain models for me of how to be a Muslim. They are the reality of American Muslim life. Through them, I learned about the history of Islam in African American communities. We estimate that at least 10 percent of the slaves brought over from West Africa were Muslim. So to take only one example, in 1730, a Muslim slave named Ayuba Suleiman Diallo, also known as Job ben Solomon, was brought as a slave to Annapolis, Maryland. This, one needs to remember, was two years before George Washington was born. Diallo's story was told in a slave narrative that was published in London in 1734.

Two centuries earlier, in 1528, another Muslim, Estevancio the Moor, landed in what is now Florida. He was a slave of Andrés Dorantes de Carranza, and they both accompanied the Spanish conquistador Pánfilo de Narváez on his expedition to the New World. Estevancio explored not only Florida but also Arizona, before he was killed in 1539 by the Zuni in what is now New Mexico. Dur-

---

5. Mahita Gajanan, "Quebec City Mosque Shooting Suspect Criticized Refugees and Supported Trump Online," *Time*, January 30, 2017.

ing the second presidential debate, Hillary Clinton mentioned that Muslims had been in America since the time of George Washington. In fact, we'd been here over ninety years before the Pilgrims arrived, and some two centuries before General Washington was born. There has never been an America without Muslims.

American Muslims, it should be pointed out, are very different from European or Canadian Muslims, other places where we are also minorities in a Western context. Canadian Muslims do not have the same history that American Muslims do. So while there was a small Muslim population in Canada at the end of the nineteenth century (the first Canadian census in 1871 listed a Muslim population of thirteen), it was nothing like the number of Muslim slaves that were present in America generations earlier. There is no comparable component in Canadian Muslim life that resembles African American Muslims, who represent at least one-quarter of American Muslims. African American Muslims, as Americans, have for centuries been part of the history of the United States.

In Europe, the situation is markedly different, both among the Muslim and the non-Muslim populations, which each tends to be much more homogeneous than they are in the United States. So in Britain, the majority of Muslims have their origins in South Asia. In France, Muslims are mostly from North Africa. In Germany, Muslims are usually Turks or Kurds. Contrast that with the American situation, where Muslims are equally African American, South Asian, or Middle Eastern (to take only the three largest groups). There are also narrower definitions of what it means to be French or English or German than what it means to be American, which incorporates all of those European identities and many others.

There is also a socioeconomic difference. American Muslims are an American success story, solidly middle class, and mostly professional. There are thousands of American Muslim physicians, for example, perhaps as many as 20,000 if one looks at information from the Islamic Medical Association of North America. European Muslims by contrast are more marginalized, often in a much lower socioeconomic class with much higher rates of unemployment. Sometimes, as is often the case in Germany, they are in the status of migrants or guest workers, not citizens.

Finally, there is a difference between American-style secularism, which doesn't seek to abolish religion but to give all religions an equal seat at the table, and various kinds of European disestablishment of religion, which seek to make the public space nonreligious. In the United States, America's seven million Muslims are free to live out their Islam in the public space. And there are so many American Muslims who do this; none did it better than my childhood hero, the Greatest of All Time. Look at the life of Muhammad Ali, and you begin to understand the contributions that American Muslims have made to what it means to be American.

Muhammad Ali was born Cassius Clay in Louisville, Kentucky, and gained national fame when he won a gold medal at the Rome Olympics in 1960 as a light heavyweight boxer. In 1964, the twenty-two-year-old Clay, by his own admission, "shook up the world" in his six-round defeat of Sonny Liston, becoming the world heavyweight boxing champion. A few years earlier, Clay had gone to Nation of Islam meetings. There he met Malcolm X, who as a friend and advisor was part of Clay's entourage for the Liston fight. Clay made his conversion public after the fight, and was renamed by Nation of Islam leader Elijah Muhammad as Muhammad Ali.

When Ali was reclassified as eligible for induction into the draft for the Vietnam War, he refused on the grounds of his new Muslim religious beliefs. Famously, he said that "war is against the teachings of the Holy Koran. I'm not trying to dodge the draft. We are not supposed to take part in no wars unless declared by Allah or the Messenger [Elijah Muhammad]. We don't take part in Christian wars or wars of any unbelievers." Even more famously, reflecting on the racism he had experienced in America, Ali said, "I ain't got no quarrel with them Viet Cong—no Viet Cong ever called me Ni**er." This conscientious objector status *was* rooted in the teachings of the Nation of Islam, and Elijah Muhammad had been jailed for his refusal to enter the draft in World War II. On April 28, 1967, Ali refused induction into the draft. He was arrested, and his boxing titles were stripped from him. Ali never went to prison, but he couldn't box for over three years. For him, as a Muslim, as a black Muslim, the Vietnam War was wrong. In 1967, that was not the popular stance that it is today, and Ali paid dearly, unable to make a living at the trade for which he was eminently qualified, at the peak of his talents.

Ali's case went to the United States Supreme Court, which ruled unanimously on June 28, 1971, to overturn his conviction. The Court did this on a technicality, since the appeal court had never given a reason for why Ali was denied conscientious objector status. But Ali was free, able to resume his work, and continue to be an American Muslim who changed America. In 1975, he followed Warith Deen Mohammed, who took his father's Nation of Islam into Sunni orthodoxy. He became a proselytizer for Islam, giving out pamphlets inviting others to Islam, autographed so that he knew they would be kept by those who received them. And as people began to see what Ali had done in the 1960s, he became a hero not just for his athletic prowess but for his work on civil rights. Who can forget in 1996, when the opening ceremonies were held for the Olympics in Atlanta? There was Janet Evans, one of the most decorated American swimmers, passing the torch to Ali, who held the torch aloft in his right hand, but whose left hand was shaking with Parkinson's Syndrome. In the hush of the crowd, it was Ali who would light the cauldron, something that he would repeat at the Winter Olympics in Salt Lake City in 2002.

Ali's funeral showed the outpouring of love and support for him. This was a beloved American hero returning home, a beloved American Muslim. The public funeral was held during the first week of Ramadan, on June 10, 2016, in his hometown of Louisville. The day before, however, Ali had also had a traditional Muslim funeral service, or *janazah*. At his passing, his body was washed and shrouded and prayed over in accordance with Islamic customs. Muslims across America and around the world were encouraged to hold *janazah* prayers for our deceased Muslim brother.

The *janazah* prayer for Ali was extraordinary, held on June 9, 2016, at the Kentucky Exposition Center in Louisville. This was next to Freedom Hall, where Ali had fought Tunney Hunsaker in his first professional fight on October 29, 1960. I watched the funeral service online from Los Angeles, on a YouTube feed from Fox 10 News, the Fox owned and operated television station in Phoenix, Arizona. The irony was rich. Here was a television station, Fox, not noted for its sympathetic coverage of Muslims, covering live the full Islamic prayer service for Muhammad Ali. On the drive home, I heard part of the Qur'an recitation from the funeral on CBS radio, the first time I ever heard coverage of a Muslim funeral on the recap of the daily news.

The service was led by Imam Zaid Shakir, a noted American imam from California and the co-founder of Zaytuna College, the first accredited Muslim liberal arts college in the United States. The coffin was brought in by pall bearers that included Shaikh Hamza Yusuf (another co-founder of Zaytuna College), and international recording star Yusuf Islam (the former Cat Stevens). The funeral prayer was performed, followed by a Qur'an recitation and a translation of the words recited by Shaikh Hamza. Then three people were invited to give short sermons to the crowd. They were Sherman Jackson, a professor at the University of Southern California and one of the most important Muslim scholars in the United States; Dalia Mogahed, the former director of the Gallup Center for Muslim Studies; and Khadija Sharif-Drinkard, a lawyer who oversees business and legal affairs for the New York offices of Black Entertainment Television (BET). That two of the three were Muslim women (who were also successful businesswomen) was important to show the leadership roles that many American Muslim women have in American society. Sherman Jackson is one of the most important American Muslim scholars, a mentor and friend for years. Professor Jackson's short sermon was brilliant, and a few lines from it captured the intertwining of American and Muslim identities in the body of Muhammad Ali:

> As a cultural icon, Ali made being Muslim cool. Ali made being a Muslim dignified. Ali made being a Muslim relevant. And all of this he did in a way that no one could challenge his belongingness to or in this country. Ali put the question of whether a person can be a Muslim and an American to rest. Indeed, he KO'd that question. With his passing, let us hope that that question will now be interred with his precious remains. . . . Ali helped this country move closer to its own ideals. He helped America do and see some things that America was not quite

ready to do or see on its own. And because of Ali's heroic efforts, America is a better place today for us all. And in this regard, Ali belongs not just to the Muslims of this country, Ali belongs to all Americans. . . . If you are an American, Ali is part of your history, part of what makes you who you are, and as an American, Ali belongs to you, and you too should be proud of this precious piece of your American heritage.

At another funeral service over fifty years earlier, on February 27, 1965, Ossie Davis gave the eulogy for Malcolm X. On that occasion he famously said, "Malcolm was our manhood, our living, black manhood! This was his meaning to his people. And in honoring him we honor the best in ourselves." Ali, as Professor Jackson pointed out, wasn't just for *his* people, but for all people. If Malcolm was our manhood, then Ali was our humanity, with a life lived for all the world to see. A life lived in complexity and contradiction, triumph and tragedy, change and metamorphosis. A life that gave the lie to F. Scott Fitzgerald's line about there being no second acts in American lives by living out its successful second and third acts. A life that showed us, in the old cliché, that it's not about how many times you get knocked down, but if you get back up, and what you do when you get back up that truly matters. An iconic American life, lived by an iconic American Muslim.

One often hears talk of "Islam *and* the West" or "Islam *and* America." This brings up an image of two mutually exclusive realities. If we change one simple word, we get instead "Islam *in* the West" or "Islam *in* America." That simple change makes all the difference. Instead of posing two warring factions, "Islam" and "America," we see the reality of their interconnectedness. Islam is, of course, a "Western" religion, sharing deep roots with Judaism and Christianity. Muslims are much closer religiously to Jews and to Christians than we are to "Eastern" religions such as Hinduism and Buddhism. Muslims are also a strong presence in the West. Islam is the second-largest religion in Canada, Britain, and France, and may well be the second-largest religion in the United States. "Islam in the West" recognizes the entwined heritage of Islam and the West. The West as we know it would not be what it is without the contribution of Muslims. Think quickly of our number system, for example, and ask yourself if it is easier to do multiplication and division with Arabic numbers or with Roman numerals. To be sure, the number system came from India, but it was the Arabs who named it. Yet we often don't see our connections, and unfortunately people here in America have at best an ignorance or at worst a fear or hatred of Muslims.

American Muslims have served in the United States military since the Revolutionary War. There were some 300 Muslim soldiers who served during the American Civil War. That's not a large number, certainly, but it also gives the lie to the oft-repeated claim that Muslims are newcomers to the United States. At the end of 2015, ABC News reported figures from the U.S. Department of Defense that some 5,896 Muslims were serving in the military. That number may be higher, since some 400,000 service members did not self-identify their faith. So almost 6,000 American Muslims serve in the armed forces, helping to defend the country.

In America, we still think of violence as something unique to Muslims and don't seem to realize the violence around us. Charles Kurzman is a sociologist at the University of North Carolina who studies home-grown Muslim terrorism. The numbers are, unfortunately, greater than zero, where they should be. But they are much lower than many people think. So, for example, in 2015, nineteen Americans were killed in mass shootings by Muslims in America, fourteen by the San Bernardino shooters (I will not glorify murderers by naming them), five by the shooter in Chattanooga. That's less than the number of American Veterans who commit suicide each *day* (approximately twenty-two), and about the equivalent of the number of Americans shot in any eight-hour period each day. Unfortunately, that changed on June 12, 2016, less than 2 days after the funeral of Muhammad Ali, when an American Muslim killed forty-nine people and injured over fifty more in the worst mass shooting in the United States.

The shooter was known to law enforcement and had been questioned multiple times about ties to terrorism. His ex-wife told the *Washington Post* that he "wasn't a stable person" and that he had beaten her. A former coworker described him to the *Los Angeles*

Times as "angry at the world," as well as being "unhinged and unstable." However, he was still able legally to purchase guns in the week before the shooting. In a horrific way, the shooter *also* represented America, taking on our worst characteristics as a society. He was homophobic, and chose to attack an LGBTQ nightclub during Pride Month. Sadly, LGBTQ Americans are the most likely to be violently attacked in a hate crime. He also attacked the nightclub on Latin night, and the majority of those killed or injured were LGBTQ Latinx. So there was a deeper tragedy: those marginalized for their ethnicity and their sexuality were the targets that the shooter chose.

On a 911 call during the shooting, the shooter pledged his allegiance to the Islamic State. He also posted extremist Islamic statements on Facebook. Clearly, his interpretation of Islam is important here, and this part of his background needs to be investigated. But people belonging to other religious traditions have also committed mass shootings, and homophobia is sadly not unique to Islam. Matthew Shepard, to take only one tragic American example, was not tortured and killed by Al-Qaeda. American Muslim groups were quick to condemn the shootings (as they always do), and remind people that their sympathies were with the murdered, not with the shooter. The shootings also caused many Muslims to think about homophobia in their communities, and perhaps to rethink their views on homosexuality.

Horrific as the shootings were, the worst in American history, they are all too often something that Americans do. It was the sixteenth time that President Obama had to do a public briefing about a mass shooting during his presidency. And he did it from a briefing room named in honor of James Brady, the White House press secretary who was shot in 1981 in the assassination attempt on President Ronald Reagan. And while there is discrimination and mistreatment of Muslims, that pales in comparison to the historic injustices of segregation, the internment of Japanese Americans, or slavery to take only the first three examples that come to mind. In a strange way, that too gives me hope. Not because we are discriminated against because we are Muslims, which of course is dreadful. But we began this country, as Jim Wallis of Sojourners famously reminded us, with the near-genocide of Native Americans and the enslavement of Africans.[6] Hatred of Islam, I remind my Muslim friends, isn't the same as slavery or Jim Crow laws. Perhaps this is simply our time to pay our dues so that we can be fully recognized as the Americans that we are. Or to use a darker metaphor, perhaps it's now our turn to be "jumped in."

For those unfamiliar with the horrors of gang life, to be jumped in means to go through a brutal ritual of initiation. One cannot fully join the gang unless one is beaten by the other members to show that one can take the pain and the punishment. Only then is one given hugs and love and full membership in the gang. Perhaps in this metaphor, America is the gang, and it is our turn as Muslims to get jumped in to prove that we belong and can have full membership. Just as Muhammad Ali represents our best ideals as a country, the Orlando shooter represents the worst. American Muslims need to live the legacy of Muhammad Ali. We need to continue to stand, as he did, for justice. "Service to others is the rent you pay for your room here on earth," Ali would often say, and we need not only to remember that saying, but to act on it. In this way, we can live out the best of our ideals, both as Americans and as Muslims.

We can deepen our interfaith connections as we resist the actions of the Trump administration. We need to get back to our shared values of taking care of our neighbor, which we are called to do by our religious traditions. As Muslims, we need to be more visible than ever in the media, given the attacks by the Trump administration on the news media. Many Muslims who have come to America from countries with authoritarian regimes know the difference between journalism and propaganda. We need to encourage more Muslims to enter the media in order to properly and honestly tell our stories. We also need to be more involved in the political process, not just to vote, but to contact our elected officials about our concerns and where possible to run for office. We, too, as the poet Langston Hughes reminded us, *are* America.

---

6. Jim Wallis, "Racism: America's Original Sin," *Sojourners*, July 29, 2013.

CHAPTER 15

Jewish Resistances
Trumpism, Holocaustic Memories, and the Paradoxes of New Whiteness

SANTIAGO SLABODSKY

Trumpism and the End of Science Fiction

Two days before the inauguration of Donald Trump, dozens of Jewish community centers across the United States were evacuated in response to simultaneous bomb threats. Images of kids escaping through manicured parking lots led some analysts to discuss that parents "were right to be afraid" for their children's safety. Some exaggerated comments even saw these threats as signs of a "new Holocaust."[1] Up until the recent wave of attacks the concerns of the American Jewish establishment were largely focused on whether the United States would keep supporting "Jewish interests" at the international level (i.e., Israel). The possibility that an active anti-Semitic agenda could coalesce at the domestic level and be adopted across the country, however, was largely reserved for science fiction. When these narratives did appear they explored time and again a counterfactual history of the Holocaust. Since the 1950s, when Jews started to be welcomed as white and Western in the American public sphere, the fear of anti-Semitism was predomi-

---

1. Elisa Strauss, "The JCC Bomb Threats Confirm that Jewish Parents Are Right to Be Afraid," *Slate,* January 19, 2017, http://www.slate.com. See public comments as a complement.

nantly justified in imagining alternative scenarios to the end of the Second World War.

Even if this counterfactual history, which functions both as an outlet for a repressed trauma and as a political stance, can be traced back several decades, it is in twenty-first-century popular culture that it finds its full crystallization. For example, Philip Roth—arguably the most important contemporary Jewish American novelist—wrote *The Plot Against America* in 2004. In this novel he explores a scenario in which the 1940 presidential election had turned out differently and led the United States to enter into an alliance with the Third Reich, leading to a massive pogrom.[2] In 2015, the distribution giant Amazon started producing the TV series *The Man in the High Castle* based on a 1962 novel of the same name. The series explores a world in which the Axis won World War II, the United States is occupied, and its rulers lead an intense persecution of Jews as a natural continuation of the Holocaust.[3] Some popular culture critics might correctly dismiss this scenario as another expression of white fear, considering that Hollywood—not only Jewish Hollywood—has tirelessly explored the fear of annihilation of the white race by barbarians (often aliens) in an attempt to mitigate fears of a revenge led by the former colonized, enslaved, or dispossessed people. Still, the actual historical antecedent of the Holocaust makes it rhetorically more difficult to dismiss this counterfactual history as just another instance of white fear.

If we eschew the tendency to read these scenarios as examples of white narratives, the question emerges as to whether, in the era of Trumpism, anti-Semitism could become part of a mainstream attitude, or even become a facet of a domestic agenda that harbors a broad spectrum of racist and misogynist forms of hatred. It is possible to make this case. The bomb threats against the Jewish community centers were preceded by a call for a pogrom against the Jewish community in Whitefish, Montana, and a number of "alt-right" attacks throughout the United States. The designation

---

2. Philip Roth, *The Plot Against America* (New York: Vintage, 2004).

3. Philip Dick, *The Man in the High Castle* (New York: Harcourt, 1962), and the TV series produced by Ridley Scott and Frank Spotnitz (2015).

of Steve Bannon, the leading voice of the refashioned Right and an avowed anti-Semite, as chief strategist and senior counselor to Trump can be seen as evidence that this anti-Semitism is more than a feature of a political climate. It may be that the new anti-Semitic agenda, along with xenophobia, racism, misogyny, and Islamophobia, will be administered from the White House.

Yet, some may argue that this is an exaggerated fear. Online tabloids, for example, repeatedly point out that the "first daughter" Ivanka converted to Judaism and that her husband, Jared Kushner, was designated a senior adviser, and, finally, that, both during the campaign and after being elected, Donald Trump pledged to support the primary interest of the Jewish establishment, the State of Israel. Since Israel has portrayed its continued existence as the guarantee that the Holocaust will never be repeated, these details and stances, particularly Trump's support for Israel, pose the question of whether critical perspectives should so readily associate Trumpism with anti-Semitism. Even the avowed anti-Semite Bannon has shown himself to be decidedly pro-Israel.

A number of commentators, however, rightly point out that neither the presence of Jews nor the international support for Israel undermines the possibility of implementing anti-Semitic policies. There have always been court Jews—even in some of the most extreme moments of history. The coexistence of right-wing (fascist and Christian fundamentalist) hatred for Jews and blind pro-Zionism shows that the equivalence between anti-Zionism and anti-Semitism has been predominantly a rhetorical chimera. So if the Jewish communities take seriously the imminent threat, the possibility that a domestic anti-Semitic agenda could be implemented in the United States within a broader framework of hatred toward minorities, one wonders what resources could be used to mount a challenge in this new stage.

In this chapter, I will demonstrate that these resources are considerably limited by the normative narrative American Jews have constructed to connect their whiteness both with the Holocaust and with the State of Israel. Furthermore, I argue that the strengthening of the Jewish contribution to the resistance against Trumpism depends on delinking these narratives about identity. Without this, the Jewish establishment and the majority of American Jews will remain blind to the reasons behind their harassment within a larger spectrum of persecuted communities.

Re-evaluating Linkages

Just a few days after Trump was elected, an article appeared in the English-speaking edition of *Haaretz*, one of the most widely read global Jewish outlets among members of the U.S. Jewish liberal intelligentsia. The title of the article was not necessarily surprising: "Trump's Election Triggers Old Nightmares for Holocaust Survivors in America." As can be expected, 80 percent of the article narrates the activated memories of octogenarian survivors and provides a basic psychological explanation of trauma. It was the hook chosen by the New York–based correspondent that was innovative. She begins the article recalling the voice of Claire Cohen, a twenty-year-old student at the New School, the university once known as "University in Exile" and populated by intellectuals who had fled Nazi Germany. Cohen was reflecting on the swastikas that appeared on the doors of a secured fifteenth floor residential hall housing "Jewish, minority and LGBT" students. Making an explicit connection with her grandmother who had survived the Holocaust, Cohen told the interviewer: "I never experienced the hate my grandmother did," but "I never thought I would see something like this happen here." And she was referring to a space where Jews became part of the normative population. The interviewer then builds a connection between the past and the present, overlooking the different roles Jews played in each society.[4]

Trumpism may have overcome its characterization as science fiction, but the link it forges between the Holocaust and Jewish persecution in the United States has remained intact. While this narrative is today considered standard, it is crucial to understand it not as a given, but as a political construction. Even acclaimed survivors such as Elie Wiesel typically narrated how difficult it was to

---

4. Marisa Fox-Bevilacqua, "Trump's Election Triggers Old Nightmares for Holocaust Survivors in America," *Haaretz*, November 18, 2016.

confront the silence about the extermination in Europe for the first two decades. This was not necessarily a surprise: Jews were just too busy becoming white. When World War II ended, the U.S. government actively pursued an agenda aimed at promoting a binary racial structure (white vs. black) by classifying Jews (along with Irish/Italian Catholics) as white. One of the key means to achieve this goal was the GI Bill, which allowed new whites to have access to higher education, establish independent businesses, and move to the suburbs, leaving African Americans behind. This was not an innocent move. Until the 1930s, Jews and African Americans had been some of the most radicalized allies against the U.S. establishment in a diversity of forums (including the Communist Party). Promoting the racial upgrade of Jews was a way to disarticulate this alliance, leaving it to McCarthyism to dismantle what economics could not accomplish.[5]

This whitening of the Jewish population did not stem from international pressures. The State of Israel, founded in 1948, had largely dismissed the relevance of the figure of the powerless European Jew and replaced it with a hypermasculine figure that very much resembled Fascist propaganda. If Jews in the United States were too busy becoming white, in Israel, they were too busy portraying themselves as invincible in relation to their "hostile" neighbors or to the memory/struggle of the displaced Palestinians to truly concern themselves with making the Holocaust and anti-Semitism central concerns. According to traditional interpretations of anti-Semitism, this transition was logical. American Jews were trying to get rid of the vestiges of anti-Semitism by becoming like any other Western citizens of a state. And citizens of Israel were trying to get rid of the vestiges of anti-Semitism by becoming like any other Western nation-state.

We can assert, then, that the standard linkage between the Holocaust, Israel, and the American Jewish community is not inevitable. The link began to emerge strongly by the end of the 1960s, when

---

5. See the book that is now the landmark in the field, Karen Brodkin, *How Jews Became White Folks & What That Says about Race in America* (New Brunswick, NJ: Rutgers University Press), 1998.

a war in the Middle East led to unprecedented solidarity among Jewish youth across the world, as they fundraised, lobbied, and even joined the armed forces in Israel, endeavoring, according to the rhetoric of the period, to prevent a second Holocaust. The next twenty years saw the gestation among intellectuals, activists, and then popular culture of what would come to be known in the 1990s and 2000s as "the Holocaust industry."[6] This refers to the complex construction of a narrative supported by educational programs, museums, media, and popular culture that places the Holocaust at the center of Western history, portraying the United States, American Jewry, and Israel as guarantors against a second Holocaust. This had a powerful outcome for each of the winners. Israel could equate any questioning of her treatment of Palestinians with anti-Semitism. An increasingly anachronistic liberal Jewish American establishment could monopolize the role of victim—even when anti-Semitism was not a problem—thereby further undermining the luck of other minorities (fundamentally African Americans). And finally, the United States could represent any event as a repetition of World War II, perpetually portraying itself as a liberator, never as the occupier, on the international stage, and as inclusive, never exclusive, in its domestic agenda.[7]

It is then that the link between the Holocaust, Israel, and the American Jewish community became a staple theme. In the twenty-first century, this narrative has been naturalized, and its American institutions—ranging from the American Israel Public Affairs Committee (AIPAC) to the Anti-Defamation League (ADL)—are at the forefront of its perpetuation. Both these organizations have been too busy persecuting pro-Palestinian students or African American movements (sometimes joining forces with Islamophobic and racist discourses) to truly measure the threat posed by what is today normalized as the "alt-right." In the Trumpist age, however, one must

---

6. See critiques in Marc Ellis, *Unholy Alliance* (Minneapolis: Fortress Press, 1997); and Norman Finkelstein, *The Holocaust Industry* (New York: Verso, 2000).

7. I advanced some of these critiques in my book *Decolonial Judaism* (New York: Palgrave, 2015).

question whether the insistence on equating the "American Jewish interest" with the energetic defense of the State of Israel—based on the threat of a new Holocaust—while ignoring how they earned their domestic privilege (via post-1950s racial reclassification as white) will limit the established Jewish community's possibilities for fighting the array of hatred that Trumpism seems to entail.

The Limitations of Jewish Resistances

For most Jews in the United States, the narrative linking American Jewish interest with the Holocaust and the State of Israel is taken as natural and not viewed as the product of a historical process that started with the Jews' newly acquired whiteness. The strength of this narrative was recently put to the test when the Black Lives Matter (BLM) movement released its platform. The great majority of Jews consider themselves to be politically liberal and were outraged by the systematic and largely unpunished murders of African Americans. But as soon as the BLM, following a long tradition of transnational solidarity, extended its hand to the Palestinian struggle, the established Jewish community reacted with vehemence. While some rejected the movement, others paternalistically pointed out that the declaration was out of place. Yet both stances asserted, explicitly or implicitly, that if transnational solidarity among the oppressed didn't ascribe a central place to the Holocaust experience, it would necessarily wind up being anti-Semitic.[8]

And this is exactly the problem faced by Jewish resistances in the age of Trump. The normative Jewish claim of persecution is tied to a reading of the Holocaust that has clear implications in the international and domestic spheres. The problem is therefore not limited to the uncritical defense of the State of Israel for its treatment of Palestinians and Jews of color. But at the root of this problem is also the tendency to naïvely support a socioeconomic status that was fabricated in order to reproduce a binary conception of race in the United States and to limit social mobility, in large part for

---

8. See Laura Adkins, "Black Lives Matter Is Not about You," *Forward*, August 8, 2016, http://forward.com.

African Americans (and eventually Latinxs). In a context in which Trumpism takes the flag of international Jewish interest but promotes anti-Semitism in the domestic sphere, the narrative that was once largely thought of as natural breaks down. As a result, the Jewish community is confused and incapable of understanding the new American racial configuration.

The consequences of this are multiple, but I want to focus on a central one: the problem of alliances. In the 1950s Frantz Fanon clearly pointed out that he was taught to pay attention to anti-Semitism because it was necessarily linked to anti-blackness.[9] Thirty years later Edward Said linked Orientalism (or Islamophobia) and anti-Semitism by pointing out their common root and mutual reinforcement.[10] Today, thirty years after Said, we should ask if we can still talk about this natural link between hatred toward Jewish, African, and Arab/Muslim communities. On the one hand, we could answer negatively, explaining that it is precisely the inclusion of Jews and Israel that made possible the continuation of racism against African Americans domestically and of Islamophobia internationally. On the other hand, Trumpism represents the full crystallization of white supremacy within the state. Jews who have been taken as pawns (at times, very willing pawns) in the reproduction of the racist struggle now see they might have lost their protection.

The problem is that their long-standing contribution to a system that benefited them for just over half a century makes their potential allies (African Americans, Muslims) suspicious and, in turn, makes Jews uncomfortable. This is when one needs to acknowledge that the racial system is constructed not just out of exclusion but of an interplay between forced inclusion/exclusion making communities struggle for recognition while the system continues to reproduce itself. This does not downplay middle-person privilege, rather, it puts in question the divisions between those affected by the systemic structure. So perhaps, and only perhaps, Trumpism is

---

9. Frantz Fanon, *Black Skin/White Mask* (New York: Grove Press, 1992 [1952]), 122 [1944].

10. Edward Said, *Orientalism* (New York: Vintage, 1978), xxiv.

not new. It may just be the continuation of a long-standing pattern of domination that has donned Trumpism as a mask. The question is: how do we confront it?

The Future of Resistances

In the midst of Nazism's rise to power, Jewish intellectuals reflected on its logic and on possibilities for resistance. Early on, in 1933, Emmanuel Levinas recommended that "Hitlerism" should not be dismissed for its simplicity and asked whether "all that we need is liberalism" to confront the rising regime.[11] A decade later Theodor Adorno and Max Horkheimer complemented Levinas, arguing that both democratic liberalism and fascism keep the wheels of the capitalist system running. They argued that omnipresent racism was just a "cheap means for distraction" for "the masses."[12]

If Jews are to resist Trumpism, a new narrative of the Holocaust should emerge. Not one that focuses on Jewish suffering as the central component of the Holocaust and whitewashes Jewish racial status in the United States and Israel/Palestine. This narrative should make the Holocaust a source of systemic reflection on what Trumpism is reproducing. The point is that Trumpism represents, as Hitlerism did, one more stage in the long-turning wheel of capitalism. In the United States, liberal democracy has espoused neo-liberal economic policies. Trumpism is leaving the aim intact, changing only two key means. Companies no longer need to lobby Washington because they have just seized the reins of power. And they have abandoned the pretension of liberal inclusion. They can let loose racist and misogynist discourses either as cheap means of distraction or direct abuse of bodies. The system, however, remains intact.

Before the Trump era, Jewish organizations could ignore the existing contradictions of their narrative. This time is now over.

---

11. Emmanuel Levinas, "Reflections on the Philosophy of Hitlerism," *Critical Inquiry* (1990 [1934]): 62–71.

12. Max Horkheimer and Theodor Adorno, "Elements of Anti-Semitism," *Dialectic of Enlightenment* (Stanford, CA: Stanford University Press, 2002 [1944]), 137–39.

The Holocaust, then, must cease to be the basis for a monopolistic blackmail between communities in struggle. It should become a (not the) source for structural reflection about the relation between capitalism and racism in a moment of full crystallization of white supremacy. Until Jews can understand that the linkage between the Holocaust, Israel, and American Jewish whiteness has been broken, they will be disoriented and their (our) resistances will fall short of their expectations. I then call on allies to recognize that the established Jewish institutions cannot collaborate in the process of resistance. I encourage resisters to find interlocutors in emergent communities. Options include Open Hillel for campus life, Jewish Voice for Peace for international discussions, or Jews for Racial and Economical Justice for urban justice. These new networks undertook the struggle to dismantle the anachronistic narrative before 2017. They are the hope for a Jewish contribution to the resistance against Trumpism.

CHAPTER 16

Cripping Donald Trump's "Crippled America"

SHARON V. BETCHER

Ironically, the election of Donald Trump as U.S. president has brought the experience of living with disability front and center in national politics. This rare moment originated with Trump's gestural mockery of reporter Serge Kovaleski, who lives with arthrogryposis.[1] Amid all of Trump's boastful misogynistic and nationalistic rhetoric, this display—one he deems a bit slapstick, while others see it as consistent with the politics of humiliation—is considered his most publicly disaffecting behavior.[2] Actress Meryl Streep consequently passionately denounced Trump's bullying in her reception of the Cecil B. DeMille award at the Golden Globe Awards of January 8, 2017: "This instinct to humiliate, when it's modeled by someone in the public platform, gives permission for other people to do the same thing. . . . When the powerful use their position to bully others, we all lose."[3] And yet this volley—Trump's affective aggression countered by Streep's well intended, if pater-nalistically tinged rejoinder on behalf of one she characterized as

---

1. Daniel Arkin, "Donald Trump Criticized after He Appears to Mock Reporter Serge Kovaleski," *Politics,* November 26, 2015. This was not Trump's first public mockery of people with disabilities (PWDs). See Gideon Resnick, "Donald Trump's War on People with Disabilities," *Daily Beast,* December 2, 2015.

2. Irin Carmon, "Donald Trump's Worst Offense? Mocking Disabled Reporter, Poll Finds," *Politics,* August 11, 2016.

3. Nicola Agius, "Meryl Streep's Golden Globes 2017 Speech in Full: Star Lashes Out at U.S. President-elect Donald Trump," January 9, 2017, www.mirror.co.uk.

"someone [Trump] outranked in privilege, power, and the capacity to fight back"—hardly sums up that which most deeply worries persons living with disabilities (PWDs).

Even entering into the Trump era, to subsist with "disability"—a category homogenizing life-onset impairments and genetically expressive variabilities—often involves countless hours patching together diverse health care specialists, weaving networks of attendant and educational care, and tapping multiple governmental welfare accounts, leaving oneself, if not one's family, indebted and exhausted. PWDs, given this patchy cultural and policy environment, which does not appear to will our well-being, and contrary to Streep's rhetoric ensconcing our vulnerability, see themselves as resilient—not fragile. In fact, Kovaleski—a reporter at the *New York Times*, whose awards include a 2009 Pulitzer for investigative journalism—is hardly one unable to speak for himself.

Yet, in another sense, Streep was correct in calling attention to vulnerability: while PWDs succeed against the odds, ecological, economic, labor, and social policies unjustly exploit the existential precariousness of some bodies more than others. "Disability," as a disqualifying judgment marinated in medical sympathy, occludes awareness of the fact that this category of bodies accrues via the politically, ecologically, and socioeconomically leveraged precaritization of flesh. That is, some bodies, made more vulnerable by economics or environment than others, become "disabled" at the interface of flesh and world, and then become subjected to cultural humiliation or, contrarily, paternalism. Once swept into humanism's racial margins as "disabled," bodies become thereby exponentially more vulnerable to further sociocultural disavowals—like Trump's aesthetic display, but more enduringly lack of health care, welfare, accessibility, education, and employment.

After assessing that which makes the lives of PWDs vulnerable in the Trump era—most specifically, policies affecting the commons of flesh, this essay challenges the dystopic narrative Trump has spun—his messianic ruse as "the only one" who can cure "crippled America."[4]

---

4. See Donald J. Trump, *Crippled America: How to Make America Great Again* (New York: Threshold Edition, 2015).

Considering Disability in the Trumpian Era

Looking into the Trumpian era, there is—because every experience of "disability" is phenomenologically singular—no one governmental policy or department toward which we can look to assess or, therefore, mobilize protest regarding policy impacts on PWDs. The ranks of "the disabled" include veterans, and hence the policies of Veterans Affairs, as much as aging boomers and the need for Medicare as well as workers displaced from mining and industry. Undocumented migrants, whom Trump threatens to deport, may serve as low-wage health care attendants for PWDs; their absence for PWDs signals an intimate loss. Equally, the undocumented may be among those doused with pesticides as they labor in tomato patches, their own disablement consequently written out of corporate responsibility. Inept environmental practices, like the spraying of certain pesticides, accrue as a "body burden" not only through direct contact but epigenetically as "disability." That "cause" can never be singularly ferreted out means that claiming federal support becomes part of the daily fight by which PWDs often gain but subsistence livelihood.[5]

Trump's intention to turn over public rights, like education and health care, to the consumer market and/or state-based welfare leaves PWDs outside the purview of federal enforcement and oversight. Trump's cabinet head for the Department of Education, Betsy DeVos, expressed during her confirmation hearings the intention to shift oversight of education for children living with disabilities to the state, where the right of PWDs to a fair and appropriate educa-

---

5. As but one example of the difficulty of receiving disability benefits, consider the case of black lung disease among coal miners. Prior to the Affordable Care Act ("Obamacare"), "miners had to prove not only that they were disabled because of breathing problems, and that they had coal workers' black lung, but their disability was [singularly] caused by their years in the mine." Because "cause" is hard to establish and company lawyers can insert the shadow of a doubt, "the vast majority of people were denied benefits." The Byrd Amendment to the ACA shifted the burden of proof from miners to the mining companies. Repeal of the ACA could change such provisions. See Eric Boodman, "Trump Promised to Bring Back Coal. Now Some Worry He Will Take Away Miners' Black Lung Benefits," *Stat,* November 28, 2016, www.statnews.com.

tion will be unremittingly subject to the paucity of state education budgets.[6] PWDs further worry about the rollback of or refusal to endorse protective regulations, even the labor regulation known as the ADA (1990 Americans with Disabilities Act). Trump himself, as a businessman, has been regularly investigated for negligence regarding ADA compliance.[7] While Trump has assured the public that health insurance companies will not be able to disallow pre-existing conditions in his still-to-emerge health care proposal, this policy consideration is a primary strut in the game of health care Jenga: given the need for dispersion of the costs involved in caring for pre-existing conditions, truly "affordable" health care requires all Americans to shoulder well-being as a people, as kin, as one flesh.

Yet as much as PWDs will worry about affordable care, supplemental income, and ADA enforcement, we'll equally worry about the northward creep of Lyme disease with climate change, diabetes and obesity in food deserts, and life downstream from coal mines. Vulnerability for bodies begins where flesh and environment inform each other; hence, the need for protective regulations, from the reach of the EPA through Labor.

Flesh and the Human Commons

"Disability" is a disqualifying cultural judgment about the discrete morphological contours or neurocognitive patterns of another body. Marginalization of this population keeps normates from having to face this truism: flesh, like water, air, and earth, is an interactive commons of life. The fact that no human body can be walled off

---

6. The Supreme Court is now deciding a case (January 2017), *Endrew F. v. Douglas County (Colorado) School District*, that suggests how vulnerable children with disabilities are to the economics of state budgets. See also Emma Brown, "DeVos Says She Will Protect Students with Disability, but Advocates Aren't Convinced," *Washington Post*, January 26, 2017.

7. Resnick reports that both the U.S. Department of Justice and the U.S. Attorney's Office for the District of New Jersey have investigated Trump's businesses—in each of these cases, the Trump Taj Mahal in Atlantic City—for noncompliance with ADA (see Resnick, "Donald Trump's War on People with Disabilities"). Also see Steve Benen, "Trump Thinks Following the ADA Is Worthy of Boasts," *MSNBC,* July 28, 2016.

from another or from its environment makes vulnerability a human universal. When damaging this commons, by running drinking water through lead pipes or spraying our food supply with chemicals causing epigenetic malformations, we unjustly, existentially leverage or precaritize the life of another, thereby causing "disability."[8]

Flesh, this tissue of intrarelational being we share with one another and the environment, constitutes every human's vulnerable flank. Yet the burden of flesh is unevenly and unjustly distributed—as, for example, where "class" implies the body burden of muscular, skeletal, and respiratory damage to those who perform heavy labor or where nuclear hazards sidle up to an economically needy community. Today flesh constitutes a newly remembered, theologically defensible commons. Persons religious may also remember that imperial policies requiring certain bodies—namely, slaves—to carry vulnerability in unjust degrees was already inconsistent with the theological values of ancient Israel.

Trump's early policy agenda, carried out by executive orders revolving around deregulation, aggravates this inherent commons. The deregulation of environmental and labor protections—like his disruption of the Clean Power Plan, his conjoint silencing of the EPA, and igniting of the Keystone Pipeline project—can only consequently generate human impairment, directly or through climate change. The economy—contrary to the vision driving the Trumpian era and in the name of which he is enacting deregulation—cannot be set in opposition to the environment without bodies becoming the vulnerable lynchpin thereof and "disability" the unjust consequence.

"Disability" may sometimes be the rhetorically strong language needed to warn of such damage. In the Trumpian context, however, "disability," given Trump's public politics of humiliation and his disdain for suffering,[9] even while invoking the plight of the work-

---

8. In week one of his administration, Trump suspended thirty protective environmental regulations issued under President Obama, despite the EPA's mission "to protect human health." See Sharon Lerner, "Protect Our Children's Brains," *Sunday New York Times* (SR 7), February 5, 2017.

9. Trump's disdain for suffering was already obvious when he, during the

ing class in terms of "crippled America," seems rather a target for that other temptation, namely, the possibility of toying with aggression, especially where life has been culturally devalued. Given that Trump's cabinet appointees seem, on first blush, to be drawn from among today's corporate "robber barons," we should be wary of his rhetorical resolve, promising to cure the crippling malaise of the middle, working class, by unraveling the protective regulations from labor through ecological standards. Protective policy regulations are means by which we've begun to secure flesh as a shared commons.

"Crippled America"

But what shall we make of the fact that sixteen of the twenty states receiving the highest Social Security disability payments are states, stretching from Appalachia through the post-industrial pockets of the Northeast and lower Midwest, that voted for a Trump presidency?[10] Recipients of Social Security disability may not be among those who lean into "the disability rights movement." But to account for how "disability" plays in the Trump era, one cannot ignore this phenomenon. As mining and industry recede, failing health doubles over failing futures: persons—knees buckling, souls despairing—stare into the haunting abyss of purposeless days and ghost towns. If there are jobs still to be had in former industrial communities, persons, backs and tendons worn out, have often become misfit to the context, for example, unable to carry fifty pounds or climb ladders or stand on one's feet all day. At that point, Social Security disability payments, an income below the poverty line, may be the economic mainstay for a household.

---

election cycle, criticized Senator John McCain, a former Navy pilot taken prisoner in North Vietnam: "He's not a war hero. . . . I like people who weren't captured." See Ben Schreckinger, "Trump Attacks McCain: 'I Like People Who Weren't Captured,'" *Politico,* July 18, 2015. It was equally in view when Trump cut off health care for his nephew's disabled son. See John Cassidy, "What Sort of Man Is Donald Trump," *New Yorker* (January 4, 2016), http://www.newyorker.com.

10. Paula Dwyer, "Trump Wins Big in Disability Country," *Bloomberg View*, April 26, 2016.

Trump's meme "Crippled America" draws attention, among other things,[11] to the suppressed pain of communities abandoned, livelihoods outclassed. Trump's intention to give full throttle to the economy, by erasure of protective environmental, banking, and corporate regulations, intends, he claims, to sympathize with this economic pain and so to circulate resources in such a way as to alleviate this unbearable identity. "Disability," marked from the get-go with that hissing "dis," is not a liberative identity. "Disability" is a disqualification, a sociocultural construction based in economics and couched in aesthetics and medicine that precedes one. To identify another as "disabled" is always already to submit that person to the politics of humiliation. In the face of cultural humiliation, Trump's implicit narrative arc, that the crippled will be cured by a messianic figure ("I alone can fix it"), may feel familiar not only to those conditioned in authoritarian family structures and/or to an evangelical audience, but even to a technoscientifically sophisticated one, since biotechnoscience assumed the miracle tradition.

The "cure of the cripple" has, however, not been a story of hope, either for PWDs or, economically, for colonized continents. It is an arc of hope plotted within "strong theology" and registering no awareness of the geotemporal rhythms of earth and the limits of flesh.[12] Such a national analytic of disablement as is "Crippled

---

11. "Crippled America" also apparently refers to the apocalyptic surmises of Steve Bannon, Trump's chief strategist. Bannon views "Judeo-Christian America" as crippled by secularism and religious pluralism. The loss of "Judeo-Christian values," including the Christian convictions informing capitalism, leaves the United States, Bannon contends, weak and unprepared for its war with Islam. "Secularism has sapped the strength of the Judeo-Christian West to defend its ideals," Bannon declared at a 2014 Vatican conference. See Paul Blumenthal and J. M. Rieger, "Steve Bannon Believes the Apocalypse Is Coming and War Is Inevitable," *Huffington Post*, February 8, 2017. But, of course, one could interpret secularism as a practice of Christian hospitality to religious difference. And one could comparably see the religious pluralism of America as comparable to "La Convivencia," the cohabitation of Islam, Judaism, and Christianity for several hundred years (711–1492) on the Iberian Peninsula. Fear of alterity tips this into an apocalyptic register.

12. Political theorist William E. Connolly observes that "the desire for consummate human agency" over uncertainty, contained or enclosed in the

America"—"disability" seemingly biomedically self-apparent and therefore sym/pathetic—was first mapped onto the African continent ahead of the colonial mission, cloaking imperialism, including massive resource extraction, under the guise of medical humanism. Resource depletion there has actually further aggravated human impairment. There, bodies, first made vulnerable by unjust economic and ecological policies, have been turned into the new medical and pharmaceutical marketplace. There is nothing innocent or compassionate about the assessment "disability." It is dangerous rhetoric, inflating the prowess of those who presume authority over it and covering up the political and economic policies aggravating the conditions that occasion disablement. Trump's salvific resolve appears no different than the early stages of colonialism, unregulated resource extraction under the guise of humanitarian repair.

For persons of faith, resisting this narrative will involve not only checking the strong theology behind the purported cure but rethinking theological anthropology. Modernity's social contract assumed that each body constitutes a natural resource; by marketing one's labor, a person might thereby participate in the cash nexus and, later, the capitalist consumer banquet. America's cultural disdain for disability, the marginalization of those held outside this labor contract, has been shaped by an implicit Puritan ethos, a sentiment lifted up from Christian Scriptures, that is, "Those who are unwilling to work will not get to eat" (2 Thessalonians 3:10). When paid labor becomes not only the means by which we belong together as a nation but a religious norm of the self, the economically precaritized may assume further harm to their own environment and bodies in the hope of jobs. Self-loathing, the introjection of public feeling, understandably seeks relief, as may account for some measure of those who hope in Trump.

Might we, theologically speaking, begin to challenge both disability as a disqualifying cultural judgment as well as the linkage between work and the value of a human life? This becomes impera-

---

economy, resonates with "the quest to surrender to an all-encompassing God." See his *Capitalism and Christianity, American Style* (Durham, NC: Duke University Press, 2008), xiii.

tive given the likelihood that PWDs are but the first inkling of an economy wherein we will be challenged to live "good lives without good jobs."[13] We need, as a nation that admits the vulnerability of flesh, to propose new ways of living so as to counter communities abandoned, the emergence of technofeudalism, and the inequality of unfettered capitalism. Policy wise, universal basic income along with affordable health care will go far to redress the racialization of the disabled as well as communities economically abandoned.

Conclusion

"Disability" is today something of a strange universal, an unexpected nexus at which persons from diverse ideological perspectives meet. Prone amid economic scarcity to horizontal violence over who among us is more deserving, PWDs nonetheless know too well how many hours and programs it takes to patch together subsistence livelihood, how hard it is to remain psychologically buoyant given culture's "dis"/missal. A raised eyebrow, a simple offer of recognition among those on the racial underside of humanism, registers appreciative awareness of the courage summoned and the indignities endured to get what one needs to make a life. Forced together by culture's refusal, PWDs may even suggestively insinuate a politics of hope behind the scrim of ideological differences. Maybe crips could become in the Trump era, given our respect for suffering, something of a strange attractor and a counterforce of hope. This essay has argued that such a liminal collectivity may be furthered by faith communities and/or persons religious who value flesh as a commons, and who today think anew about how, given the loss of work, we will as a nation distribute the benefits needed to make a life. For contrary to the messianic narrative borrowed by Trump, the politics of hope requires learning how to keep faith with one another in our differences.

---

13. Michael Lind, "Good Lives without Good Jobs," *New York Times,* Sunday Review/Opinion (SR1), September 18, 2016.

CHAPTER 17

Draw the Circle Queerly, Then Draw It Queerer Still

MARVIN M. ELLISON

And always remember: If Donald Trump can become president, nothing is impossible.
—Eugene Robinson, *Washington Post*

During the sorrowful week of Donald Trump's inauguration as president, I also mourned the death of Mitzi Lichtman, a lesbian friend and justice advocate in Maine whose obituary stated that her "friends and relatives marched in her memory at the Women's March on January 21, 2017, in many cities nationwide. She showed us that there is *nothing wrong with hoping for something that seems unlikely and nearly impossible.*"[1] The queer justice movement, in which Mitzi and countless others have been engaged for decades in the United States and beyond, has long dared to seek the "nearly impossible."

Queer activists, including queer activists of faith, have earned our reputation as disruptive nonconformists by questioning the normal and conventional whenever the prevailing cultural habits and norms of the day have reinforced social hierarchies of privilege and value. We have proudly embraced maladjustment as a moral virtue, especially our refusal to rest quietly in the face of injustice and oppression whether our own or that of others. The

---

1. *Penobscot Bay Pilot*, January 23, 2017. Emphasis added.

moral struggle is not narrowly about the inclusion of any particular out-group within a messed-up, inequitable status quo, but rather the far more demanding struggle to end oppressive power relations through personal and institutional transformation so that all might freely live in communal right relations of mutual respect in which power and resources are broadly and fairly shared.

This justice work, perennially challenging and perennially necessary, has become even more urgent as the Trump-Pence administration begins to unfold policies and practices that have already increased suffering among Muslim immigrant and other marginalized communities. By all the signs, what lies ahead is further dehumanization of queer people, poor people, non-Christians, and people of color. As John Cassidy has observed, "Although Trump poses as a champion of the common man, he is a prime exemplar and beneficiary of oligarchical capitalism." As "an inveterate bully who views the world exclusively in terms of winning and losing,"[2] Trump shows contempt for the weak and marginalized and seeks to wall off those who are racially and culturally other. After all, didn't the November 2016 presidential election place in the White House a self-professed "Assaulter in Chief," a deeply flawed, self-aggrandizing man who has publicly boasted about hitting on women with impunity, has relished playing the bully in business and on reality television, and now has gained access to the U.S. nuclear codes?

Soon after the inauguration, in a *New York Times* guest editorial, lifelong Republican Peter Wehner argued that the trouble with Trump is less ideological and more a matter of temperament and character. "Donald Trump is a transgressive personality," Wehner acknowledged. "He thrives on creating disorder, in violating rules, in provoking outrage. . . . For Mr. Trump, *nothing is sacred*." How does this bode for the country and world? Wehner's reading, by many estimates not his alone, is that "a man with illiberal tendencies, a volatile personality, and no internal checks is now president. This isn't going to end well."[3]

---

2. John Cassidy, "Donald Trump's Alarmingly Trumpian Transition," *New Yorker,* January 4, 2017.

3. Peter Wehner, *New York Times Sunday Review,* January 22, 2017.

While it is tempting to focus on Trump's disordered personality as if the problem at hand is primarily psychological, it is imperative to pay even closer attention to Trump's disordered politics of fear and contagion and his administration's authoritarian agenda. It is no exaggeration to speak of Trump's ascendency in terms of rising fascism, a trend well underway in Europe as well as the United States. Trump's "Make America Great Again" movement is authoritarian in tone and worldview. It unashamedly promotes a white nationalist agenda and truncated vision of America that puts communities of color in the gravest danger, including blacks in so-called inner city wastelands, Mexicans at the border, and immigrants from Muslim-majority countries. By insisting on "America first," Trump is deploying code language that resonates with his supporters about exercising a preferential option for all things white, male, heterosexual, and rich within a Christian-supremacist social order. Even in the early days of his administration, as Trump issues a barrage of executive orders and pushes Congress to follow his policy directives, we see an authoritarian impulse at work, rewarding loyalists, punishing dissenters, and consolidating power in a monarchical presidency.

Trump-style authoritarianism endangers democratic institutions by threatening to upend delicate systems of checks and balances, undermine respect for the rule of law, and delegitimize the media in its watchdog role. All dictatorial leaders seek to alienate followers from investing in the common good and to discredit the cultural values necessary for sustaining cultural diversities, including a robust religious pluralism. In Trump's case that means castigating "political correctness" and multiculturalism, heightening fears about "hoards of illegals" overwhelming national borders, scoffing at climate science, denouncing wealth redistribution, pandering to right-wing religion, and feeding nostalgia for a long-ago discredited vision of a white, culturally homogenous America.

Maintaining proper perspective requires keeping foremost in mind, as Henry A. Giroux argues, that "Trump's entire movement is rooted in an ethnic, racial, and linguistic nationalism that sanctions and glorifies violence against designated enemies and outsiders, is animated by a myth of [national] decline and nostalgic renewal, and [is] centered on a masculine cult of personality."[4] By asserting himself as the victorious "strong man" who exaggerates his self-proclaimed mandate as the long-awaited savior to restore national prosperity and safety where "all others have failed," Trump is responding to, and at the same time deftly cultivating, the pervasive sense of fear, powerlessness, loneliness, and vulnerability found among increasing numbers of people within a neoliberal social order that has, for at least four decades, been casting off its own members as expendable "losers" and still today "derides dependency, solidarity, community, and any viable notion of the commons." Under a Trump regime, what Giroux calls the "savagery of neoliberalism" will very likely intensify. Confidence will further erode in the capacity of citizens, through their democratic institutions, to contain the super-rich or hold those who abuse power accountable. Therefore, be prepared to grasp how under the Trump presidency, as Giroux summarizes, "the worse dimensions of a neoliberal order will be accelerated and will include deregulating restrictions on corporate power, cutting taxes for the rich, expanding the military, privatizing public education, suppressing civil liberties, waging a war against dissent, treating Black communities as war zones, and dismantling all public good."[5]

LBGTQ activists agree that Trump is, at best, indifferent about our justice concerns and human rights struggles and, at worst, hostile. Throughout the presidential campaign, he indicated his readiness to roll back LBGTQ gains achieved over the past decades, including marriage equality, the right of gay adoption, nondiscrimination protections, support for transgender youth and adults in securing access to health care and public accommodations, and President Obama's executive orders to protect federal LBGTQ workers. Presidential power to nominate one or more ultraconservative Supreme Court justices gives additional weight to Trump's threats. Headlines from the LGBTQ press and other sources reflect the rising anxiety within LBGTQ communities: "LBGT Activists

---

4. Henry A. Giroux, "Militant Hope in the Age of Trump," *Tikkun,* January 18, 2017.

5. Ibid.

Brace for Efforts to Undermine Recent Progress,"[6] "Under Trump LGBT Student Rights Could Be in Trouble,"[7] and, again, "Trump Win Seen as 'Devastating Loss' for Gay and Transgender People."[8]

Perhaps the most poignant indictor of present and future troubles is the negative impact of Trump's demeanor and policies on the safety and well-being of queer youth. The Human Rights Campaign (HRC) recently conducted a postelection survey across the United States of more than 50,000 queer youth ages thirteen to eighteen representing diversities in gender, sexual orientation, race, ethnicity, and religious affiliation. During or since the 2016 election, 70 percent of these youth reported witnessing or directly encountering bullying, hate messages, or harassment; 79 percent said that these incidences escalated throughout the presidential campaign. When asked what motivated these acts of violence, youth see the bullying and harassment directed at them as hostile efforts to police and keep under strict surveillance not only gender presentation and sexual orientation, but also race and immigration status. The rancorous Trump campaign gave ample encouragement for such public bullying, and few if any Trump supporters (or critics) have misunderstood either the intended message or target audiences. Accordingly, it is not surprising that one-third of the queer youth responding to the HRC survey, especially queer youth of color and non-Christian religious identity, have shared that they have felt hopeless during most or all of the postelection period.

While the bad news is undoubtedly the widespread fear and anxiety registered among these vulnerable youth, the good news is that the majority of these youth also say "they are more committed than ever to supporting others who are targeted for discrimination and harassment."[9] The HRC findings about queer youth are in sync

---

6. *Portland Press Herald,* January 19, 2017.

7. *The Nation,* January 11, 2017.

8. *New York Times,* November 11, 2016.

9. "Key Findings," *Human Rights Campaign Post-Election Survey of Youth,* Human Rights Campaign Foundation, January 2017. Chris Sommerfeldt, "American Teens Report Sharp Spike in Bullying since President's Trump's Election, Survey Finds" (*New York Daily News,* January 25, 2017), shares a vignette about a transgender youth who participated in the HRC

with similar research conducted by the Gay, Lesbian, and Straight Education Network (GLSEN), which concludes that "life may have gotten better for many in the LGBT community in the last decade, but for LGBT youth in middle and high school, there is much room for improvement."[10] Teachers often wish to help, but lack training in appropriate response. Again, youth experience oppression daily, but many resist and encourage others to do so. As one trans youth reported, "On days I am really sad, I give myself five minutes to cry. Then I make myself do something proactive for the community."[11]

Doing something, making a difference, happens through communal acts of resistance and by keeping alive what Rev. Dr. William Barber II of the Forward Together/Moral Mondays movement lifts up as "dangerous memories," not only memories of injustices borne but also life-affirming visions of a radically different, more humane world.[12] In addition, mounting resistance to authoritarianism requires adopting an intersectional justice analysis that is attentive to class, race, and religious diversity as well as to gender and sexuality, and it also involves exploring effective strategies for embodying a communal solidarity with those disproportionately harmed because of rising economic inequality, white supremacy, and Christian cultural hegemony.

It is important to notice how, within the last forty years, there have been significant gains for the LBGTQ communities in terms of greater cultural acceptance of gender equality and sexual diversity as well as enhanced legal recognition and protection of same-sex relationships and families. Much good has been accomplished because LBGTQ folks, courageously and often at great

---

survey: "A transgender teen from Idaho, whose identity was kept anonymous by the HRC, said they and a Latin friend were confronted at school by a classmate who said, 'Donald Trump is gonna deport wastes of space like you, and hopefully he does something about freaks like you too.'"

10. Marissa Higgins, "LGBT Students Are Not Safe at School," *The Atlantic*, October 18, 2016.

11. Ibid.

12. William J. Barber II, *The Third Reconstruction: Moral Mondays, Fusion Politics, and the Rise of a New Justice Movement* (Boston: Beacon Press, 2016).

cost, became publicly visible and organized locally and nationally, pressed for legislative and judicial change, and formed a vibrant change movement that honored LBGTQ lives, celebrated our spiritual and moral capacity to love and be loved, and worked diligently, though not always successfully, at connecting across our many racial, class, and cultural differences. Our mantras have been "love wins" and "difference without dominance."

At the same time, we should be sobered that during those same forty years, there has also been the ascendance of right-wing populism in the United States, certainly fueled by resistance to these same cultural changes that have benefitted LBGTQ and other communities, but also fueled by the economic dislocation of white working- and middle-class Americans who have been suffering stagnant or declining wages, increased unemployment, and the painful disruptions caused by globalization, automation, and deindustrialization. As Thomas Edsall observes, because of increasing economic inequality within the United States, accelerated by the 2008 economic meltdown, "the number of those left behind has grown steadily. Those who do not experience the benefits of prosperity . . . can see 'others'—'an influx of foreigners,' for example—as the culprit causing their predicament."[13] This tendency is particularly true when white men who are socialized with an expectation of entitlement—their "God-given right" to be on top—become resentful and enraged when they experience a humiliating decline in fortune and status, and display what sociologist Michael Kimmel calls "aggrieved entitlement." As Kimmel writes, "The new American anger is more than defensive; it is reactionary. It seeks to restore, to retrieve, to reclaim something that is perceived to have been lost. Angry White Men look to the past for their imagined and desired future. . . . Theirs is the anger of the entitled: we are entitled to those jobs, those positions of unchallenged dominance. And when we are told we are not going to get them, we get angry."[14]

---

13. Thomas B. Edsall, "The Peculiar Populism of Donald Trump," *New York Times*, February 2, 2017.

14. Michael Kimmel, *Angry White Men: American Masculinity at the End of an Era* (New York: Nation Books, 2013), 21.

Rising economic insecurity and displacement, coupled with confusion about cultural change and fears about immigration, have created the conditions for authoritarian populism to emerge. Add racism and white supremacy to this mix, and the brew is toxic. Sociologist Arlie Russell Hochschild, in her 2016 study *Strangers in Their Own Land*, examines the persistence of white racism in fomenting the alienation of many white voters from contemporary American culture. Hochschild's findings can be summarized this way: "Less-educated white Americans feel that they have become 'strangers in their own land.' They see themselves as victims of affirmative action and betrayed by 'line-cutters'—African-Americans, immigrants, refugees and women—who jump ahead of them in the queue for the American dream. They resent liberal intellectuals who tell them to feel sorry for the line-cutters, and dismiss them as bigots when they don't."[15]

Womanist theologian Kelly Brown Douglas amplifies this analysis by explicating how Anglo-Saxon exceptionalism undergirds white supremacist ideology and social structures in this nation, maintaining exclusive white control of place and border crossings. When nonwhites step out of place or attempt to cross borders without white permission, as Trayvon Martin and many other youth of color have experienced, they are subject to threats of violence and, increasingly, to killing violence itself.[16] White fears of losing control and of cultural displacement were much in play in the 81 percent of white evangelical Protestants and the 60 percent of white Catholics who voted for Trump. While Robert P. Jones argues that the "end of white Christian America" is in process, its demise has not yet happened, and its flaws are quite evident: its "arrogant assumption that it spoke for the country or its complicity in racism, its mistreatment of LGBT people and mischaracterization of their lives, and its willingness to compromise its theological integrity for partisan ends."[17]

---

15. Edsall, "The Peculiar Populism."

16. Kelly Brown Douglas, *Stand Your Ground: Black Bodies and the Justice of God* (Maryknoll, NY: Orbis Books, 2015).

17. Robert P. Jones, *The End of White Christian America* (New York: Simon & Schuster, 2016), 227.

What does living with theological integrity look like in an age of Trump? That's the question of the hour, and one that must be answered not in the abstract but concretely. I wager there are lived examples of profound moral and spiritual integrity that we should attend to for insight and inspiration. In closing, I mention only two.

In "Lessons from the Last Fight," lesbian activist Sarah Schulman remembers that during the first half of his presidency, Ronald Reagan refused to say the word "AIDS," even though that health crisis was escalating at the time and costing tens of thousands of lives. Grassroots queer activists in ACT UP (the AIDS Coalition to Unleash Power) and the Lesbian Avengers demonstrated, agitated, and publicly pestered civic and religious leaders and refused to stay silent or be cowed by the established powers. "Against all odd," she writes, "a despised population, abandoned by their families and government and facing a terminal disease for which there was no treatment, joined together and forced this country to change against its will."[18] Join together, act up, and don't be silenced.

The second example is also communal, this time about radically inclusive table fellowship as a spiritual practice. In the United Church of Christ congregation to which I belong, we begin public worship by saying together, "No matter who you are, and no matter where you are on life's journey, you are welcome here." That vision of inclusive wholeness is celebrated in the sacrament of communion, constructed as an open table where all are welcome, without distinction, to share nourishment and life together. The only rule of exclusion is this: each is welcome as long as each welcomes all others.

In the age of Trump, we need vision, we need to stay in the struggle, and, I would argue, we need a grounding spirituality to claim—and be claimed by—a fierce, holy power that is life giving and life transforming. This transformative power is not empire's power to "use, abuse, own, and discard," but rather the "powers of the weak,"[19] to use Elizabeth Janeway's felicitous phrase, which are

18. Sarah Schulman, "Lessons from the Last Fight," *Harper's Magazine,* January 28, 2017.

19. Elizabeth Janeway, *Powers of the Weak* (New York: Morrow Quill Paperbacks, 1981).

twofold: the power of disbelief and the power of coming together. Disbelief encourages the questioning of official interpretations and of so-called alternative facts that falsely claim legitimacy, but only bolster the status quo and further mystify. Coming together grants the disenfranchised voice and power. Here power refers to the subversive power "from below," which includes queer folks and other outcasts, nobodies, and the maladjusted, all of whom pledge, against the odds, to connect in rising self-respect, to steadfastly commit to justice making as the rebuilding of community, and all the while to refuse to turn others into enemies. Our queerest, most subversive claims are to insist that, no, Trump is not lord, and, yes, change is possible.

CHAPTER 18

White Christian Complicity in Trump's Victory and Responsibility Now for Faith, Resistance, and Healing

JIM WALLIS

The "Why" of Trump—The Complicity of White Christians

Faith leaders shouldn't predict elections. But our Sojourners team can tell you that when Donald Trump announced he was running for president in 2015, I thought he would win the Republican nomination and could run 50-50 with the most likely Democratic nominee, Hillary Clinton. I knew all the conventional wisdom would prevent that if it worked, and I hoped that I would be proved wrong; but it seemed to me that many of the traditional political assumptions might not apply for this election It was an unprecedented election cycle with an unprecedented candidate.

I thought he might win for two reasons:

1. Donald Trump embodies the worst of American values—the consummate attractions of money, sex, and power—which many Americans are drawn to. He was the Reality Television Candidate in a reality TV era with many Americans watching.
2. We're at a crossroads of race in America, and I could see from his first speech how Trump was going to use white discomfort with rapidly changing American demographics to foment anger at "the others" they blamed for their grievances.

It was a *perfect storm* that elected Donald Trump. It combined flawed candidates and a populist impulse on all sides against a system that truly is rigged—both economically and politically—as candidates from both sides said, Bernie Sanders along with Trump. It showed the skillful turning of economic anger into racial anger about cultural change by a candidate who is and always has been a master message marketer, with no compelling message from his opponent.

At the heart of the storm was a clear racial division. Let's be frank here: This was, as Van Jones put it, a "white-lash" election. It was a race election. Contrary to all the data and demographics about a changing America, Donald Trump defied the conventional wisdom and won by mobilizing the white vote and turning out angry white voters in ex-urban and rural parts of key swing states in greater numbers than others believed was possible—all while depressing the turnout for his opponent through tactics ranging from capitalizing on Russian-aided leaks of politically embarrassing emails and the unprecedented public letters from FBI Director James Comey, to a variety of voter suppression tactics used in many states, including Wisconsin and North Carolina.

This wasn't only noncollege-educated white voters (whom the elites and pundits like to pick on); it wasn't only white male voters or older white voters. A vast majority of white voters of all education levels, classes, and genders came out to put Donald Trump in the White House.

Donald Trump *ran on racial bigotry, xenophobia, and misogyny*—not implicitly and covertly, but explicitly and overtly. In an America that is rapidly changing demographically and culturally, Donald Trump chose to run on white identity politics and to bring white nationalism back into the mainstream of American public life. And white people from all walks of life voted for him, including a clear majority of white Christians—Catholics, mainline Protestants, and an overwhelming majority of white evangelicals. Some white voters told themselves and others that they were voting for Trump in spite of his bigotry, rather than because of it—but the bottom line is that racial bigotry wasn't a deal breaker for a majority of white voters, including white Christian voters.

Most white evangelicals didn't seem to mind that they gave their votes and, some would say, sold their souls to a man who embodies the most sinful and shameful worship of money, sex, and power. Donald Trump—perhaps more than any other public figure in America—represents the very worst values of what American culture has become. We have never witnessed such religious hypocrisy as we saw in this election, with the majority of white Christians voting for a man like Donald Trump, including an overwhelming number of white evangelicals: 81 percent, 8 points better than Romney, including 75 percent of *white evangelical women.*

It is a real tragedy that most of America's well-known white megachurch pastors were not heard from in this election, and their silence in the face of Trump's racial politics may end their own moral credibility. The Religious Right's leaders, who supported Trump politically over all their previously expressed religious values, showed once and for all that they have always been primarily right-wing political operatives and should never be taken as "religious" again.

Indeed, the vast majority of white evangelicals acted more white than evangelical, putting their white identities ahead of their Christian identities, and choosing their identities as Republicans over their identities as Christians. They prioritized the strategic idol of a conservative Supreme Court and were willing to look the other way not only on their candidate's bigotry but his shocking lack of personal morality. As Andy Crouch, the editor of *Christianity Today*, said in October:

> But there is a point at which strategy becomes its own form of idolatry—an attempt to manipulate the levers of history in favor of the causes we support. Strategy becomes idolatry, for ancient Israel and for us today, when we make alliances with those who seem to offer strength—the chariots of Egypt, the vassal kings of Rome—at the expense of our dependence on God who judges all nations, and in defiance of God's manifest concern for the stranger, the widow, the orphan, and the oppressed. Strategy becomes idolatry when we betray our

deepest values in pursuit of earthly influence. And because such strategy requires capitulating to idols and princes and denying the true God, it ultimately always fails.[1]

Admittedly, there were issues of principle involved for many Christians like abortion and religious liberty. But as Russell Moore, the president of the Ethics and Religious Liberty Commission of the Southern Baptist Convention put it:

> In a time when racial tensions run high across the country, Mr. Trump incites division, with slurs against Hispanic immigrants and with protectionist jargon that preys on turning economic insecurity into ugly "us versus them" identity politics. When evangelicals should be leading the way on racial reconciliation, as the Bible tells us to, are we really ready to trade unity with our black and brown brothers and sisters for this angry politician? Jesus taught his disciples to "count the cost" of following him. We should know, he said, where we're going and what we're leaving behind. We should also count the cost of following Donald Trump.[2]

When the videotape emerged of Donald Trump bragging about adultery and sexual assault, some white evangelicals initially said "enough." But in the end, the votes of white evangelicals demonstrated the truth as many of them came back to the Republican candidate. Because of this politicizing of the term "evangelical," many younger evangelicals no longer are comfortable using the word to identify themselves.

Because of all this, the distrust now between people of color and white people—including Christians of color and white Christians—is greater than I have seen since the civil rights movement and legislation of the 1960s.

---

1. Andy Crouch, "Speak Truth to Trump," *Christianity Today*, October 10, 2016.

2. Russell Moore, "Have Evangelicals Who Support Trump Lost Their Values?" *New York Times*, September 17, 2015.

Responsibility of White Christians to Engage in Faith, Healing, and Resistance on Behalf of All Vulnerable People

Many of our *Sojourners* readers are asking themselves and us: What can I do? Maybe more importantly, for white Christians, What *must* I do? What's my responsibility in this new political reality that I, or at the very least people who look like me, created? The politics going on now are to some extent beyond our control, but we can control what we do with our own faith and with our own actions. There are two clear and critical roles for the faith community.

First, we are instructed to always protect vulnerable and marginalized people. We are always to include and welcome "the other"—we, people of faith, whom our Scriptures instruct to preach and practice racial justice and reconciliation. That commitment is already coming from many quarters, at the grassroots and at many levels of leadership in faith communities. In February, a broad group of Christian leaders from many denominations and ethnic backgrounds launched the Matthew 25 Pledge—a unifying commitment for those on different political sides to join together to defend those who feel and *are* most vulnerable in the Trump era.

In Matthew 25, Jesus says, "I was hungry and you gave me food, I was thirsty and you gave me something to drink, I was a stranger and you welcomed me, I was naked and you gave me clothing, I was sick and you took care of me, I was in prison and you visited me. . . . Truly I tell you, just as you did it to one of the least of these who are members of my family, you did it to me." In this text, Jesus is literally saying to us: How you treat the most vulnerable is how you treat me. He is saying I will know how much you love me by how you respond—or don't respond—to them. This gospel passage, which was my own conversion text, is coming up again and again right at the time when so many people are feeling vulnerable *and* so many others don't know what to do.

Here is what we all must do—and no group more so than white Christians, who bear the greatest responsibility for bringing Trump to power: stand up and defend those most at risk at this crucial moment in America's political history. Matthew 25 is answering our question. *Matthew 25 is rising up in the face of a new political regime that is making many people feel so afraid.*

The Matthew 25 Pledge simply says: "I pledge to protect and defend vulnerable people in the name of Jesus." It's the outcome of a retreat just after the election that brought together a broad spectrum of pastors, heads of churches, grassroots activists, and the leaders of national faith-based organizations and networks who prayed and discerned together about the election results, reaching consensus to act in solidarity with those most at risk in the new administration.

No matter how Christians might have voted, it is absolutely clear that Christians are always called to serve Jesus by sheltering those most in need. *This could be a unifying commitment between people of faith on different sides of the aisle—to protect the most vulnerable together.* Clearly, many people in America are feeling quite vulnerable right now—racial and religious minorities, women, and LGBTQ people—and especially those who sit at the intersections of marginalized groups. We should be committed to protecting the lives and rights of all those who feel threatened. The starting point should be the three groups most consistently attacked during the campaign, as the early weeks of this administration have clearly indicated they continue to be targets. Here are some concrete action steps:

1. Support undocumented immigrants threatened with mass deportation.

Arresting and deporting hard-working and law-abiding people who have lived in America for decades would break up families and potentially put people's lives in danger. Many at risk are the young "Dreamers," who were brought here as children and who turned in their names and contact information to the administration in response to executive orders that allowed them to study and work.

Already, prayerful networks of support are being set up in faith communities to offer love, welcome, assistance, and ultimately, resistance to block and obstruct such mass deportations. If massive arrests of the people Jesus calls "the stranger" are ordered, immigration police will be forced to arrest many of those immigrants in our churches, seminaries, schools, and homes. Faith communities must continue to make it clear that they have the capacity to impose a clear domestic cost on any efforts aimed at massive deportation of undocumented immigrants who have become our neighbors and fellow churchgoers.

2. Stand with African Americans and other people of color threatened by racial policing.

Black pastors and parents are especially concerned about how their young people will be treated under an administration that has fueled racial bigotry and continued to stoke those fears by its White House and cabinet appointments. The new president promotes "law and order" and "stop and frisk" in an uncritical code language that racial minorities understand. But if there is little or no accountability from the federal government under the Jeff Sessions Department of Justice to excessive force against our citizens of color, and especially young people, local clergy are committing to hold their police departments accountable.

For Christians, when one part of the body suffers, as it says in 1 Corinthians 12:12-26, the whole body should feel that pain and respond. So racially diverse local clergy from ecumenical and interfaith associations must join together and go to their sheriffs in every community to help support healthy community policing. But they must also promise to watch, monitor, and resist any racial policing by standing against such practices and standing with those who they are aimed at, promising to hold law enforcement accountable to racial equity and healing in our communities.

3. Defend the lives and religious liberty of Muslims, threatened with travel restrictions, monitoring, and even registration.

Citizens of the United States and immigrants who practice their Islamic faith in this country—our friends and neighbors—are our brothers and sisters as fellow human beings and children of God. Many Christians, Jews, and others who believe in religious liberty are promising that if Muslims living in America, whether citizens or immigrants, are ever asked to register based on their religious identity, we will deliberately line up before them to declare ourselves to be Muslims, too. We will also never accept a religious test for entry into the United States. Now more than ever, as we've already witnessed the Trump administration's clear efforts to discredit and suspect Muslims, our Christian faith should *compel* us to act—to advocate for welcoming refugees and immigrants of all faiths into our country instead of turning them away. Religious tests, in addition to being morally repugnant, would threaten our nation's democratic principles and the constitutional rights of every American. The violation of the religious freedom of our Muslim brothers and sisters should not be accepted by any people of faith.

Rather than just watching, grieving, and feeling sorry for what is happening to the most marginalized, who are named in the twenty-fifth chapter of Matthew, we can pledge to join together in circles of support in the name of Jesus. In unjust times, justice often starts in the small places and personal decisions that challenge the big places and structural injustice. As Brittany Packnett, a leading Black Lives Matter activist, said in *Sojourners* magazine: "The Christ I serve did not sit idly by in times like these—for in eras like this one, inaction is a sin."[3]

The second role and responsibility for Christians in the Trump era, especially white Christians, is that faith communities and congregations at the local level must become safe and sacred spaces for deeper conversations about race in our history and in our communities today. We should talk about our original sin, how it still lingers, and what repentance from our continuing racial sins might look like. In a divided nation, people of faith must help lead the way, learning and showing how faith can and must triumph over race, that "Christian" must come before "white" and not the other way around.

In this new age of Trump, many people of color are losing hope for an America that values diversity—and them—and are losing trust in white Christians who loudly claim not to be racist but who

---

3. Brittany Packnett, "Resistance is Holy Work," *Sojourners*, January 2017.

clearly decided that Trump's racial bigotry was not a disqualifier for their vote. White Christians ignored Trump's bigotry with no seeming understanding of or empathy toward families of color. Further, when white people dismiss the real fears that parents of color have for their children after this election, it painfully reveals the distance of the white majority from people of color in America and the realities of their daily lives.

What in the world do we do about that? In our homes and in our churches, we must answer the question: "What should white Christians and white churches do in the Trump era?" Repent of the sin of racism. It's time for a serious study of the history of racism in America and the narrative that must be changed. It's time for much more direct proximity between white Christians and Christians of color. It's time for uncomfortable but honest listening and conversations with one another. It's time to change our relationships and racial geography, time for prayer, and, most of all, for action to change our practices and our policies. Studying racism in the era of Trump will be an act of reconciliation and resistance.

Perhaps the value that our country needs most right now, in an age of almost complete cynicism about politics, is the power and promise of *hope*. We can decide to spend our time, energy, and the gifts of our lives to make this a better world—for those around us, especially for those on the edges, and to be good stewards of the creation itself. That's who people of faith are supposed to be; that is what we are supposed to do. And there is no better time to do that than right now. No matter what politics says and does, it is always time for faith to flourish and move forward.

CHAPTER 19

Feminism in a Reactionary Time

SUSAN BROOKS THISTLETHWAITE

It is absolutely crucial for feminism to resist not only the rise of Donald J. Trump, but also the kind of global reactionary politics of which he is a part. In the United States, however, unless white feminists confront and reject the deformations of white privilege in themselves and in protest movements, this will continue to be an insurmountable barrier to their joining with effective movement politics.

Global Trajectories and Feminism

I work out of a liberation theological method, and the first step in that method is contextual analysis, from global to local to personal.[1] The global context is defined by the rise of the "Strong Man" as a reaction to disruptive forces of globalization, and we must see the rise of Trump as part of that trajectory. The rise of the "Strong Man" phenomenon has been years in the making. These types of leaders are Vladimir Putin (2012) in Russia, Abdel Fattah al-Sisi (2013) in Egypt, Recep Tayyip Erdogan (2014) in Turkey, Rodrigo Duterte (2016) in the Philippines. And now Donald Trump (2016). Turkey is perhaps the closest analogy since Erdogan was democratically elected.

---

1. Susan Brooks Thistlethwaite and Mary Potter Engel, *Lift Every Voice: Constructing Christian Theologies from the Underside* (Maryknoll, NY: Orbis Books, 1998).

Pollsters and many in the American public may have missed this pattern, but economists have to pay attention to global trends and global markets. In May of 2016, the *Financial Times* ran an article, "Donald Trump, Vladimir Putin and the Lure of the Strongman":

> All these men have promised to lead a national revival through the force of their personalities and their willingness to ignore liberal niceties. In many cases, the promise of decisive leadership is backed up by a willingness—sometimes explicit, sometimes implied—to use illegal violence against enemies of the state.[2]

It is both shocking and yet not surprising that an article about the rise of the "Strong Man" thesis does not explore the obvious heteropatriarchalism of the "strong" and "man" phenomenon. Objections to the misogyny and the homophobia that are such striking characteristics of the described "strongman" regimes are reduced to "liberal niceties." In addition, the role of conservative religion in the rise of reactionary regimes is often ignored. Vladimir Putin's control in Russia owes much to his embrace of the Russian Orthodox Church and appeals to the glorious myth of "Mother Russia." White evangelical Protestant support was essential to the Trump win.[3] Conservative religion provides the "Strong Man" a "moral" case for misogyny and heterosexism. Putin has persecuted LGBTQ people in both law and custom. Every member of the Trump cabinet is strongly opposed to LGBTQ equality.

Putin and Trump also share a deep-seated misogyny. Putin is both crudely sexist, especially in regard to women who oppose him, and promotes women who are "showgirls" for his regime.[4] Trump's daughter Ivanka is a trusted advisor, and several cabinet appointees are women. Yet, as is well known, Trump was recorded talk-

---

2. Gideon Rachman, "Donald Trump, Vladimir Putin and the Lure of the Strongman," *Financial Times*, May 16, 2016.

3. Daniel Cox, "White Christians Side with Trump," PPRI.org, November 9, 2016, http://www.prri.org.

4. Janet Elise Johnson, "Putin's Russia Promotes both Women and Misogyny in Politics. Wait, What?," *Washington Post*, November 6, 2016.

ing about how he could get away with sexually assaulting women because he was rich and famous. Trump: "Grab 'em by the pussy. You can do anything."[5]

It is striking, therefore, that Putin's sharpest critics, who have been hounded and some members jailed, are a Russian feminist punk rock group named Pussy Riot. The group's most famous action, for which they were arrested, was a performance in Moscow's Cathedral of Christ the Savior to oppose Putin as a dictator and expose his ties to the Russian Orthodox Church. After being released from prison, members of Pussy Riot released their first song in English in 2015 called "I Can't Breathe." It is a tribute to Eric Garner, the Staten Island man whose last words were "I can't breathe" as he was held in a choke hold by New York City police.[6] There is a repeated refrain in this Pussy Riot song: "It's getting dark in New York City." Also in 2015, Pussy Riot members warned Americans against taking the rise of Donald Trump too lightly. "Everybody [is] joking about Donald Trump now, but it's a very short way from joke to sad reality when you have a really crazy president speaking about breaking every moral and logic norm. So I hope that he will not be president. That's very simple."[7]

Clearly, feminist analysis and action are required in the United States to combat the dangerous racist, heteronormative patriarchalism that has the country in its grip. But unless feminism undergoes substantial self-examination and re-invention, this much-needed form of resistance will be ineffective.

Yes, Ivanka Trump Feminism Is Really a Thing

A feminist liberation analysis of the U.S. domestic context must begin with the fact that 53 percent of white women voted for Donald Trump. White women who roundly reject feminism

---

5. "Transcript: Donald Trump's Taped Comments about Women," *New York Times*, October 8, 2016.

6. Abby Ohlheiser, "'I Can't Breathe': Pussy Riot's First Song in English Is about Eric Garner," *Washington Post*, February 18, 2015.

7. Lance Gould, "Pussy Riot on Trump: We Laughed When Vladimir Putin Rose to Power, Too," *Huffington Post*, December 18, 2015.

were, of course, a big part of the Trump demographic, but white, college-educated women who self-identify as feminist were also Trump voters.[8] An article with interviews with this demographic appeared shortly after the election. Trump's business record—the fact that he bounced back despite bankruptcies—initially attracted a white woman with two adult daughters. The mother said she admires Ivanka Trump and felt she was one of the campaign's "top three assets." She sees Ivanka as a role model for one of her daughters in her own entrepreneurial interests. It's not Hillary's "Gloria Steinem feminism," she insists, but Ivanka's sleek version of female success.

Evangelical Christianity also played a role for these three women. They indicated they were Christians and anti-abortion, but other white women who called themselves feminist and pro-choice also backed Trump, saying they didn't think he really opposed abortion or thought the law in states like theirs wouldn't change even if he chose future Supreme Court justices with an eye to overturning *Roe v. Wade*.[9] What these women have in common as Trump voters is whiteness. They said they did not believe the election was about gender or race. It was a victory of "Middle America." "Middle America," however, means white, middle-class America. This brand of white feminism is decisively rooted in the history of how class in America is constructed on the basis of race.[10]

It's Not All Ivanka: My Family History of Whiteness

For decades, feminists have insisted the personal is political, but in terms of contextual analysis, it is also important to realize that the political shapes the personal. In this instance, it means I must look more deeply into my own context and connect that to the larger

---

8. Robert Jones and Daniel Cox, "Still Live Near Your Hometown? If You're White, You're More Likely to Support Trump | PRRI/The Atlantic Survey," PRRI. 2016, http://www.prri.org.

9. Emily Bazelon, "Why Did College-Educated White Women Vote for Trump?," *New York Times Magazine* (November 15, 2016).

10. See Nancy Isenberg, *White Trash: The 400-Year Untold History of Race in America* (New York: Viking, 2016).

context of how white feminism gets constructed.[11] The story of my American immigrant family begins when several in my grandparents' generation arrived as starving teenaged refugees from Hungary. They worked as children in the sweatshops of the garment district of New York City. They faced systemic discrimination as despised Central European "honkeys" as well as grinding poverty. But the racism against them did not become part of their struggles for economic justice and, for my great-aunt and grandmother, in turn in their struggles for suffrage.

The role of race in white ethnic history is, as so well argued by David Roediger in *Working Toward Whiteness: How America's Immigrants Became White. The Strange Journey from Ellis Island to the Suburbs,* strenuously ignored, poorly understood, and continuously mystified.[12] My Hungarian ancestors fought to survive in the best way they could, through joining unions and struggling for safety at work and better wages. But while my great-aunt was a union organizer and she fought for economic justice, she was also staunchly against "them coming north and taking our jobs." Her experience of the prejudice she and her siblings experienced as new immigrants to the United States did not translate into solidarity with African Americans. Far from it. She learned whiteness.

My female ancestors cut their hair and they marched for suffrage. But their commitment to votes for women, given their work in keeping African Americans out of unions, was clearly meant as a way to acquire white privilege, in terms of both voting and economic gains. For these women in my family, getting into the middle class definitely meant achieving whiteness. My family history is connected to the larger context of how the American women's suffrage movement traded away its early origins in abolitionism to get

---

11. I want to emphasize, however, how variable the results are of the way individual identities are structured. "One size *does not* fit all" in a critical approach to identity formation in liberation analysis. Each context needs a specific analysis.

12. David Roediger, *Working Toward Whiteness: How America's Immigrants Became White. The Strange Journey from Ellis Island to the Suburbs* (New York: Basic Books, 2005), 47.

across the message that votes for white women would be a strategic gain against African American men voting. Suffrage leaders such as Elizabeth Cady Stanton appealed to white race solidarity in their effort to secure the vote for *white women*, as Barbara Andolsen so well analyzes in her book about racism and the women's suffrage movement, *"Daughters of Jefferson, Daughters of Bootblacks": Racism and American Feminism.*[13]

These histories are part of the context we must analyze to understand the deep divide in the history of feminism, and one that is, in some ways, still being carried along today. Real social change is sabotaged when we separate gender, and only one gender at that, from race from class from religion from national origin. Yes, Ivanka Trump feminism is really a thing, but it is not the main thing right now. The "I didn't vote for Trump" does not give white feminists a pass. White women who would be part of a movement today to confront the rise of reactionary politics need to deeply and consistently engage the complexity of the issues we face, and consistently confront our own white privilege.

A Conflict That Cannot Be Seen Cannot Be Resolved

There is no way to go forward without conflict, and efforts to push out diversity in an effort for "unity" ultimately fail. In this past election, women of color saw what was coming far more than white women. As a sign at the #WomensMarch so pointedly said, "Black Women Tried to Save Y'All. 94%."[14] The #WomensMarch on Washington and its sister marches illustrate well the changes needed. It began badly when a call went out for a "Million Woman March," coopting the names of previous African American marches. Then three women of color, Tamika Mallory, Carmen

---

13. Barbara Andolsen, *"Daughters of Jefferson, Daughters of Bootblacks": Racism and American Feminism* (Macon, GA: Mercer University Press, 1986), cited in Jessie Daniels, "Trouble with White Feminism: Racial Origins of U.S. Feminism," *Racism Review*, February 18, 2014.

14. Zahara Hill, "11 Profound Photos from Black Women at the Women's March," *Huffington Post*, January 23, 2017.

Perez, and Linda Sarsour, all experienced activists, became the national co-chairs.[15]

Conflicts continued to abound, however, as there was not a consistent emphasis nationwide on diversity. For example, the NAACP in Portland, Oregon, withdrew its support because "queer and trans people and people of color felt as though they were being shut down when they tried to address their concerns with the event's leadership. The feeling was that those original leaders wanted the event conflict-free and tried to accomplish that by deleting comments of people they disagreed with." The national organization replaced the leadership, and the march became more inclusive. Conflict free? That's the illusion of white privilege in a nutshell. It renders all but the privileged white woman invisible. The only way forward is when these conflicts become more visible, and *it must not have to be the queer and trans people and women of color who bear the burden of bringing that up over and over.*

I interviewed a number of women while I was at the #Women'sMarch in Washington, DC, on January 21, 2017, and afterward. Older white women tended to emphasize gender solidarity as overcoming racial difference. Younger white women, on the other hand, talked to me about the importance of "intersectionality" as the future of feminism. Intersectionality as a term came from an analysis of how not only black women but also many marginalized women are rendered invisible and powerless. The "intersections" are the multiplicities and often the mutually reinforcing vulnerabilities that arise from racism, sexism, class oppression, transphobia, ableism, religious and secular diversities, and so forth.[16] Ultimately, these lead to the virtual erasure of these women within society and within movements.

When a white, cisgender, middle-class woman (such as myself!) uses the term "intersectionality," what concerns me is that this can be a leveling of the playing field, so to speak. Speaking from my own

---

15. The Women's March website, https://www.womensmarch.com.

16. Kimberlé Crenshaw, "Why Intersectionality Can't Wait," *Washington Post*, September 24, 2015.

social location, I might consciously or unconsciously be including myself in these intersections and thus ducking the power analysis. As a white feminist, I dare not skip the crucial examination of how our identities get constructed and therefore how power is distributed unequally in society and in protest movements. Contextual analysis is just the beginning. We have to move from context to action in a praxis model.

A Few Crucial Actions for White Women to Take Now

Drop the Language of Sisterhood: "Sisterhood" itself has a suppressive effect. It subtly (or not so subtly) prioritizes a particular gender and race history and experience over the multiple formations of race, class, religion, national origin, sexual identities, and their intersections in how power is constructed in this society. Instead of "sisters" or "sisterhood," I use the term "allies" because it recognizes multiplicities as well as the necessity of solidarity in action.

Focus on Actions Rather Than Words: Showing up for racial justice, for sexual justice, for a living wage, for religious tolerance, and adding your body to those movements without assuming you are in the lead ultimately says more than any words can do. I am not suggesting that this path for white cisgender women needs to be one long *mea culpa*. Your identity does change with showing up for justice over and over and over. As queer theory has taught us, identities are formed in and through cultural performances that shape you. But don't forget that however you may change through praxis, the larger society reads you as white and always will.

Make a Commitment to Be There Over and Over Again: Doing the work of confronting white heterosexual privilege in oneself and in our society is hard, and it never, ever stops. One does not arrive at a place of nonprivilege. Not ever. It is always there and must be continuously strategized against. Trust, however, can be built through long-term commitments.

Recognize Your Own Stake in these Changes: I, as a white, cisgender, educated, middle-class feminist have a stake in exposing these power conflicts because unexamined they are corrupting of any liberation theology I could possibly try to do. As Gustavo Gutiér-rez, the famous Latin American liberation theologian, once said, "I am suspicious of those who are not in the struggle for themselves." White cisgender women need to recognize that their own liberation is at stake in bringing this to consciousness and committing to this praxis.

A Very Brief Conclusion

The age of the "Strong Man" is upon us, and feminism needs to play a central role both in analyzing that and effectively countering it. But this needs to be a critically conscious feminism that priori-tizes the power deformations that whiteness always brings, and it must include continuous work on all the multiple formulations of how oppression is constructed in this society. But believe me. That is the good news. That is a way we can create an effective move-ment of resistance. And we must. The rise of the "Strong Men" around the world is incredibly dangerous.

CHAPTER 20

The Earth, Property, Pipeline, and Resistance
Waylaying Treaties

GEORGE "TINK" TINKER

> Article VI: . . . This Constitution, and the Laws of the United States which shall be made in Pursuance thereof; and all Treaties made, or which shall be made, under the Authority of the United States, shall be the supreme Law of the Land. . . .

The rash of police killings of people of color over these past few years has signaled a growing impunity of police in America. Already seventeen years ago, Michael Hardt and Antonio Negri associated the global increase in police impunity with the rise of a postmodern globalization empire, something that took a visceral step forward in the United States with the 2001 Patriot Act, passed right after the 9/11 attacks. In spite of ongoing Black Lives Matter protests, Trump's executive orders on February 9, 2017, took police impunity to a new level. At the swearing in of Jeff Sessions as U.S. Attorney General, in a moment strangely unnoticed by the press, Trump signed executive orders rhetorically couched in terms of public safety that clearly intend to increase the powers of police at all levels of society. While this auspiciously took place in the midst of Black History Month, it has immediate import for American

Indian Peoples who actually suffer a higher per capita rate of police killings than do blacks.[1]

As I write this essay, a small-time rural sheriff's heavily militarized battalion, outfitted in prime U.S. military battle gear, has geared up to squash Indian aspirations for life—one more time.[2] This time it is on behalf of Big Oil, a $3.8 billion-dollar pipeline that the company is poised to tunnel under Lake Oahe on the Missouri River right adjacent to but still on the treaty lands of the Standing Rock Indian Reservation. Indeed, at the height of the late fall 2016 defensive resistance on the part of Indian People and their allies, there were forty-two different law enforcement agencies on the ground functioning under the command of this small-time sheriff with his seemingly unending supply of U.S. military warfare equipment. Surely he should be able to hope for some kind of promotional opportunity under a Trump regime—having proved himself patriotically faithful to Big Oil fossil-fuel development.

Anyone who attempted to exercise their First Amendment rights at the job site, voicing their resistance with their bodies, were immediately cast by police rhetoric and by early press reports as violent, which rationalizes all sorts of violence on the part of a militarized police army. Moreover, there is little clear distinction between police and private pipeline security. Pipeline security personnel have used pepper spray on Defenders, and at one point even sicced trained attack dogs on unarmed Defenders.[3] Police attempts to control the Water Defenders extended to the use of dangerous "non-lethal" weapons that caused a high rate of serious injury. Rubber bullets actually pierce the skin and even killed one Defender's horse. On a particularly cold, sub-freezing temperature night, the police chose to use water cannons to try to disperse the crowd,

---

1. Graphiq Staff Research, "Visualizations Related to People Killed by Police in 2016 by Race," *The Guardian*, as of February 13, 2017.

2. Morton County, North Dakota, listed a population of 27,471 for the 2010 U.S. Census. The population includes a relatively high percentage of American Indians (3.9%).

3. "Video: Dakota Access Pipeline Company Attacks Native American Protesters with Dogs and Pepper Spray," *Democracy Now*, September 4, 2016.

soaking Defenders. Old people, who are heavily represented among the Defenders, were particularly susceptible to life-threatening hypothermia, and while hypothermia was widely experienced, a number of elders in particular had to be rushed to medical facilities over an hour away. Indeed, a U.N. "special rapporteur" named the treatment of Defenders as inhumane.[4]

The Water Defenders, on the other hand, have persistently declared their resistance movement to be nonviolent, and there was no evidence of weaponry on their part—except for a very suspicious arrest of a key Defender who was charged with having a weapon. No friends or community people know of this woman ever having had a weapon in her life. That arrest suspiciously smacks of chicanery and pure intimidation as well as a convenient raison d'être for police violence. To combat this nonviolent resistance this small-county sheriff mustered top level military equipment, including armored personnel carriers and at least one missile launcher, enough to fully arm his huge battalion mobilized from forty-one other police jurisdictions across the Midwest.

The Water Defenders at Standing Rock had to wait until the last possible moment (December 4, 2016) before the Obama administration stepped up and halted, temporarily at least, the construction of the Dakota Access Pipeline—just as it was poised to tunnel under the lake. Standing Rock, whose people get the bulk of their fresh water from Lake Oahe, had been formally resisting pipeline construction under the lake for more than two years, and the emerging camp of Water Defenders at the construction site had become very public by April 2016 and very large by late fall. Under intense pressure from American Indian resistance and their allies, the U.S. Army Corp of Engineers issued an order denying DAPL the necessary permit to dig their tunnel. Yet, with the election of

---

4. "UN Condemns 'Inhumane' Abuse of Standing Rock Water Protectors: The U.N. Special Rapporteur Says Treatment of Water Protectors Is 'Inhumane and Degrading' and a Violation of Fundamental Human Rights," *Telesur*, November 18, 2017; and Julia Carrie-Wong, "Standing Rock Protest: Hundreds Clash with Police over Dakota Access Pipeline," *The Guardian*, November 21, 2016.

Donald Trump the task of Indian resistance to this behemoth oil industry project has become even more precarious. Trump himself had been a heavy investor in the parent corporation for the DAPL, and Governor Rick Perry, his choice for energy secretary, held a seat on the company's board of trustees.[5] Indeed, only two months later under the leadership of a new commander-in-chief, the Army Corps of Engineers reversed its previous action and summarily granted DAPL the necessary easement without any hint of the full environmental study it had mandated in December.

In terms of modern survival, American Indians have generally fared only minimally better under Democratic administrations than Republican ones, characterized most often perhaps as the difference between neglect and benign neglect. Indeed, ironically enough, one of the better administrations for Indian fortunes was under a Republican president, Richard Nixon. Nixon did away with the social engineering projects of "relocation" and "termination"[6]—both Eisenhower erasure strategies aimed at trying to force assimilation of Indians into the dense, miscegenated urban landscape of america, where Indians need no longer bother the christian conscience of american peoples or their political structures.

But let's be clear; neglect is never really benign. By using the word neglect, I mean to charge it with relatively deleterious effect, related to the more or less casual ways in which the political system has learned simply to bypass Indians and their concerns, blithely ignoring treaties promising the well-being of Native Nations. A self-conscious neglect characterizes the sorts of development projects that simply ignore the presence of Indians in the rush to capitalize dollars for the barons of industry and to wrest land and resources from the Natives. Relieving the Natives of their land has been and continues to be important in those continuing euro-christian development schemes, all under the sweeping euro-christian banner of

---

5. Tom DiChristopher, "Trump Pick for Energy Secretary Sits on Dakota Access Pipeline Company's Board," *CNBC*, December 13, 2016.

6. Donald Lee Fixico, *Termination and Relocation: Federal Indian Policy, 1945–1960* (Albuquerque: University of New Mexico Press, 1986).

progress. And the power brokers have always found a way to make it legal. Hence, it always comes under the dominating banner of the Rule of Law, which all too regularly works in the favor of the already powerful. In the case of Standing Rock and the DAPL pipeline project, the trick politically and legally has been to circumvent Indian jurisdiction using sleight of hand, racialized arrogance, bullying, and outright deception.

While the resistance movement of the Water Protectors (and the public spectacle of police violence against the Defenders) finally won over Mr. Obama and his administration, Donald Trump has persistently announced his resolute and unwavering intent to support all fossil fuel development projects, including this one. The complexities of the resistance, already blurred by corporate rhetoric, became suddenly even more difficult to explicate to a larger public that suddenly seems dominated and emboldened by Trump voters.

But wait, they may object. The construction is on private and BLM federal lands, and not on Indian lands, isn't it? Wasn't it the U.S. Army Corp of Engineers who actually built the lake? Why are the Indians "protesting" (even though they call themselves Water Protectors)? This line of argumentation reflects the standard erasure of Indian Peoples on the american continent, an erasure that ignores virtually all treaties signed with Indian Peoples, and in this case with the Standing Rock Lakota People.

First of all, tunneling under the lake poses a huge threat to the water supply, not just for the Standing Rock Reservation community but for a number of other reservation communities downstream from Standing Rock, all of whom rely on the Missouri River and Lake Oahe for their communities' drinking water. Second, the lake itself was built in the middle of the last century by displacing hundreds of reservation families and flooding the most fertile acreage on two reservations, Standing Rock and Cheyenne River Sioux Reservations. This best of the reservations' land (some 206,000 fertile acres) was grabbed in accord with the legal principle of eminent domain. Moreover, the promised monetary compensation for loss of land was never paid. Somehow, we Indian Peoples have heard that story before. In any case, the lake bottom and the land around it still belong to Lakota, Nakota, and Dakota Peoples by treaty promises.

Third, in the Defenders' argument is their defense of culturally important sites in the path of pipeline construction. These sites include ancestral burial and other ceremonial sites. On one occasion in late summer, in good faith, the Standing Rock national government identified one particularly important site near the pipeline's path. By early the next day, in an act of utter meanness, DAPL had their bulldozers at exactly that site destroying ancestral treasures forever.[7]

Finally, and most important, for Indian Peoples the biggest issue involved is a legal concern for treaties. To put it bluntly, Indian resistance to the Dakota Access Pipeline is fundamentally about the historical treaties signed with the United States; and the land where the Dakota Access Pipeline is being tunneled is still today contested land under two treaties that the "Great Sioux Nation," including the Lakota People at Standing Rock, have with the United States, signed at Ft. Laramie: one in 1851 and the other in 1868. Yes, of course, it is about Standing Rock's fresh-water supply under which the pipeline is slated to tunnel. At one level, that is the up-front social justice issue that everyone ought to pay attention to. More important, however, if legally and politically more complex, are the underlying foundational legal issues pertaining to these two treaties. Those treaties made particular guarantees to Native Peoples that established very specific boundaries to their lands. Under the terms of those treaties, the construction site is on "Unceded Indian Territory." This means that the construction should be pursued only with the full consent of the Lakota, Nakota, and Dakota Peoples. It bears reiterating that treaties, according to Article VI of the U.S. Constitution, are the highest law of the land.

The great fear today is that a Donald Trump administration will be even less disposed than a Democratic Obama administration either to recognize those federal treaties or to hear the voice

---

7. Robinson Meyer, "The Legal Case for Blocking the Dakota Access Pipeline: Did the U.S. Government Help Destroy a Major Sioux Archeological Site?," *The Atlantic*, September 9, 2016.

of Indigenous Peoples naming the injustice. And we should note that it was no easy task, and never a completed one, to win the day with the more liberal Democrats. Indeed, the expectation was that a potential Clinton administration would have sided ultimately with the oil industry and pipeline development. Even in the case of Obama, it was not until the fading moments of his presidency that this announcement came—after several months of vigorous resistance at Standing Rock on the part of Indian Water Protectors and their allies and the public displays of violence against the Defenders by police and pipeline security personnel. With a new administration taking power, Donald Trump is clearly making the DAPL a priority.[8] One early Trump-aide memo reported that the president-elect "intends to cut the bureaucratic red tape put in place by the Obama administration that has prevented our country from diversifying our energy portfolio" (December 2, 2016). The new Army Corps of Engineers action in North Dakota makes that new power structure very clear.

The danger lurking for Indian Peoples in this Trump administration, however, is not the usual sort of neglect. Donald Trump has already publicly voiced his deep animosity for American Indians. Indeed, it has been a long time since there was a president with greater animosity toward Indian Peoples—going back to Abraham Lincoln (perpetrator of the largest mass execution in american history—of Dakota Indians) and even beyond to Andrew Jackson and his murderous policy of Indian Removal. Trump's rancor toward Indians surfaced a quarter century ago over Indian casinos. Not understanding treaty law and the treaty-based status of Indian Peoples in the United States, Trump complained bitterly that Indians got a better deal than he and his casino operations. Historically, since Indian Reservations are "federal" land, they are not under the legal jurisdiction of the states that surround them. Hence, in the

---

8. Devin Henry, "Obama Puts Dakota Pipeline on Trump's Desk," *The Hill*, December 5, 2016; Keith Goldberg, "Trump to Nix Climate Regs, Boost Fossil Fuel Development," *Law360*, November 8, 2016; and Ashley Parker and Coral Davenport, "Donald Trump's Energy Plan: More Fossil Fuels and Fewer Rules," *New York Times*, May 26, 2016.

1980s economically poor reservations near cities found a loophole in those states' laws against gambling and began opening tribally owned, reservation-based casinos. Initially, the states had no jurisdiction to prevent their operations, nor did states have any recourse for collecting taxes from Indian casinos.

In 1993 an infuriated Donald Trump brought a lawsuit against the United States and Indian Nations that ran nationally owned casinos charging them with unfair competition and discrimination against himself.[9] Then that same year Trump testified before a congressional committee that these casino Indians were not Indians because they failed to pass his own "look-like" test: "They don't look like Indians to me." In other words, Trump replaced the international treaties to which Indian Nations and the United States are cosignatories with some sort of racialized skin-color test. Trump's total ignorance of the complex corpus of Federal Indian Law deterred him not the least from making an all-out attack. Trump did not stop with the mere legalities of a lawsuit, but went on to engage in a "fake news" advertising campaign against Indian People in upper state New York. He is reported to have "secretly paid for more than $1 million in ads" attempting to portray members of a tribe in upstate New York as drug dealers and career criminals. Mr. Trump has proven again and again that he will stop at nothing to get what he wants, including bending rules and reciting made-up facts.

The problem facing American Indian folk most acutely now is our continued but heightened struggle to get society as a whole and especially the federal government to recognize and respect Indian sovereignty and to interact with Indian Peoples with full attention to the treaties they signed with us. Either the rule of law must mean something when it comes to protecting the treaty rights of Indian Peoples in north america, or we have to conclude finally that the so-highly vaunted rule of law is merely another euro-christian fiction

---

9. Shawn Boburg, "Donald Trump's Long History of Clashes with Native Americans," *Washington Post*, July 25, 2016; and Wayne King, "Trump, in a Federal Lawsuit, Seeks to Block Indian Casinos," *New York Times*, May 4, 1993.

for empowering the wealthy: they make the rules, and that's the law. Yet we seem to be entering a new stage in american democracy where the racial character of american law is more openly exposed as punitive for all People of Color, but especially for Native Peoples who continue to have some legal and moral claim to american lands.

The final crushing blow to Indian Peoples is the brewing sentiment to finish off the colonial project of privatizing Indian lands. The Trump administration has expressed its interest in privatizing Indian reservation lands in the interest of making access to natural resources on Indian lands much more efficiently accessible to extraction industries.[10] This would be a twofold win for Whiteness and a twofold loss for Native Peoples. Not only does it result in an immediate financial windfall for corporate america, but it finally succeeds in converting Earth into the euro-christian category of "property." As an added bonus, then Donald Trump would finally have full control of Indian gaming operations and the casinos of those few more economically successful Native Nations.

Yascha Mounk, a German Jewish scholar, captures our moment well: "When a candidate who promises to inflict extraordinary cruelty on the despised and the abject wins high office, he will (surprise, surprise) use his new-won powers to inflict cruelty on the abject and the despised."[11]

---

10. "Trump Advisors Aim to Privatize Oil-Rich American Indian Reservations," *CNBC*, December 5, 2016.

11. Yascha Mounk, "Democracy Is Holding Up, for Now, Despite Trump's Blatant Assaults on American Ideals, Our Institutions and People Are Refusing to Give In without a Fight," *Slate*, February 2, 2017.

CHAPTER 21

Black Lives Matter and the New Politics
The Search for Politics Beyond Categorical Politicization

ASANTE TODD

The controversy over the politics of Black Lives Matter emerged with the network itself. In this chapter, I want to analyze the controversy by discussing three contemporary political options: the politics of pricing, the politics of respectability, and class politics. Black Lives Matter rejects each of these options and with good reason because each politicizes life and creates categorical distinctions in the value of human life. I begin with a brief historical account.

Black Lives Matter

Black Lives Matter was born and developed over time primarily as an empathetic response to the deaths of seventeen-year-old Trayvon Martin (February 26, 2012) and eighteen-year-old Michael Brown (August 9, 2014).[1] Martin was gunned down on a cool February night in Sanford, Florida, as he walked back to his father's house from a local convenience store. He was armed only with a bag of candy and a bottle of iced tea, and was thus no match for

---

1. See Keeanga-Yamahtta Taylor, *From #BlackLivesMatter to Black Liberation* (Chicago: Haymarket Books, 2016), chapter 5.

George Zimmerman, a licensed, experienced shooter and neighborhood watch coordinator with a penchant for targeting African Americans: "These assholes, they always get away." Zimmerman was not immediately arrested. Local authorities assumed that Martin was the aggressor and prepared to close the case, and Zimmerman was only arrested after forty-five days of local and national marches, demonstrations, and protests. Zimmerman was tried, but ultimately acquitted (July 13, 2013), and in the cruelest of ironies an innocent Trayvon Martin was posthumously placed on trial for his own murder.

If Trayvon Martin's death signaled the birth moment of Black Lives Matter, the moment became a movement in 2014 after Michael Brown was shot and killed by police officer Darren Wilson. The Ferguson, Missouri, officer had received calls of a "robbery in progress," and had somehow gotten into an altercation with the unarmed Brown once he arrived on the scene. There are conflicting accounts regarding what exactly transpired (did Brown charge at Wilson or not?), but the result was similar to the Martin case: another unarmed young African American had been killed, and without legal consequence. These, and hundreds of cases like them, were the catalysts for founding efforts of Black Lives Matter contributed by Alicia Garza, Opal Tometi, and Patrisse Cullors. Black Lives Matter emerged as a "call to action for Black people" as "a response to the anti-Black racism that permeates our society and also, unfortunately, our movements."[2]

Although Black Lives Matter experienced success during its first two years, its momentum declined in 2015. Historian Keeanga-Yamahtta Taylor notes that Black Lives Matter's popularity soared in 2014 upon the publicized deaths of African Americans at the hands of "white" American (police officers).[3] Twelve-year-old Tamir Rice was shot and killed for playing with a toy gun (November 22); thirty-seven-year-old Tanisha Anderson was slammed to her sudden death on the hard Cleveland concrete by an officer

---

2. Alicia Garza, "Herstory," on the #BlackLivesMatter website, http://blacklivesmatter.com.

3. Taylor, *From #BlackLivesMatter to Black Liberation*, chapter 4.

(November 13), and Eric Garner was choked to death by police officers on video (July 17). These and other deaths spurred the nation to action against police brutality on behalf of black life. Waves of protests and marches washed across the United States in a moving display of empathy and discontent. By "December and January [2014]," says Taylor, "'Black Lives Matter' was the rallying cry from every corner."

"A week after the [Eric] Garner decision [December 3], several hundred congressional aides, most of them Black, walked off the job in protest."[4] However, the Black Lives Matter buzz soon died. This occurred at midsummer, when disgruntled Micah Xavier Johnson shot and killed five police officers in Dallas, Texas, on July 7, 2016. These and other police deaths, many in response to black deaths, have "changed the nation's . . . conversation about race, unearthing much more negativity against the Black Lives Matter movement."[5] Analyst Sarah Mervosh notes that "the days before the police shooting July 7 . . . 87 percent of tweets mentioning #BlackLivesMatter were supportive. . . . However, [f]rom July 8 to July 17, [2016], support for #BlackLivesMatter dropped to just 28 percent of tweets. And 39 percent of tweets using the hashtag were critical, compared to just 11 percent in the previous time period." Black Lives Matter was losing favor in public opinion, and for most, the primary problem is its politics.

Respect, Price, Class and the Politics of Black Lives Matter

The debate concerning the validity of Black Lives Matter centers on their politics, that is, on the appropriate art or science of government, exercise of authority, and management of interests, representation, and the like. The controversy over the politics of Black Lives Matter began almost immediately, and has been the bane of its existence to date. It started with disagreement between the

---

4. Ibid., 173.
5. Sarah Mervosh, "How the Dallas Police Shooting Upended #Black-livesmatter on Twitter," *Dallas News*, August 15, 2016 (brackets mine).

"old civil rights" guard (e.g., Jesse Jackson, Al Sharpton) and the "new" (Alicia Garza, DeRay McKesson) at rallies and protests. For example, they differed over whether this "new politics" should be gradualist and more "patient" or more radical and defiant. There was also contention between preferred models of leadership. The older generation showed an inclination toward a leader-centered group pattern of organization while the younger generation prefers group-centered leadership. The "old guard" criticizes the younger generation's politics of personal representation. For example, Reverend Al Sharpton argues, "Blackness was never about being a gangster or a thug. Blackness was no matter how low we was pushed down, we rose up anyhow. . . . Blackness was never surrendering our pursuit of excellence. . . . Now in the 21st century, we get to where we got some positions of power. And you decide it ain't black no more to be successful."[6]

Younger blacks like Ferguson protester Dontey Carter highlight the weaknesses of the old guard. "They're the reason things are like this now. They don't represent us. That's why we're here for the new movement."[7] The debate was over politics, and the old guard criticized the new for their lack of "respectability politics." As analyst David Love notes, in the view of the old guard, "liberation can only be achieved for and by people who are respectable enough to deserve it."[8] From the perspective of respectability politics, Black Lives Matter doesn't deserve respect, but condescension: "pull your pants up."

A second criticism comes from those who embrace the politics of pricing, whose ultimate goal is to create a more productive and efficient economy at lower prices. One everyday example comes from activist Carmen Rios, who traveled from New York to Denver, Colorado, to attend a pro-cop rally on December 19, 2014. "'Get a job, for Christssake,' Carmen Rios shouted at a group of

---

6. Taylor, *From #BlackLivesMatter to Black Liberation*, 160.

7. Ibid., 161.

8. David Love, "Jesse Jackson and #BlackLivesMatter: The Rift between Respectability Politics and the New Protest Movement," *Atlanta Black Star*, August 8, 2015.

counter-protesters holding signs bearing Eric Garner's name. 'He resisted arrest. . . . Isn't he breaking the law? Why is that so difficult to understand?'"[9] Rios's message was powerful enough to be pinned to columnist Christopher Robbins's headline: "Pro-Cop Rally Clashes with Black Lives Matter: 'Get A Job!'" In Rios's perspective, Black Lives Matter's path to freedom is through work, and Rios isn't alone.

One significant, like-minded person is President Donald Trump, who claimed that he would bring so many working-class jobs to African Americans that "Black Americans are 'going to like me better than Obama.'"[10] For Trump, Rios, and others, Black Lives Matter should be participating in economic activities such as entrepreneurialism and exchange instead of advocacy. Tough times require increased productivity and decreased consumption rather than increased protest and civil disobedience. Theoretically, disciplined work generates profit, and thus freedom, by making an economy (or individual) more productive at lower prices.[11] Yet, there are problems with this seemingly noble politics. For example, this politics downplays issues raised by Black Lives Matter, including fair wages, fair working conditions, and state regulation of production lines, as businesses seek to acquire resources at low costs. In addition, the fruits of collective production are rarely distributed equitably. In everyday language, this means that no matter how hard blacks work, it is often "white people in the office, and black people working the floor."[12]

Beyond the politics of respectability and the politics of pricing, class politics also presents itself as a strategic option for Black Lives Matter. For historian Barbara Ransby, class politics, or a politics that understands that economic and racial justice are connected,

---

9. Christopher Robbins, "Pro-Cop Rally Clashes with Black Lives Matter: 'Get A Job!,'" *Gothamist*, December 20, 2014.

10. Aaron Morrison, "On Jobs, Blacks Are 'Going to Like Me Better Than They Like Obama,'" *International Business Times*, January 25, 2016.

11. Friedrich Hayek, *The Fatal Conceit: The Errors of Socialism* (Chicago: University of Chicago Press, 1988), 14.

12. Marla Frederick, *Between Sundays: Black Women and Everyday Struggles of Faith* (Los Angeles: University of California Press, 2003), 52.

seems appropriate for the movement. Ransby appeals to the movement's belief that "police brutality should be exposed as part of a much larger system of oppression" and web of inequality, as well as the fact that many of the lead organizers in the movement have "roots in labor and other economic justice campaigns. . . ."[13] "The three women who launched the original Black Lives Matter hashtag in 2012 . . . are all professional organizers working with domestic workers, with immigrants, and against prisons . . . ," she says. For her, these features of the movement are determinate enough to typify Black Lives Matter's politics as class politics. "Black Lives Matter, which includes nearly a dozen black-led organizations, is as much an example of a U.S.-based class struggle as Occupy Wall Street was. . . . In speech after speech, the leading voices of this movement have insisted that if we liberate the black poor, or if the black poor liberate themselves, we will uplift everybody else who's been kept down."[14]

For Ransby, class interest determines Black Lives Matter's politics, and this explains the rift between them and the "old guard" of the civil rights movement. Yet, while Black Lives Matter does possess class consciousness, Taylor has convincingly shown that the black freedom struggle should not be conflated with communism but understood as emerging from its own organic particularity. Quoting black Caribbean revolutionary C. L. R. James, Taylor notes, "[T]he Negro struggle . . . has a vitality and validity of its own; . . . it has deep and historic roots in the past of America and in present struggles. It has an organic political perspective, along which it is traveling. . . ."[15]

The Politicization of Life and the Search for a New Politics

Black Lives Matter has rejected each of these options for politics, and with good reason, because each approach "politicizes" life itself. According to philosopher Giorgio Agamben, the "politicization of

---

13. Barbara Ransby, "The Class Politics of Black Lives Matter" *Dissent* (Fall 2015): 31.

14. Ibid.

15. Taylor, *From #BlackLivesMatter to Black Liberation*, 204.

life" is the process of distinguishing between so-called authentic or respectable life and life lacking political value.[16] One isolates certain character traits as marks of political value and citizenship and simultaneously marginalizes those who deviate from these norms. "Deviants," thus marginalized, stand "at risk" of being abandoned by the law to the exception, where the logic of sovereignty pervades the state's techniques of governance such that one is either disciplined into conformity or punished for failure to conform. "It is as if every valorization and 'politicization' of life," says Agamben, ". . . necessarily implies a new decision concerning the threshold beyond which life ceases to be politically relevant, becomes 'sacred' life, and can as such be eliminated without punishment."[17]

Black Lives Matter wants political change, but it also wants to avoid categorical politicization. Thus it resists being identified as a class movement that draws a categorical divide between the proletariat and capitalists.[18] Likewise, Black Lives Matter rejects respectability politics, politicized by philosopher Paul Ricoeur. For Ricoeur, respectability politics is rooted in a categorical distinction between those with distinctive personalities able to practice autonomy (*ipse*) and general humans more inclined to disobey the law and do evil (*idem*). Respect is reserved for "anyone who has the right to expect his or her just share in an equitable distribution."[19] Even the politics of pricing politicizes life; for economist Friedrich Hayek, freedom is the exclusive property of the entrepreneur. The "collectivist savage" remains a slave.

Black Lives Matter stormed onto the public stage in 2012, only to be silenced a brief four years later by controversy surrounding its politics. In predictable fashion, various authorities, usually male, have attempted to impose political advice upon Black Lives

---

16. Giorgio Agamben, *Homo Sacer: Sovereign Power and Bare Life* (Stanford, CA: Stanford University Press, 1998), 81.

17. Ibid.

18. Hannah Arendt, *Totalitarianism: Part Three of the Origins of Totalitarianism* (New York: Harcourt Bruce Jovanovich, 1968 [1951]).

19. Paul Ricoeur, *Oneself as Another*, trans. Kathleen Blamey (Chicago: University of Chicago Press, 1992), 204.

Matter, defacing the movement's queer and organic nature in the process. "[O]rganizing and struggle have . . . for the most part, had a male face," says Taylor, "[yet it] should go without saying that Black women have always played an integral role in the . . . Black freedom struggle."[20] Black Lives Matter thus continues the search for an appropriate politics, one that can account for the cultural politics of difference, and current political conditions suggest that we join them.

Under President Trump, we now witness an ascendant politics of pricing along with its requisite militarized police state. This mode of governance has little regard for *habeas corpus* (protection against unlawful arrest), and its goals are to institute authoritarianism and liquidate democracy. Such governance is problematic not only because market-based policies raise so many quality of life issues (gentrification, worker's rights after the globalization of corporations and production, deteriorating state infrastructure and public institutions). The politics of pricing is also problematic from a theological perspective because of its parochial philosophy of (the good) life, which is always already determined by the market's sovereign laws of supply and demand. Perhaps here is where Black Lives Matter and African American religious politics find common ground. Each attempts to practice a politics toward a world beyond the good life as we know it. For some black women, such politics is rooted in spirituality, one organically forged in the everyday struggles of life between Sundays and informed by their relationship with God.

---

20. Taylor, *From #BlackLivesMatter to Black Liberation*, 164–65.

CHAPTER 22

The Asian American Urban Vote
Why Geography Trumped Race and Religion

IRENE OH

On Thanksgiving 2016, I learned that Mike Pence, Donald Trump's vice president, was renting a house until Inauguration Day in my typically quiet suburban neighborhood in Washington, DC. A week and a half later, Edgar Welch drove up from North Carolina to my local pizzeria, Comet Ping Pong, believing fake news on the internet that the restaurant had underground tunnels for smuggling children as part of a sex ring operation conducted by Tony Podesta and Hillary Clinton. Before being arrested by the police, Welch shot an assault rifle in the popular family restaurant and demanded to be shown the tunnels so that he could save the children. As the winter break neared, a rumor emerged among the parents at my children's school that Barron Trump, the ten-year-old son of the president-elect and his wife, might be considering enrolling their child for the following school year. Lively discussions ensued about what it meant for an overwhelmingly liberal, progressive school to accept this child and his family into the community.

What is the point of these anecdotes, other than to amuse—or horrify, as the case may be—my friends and colleagues who wonder what it is like living in Washington, DC, during this roller-coaster election season and now presidency of Donald Trump? My point is, simply, that where we live matters when it comes to how we experi-

ence politics. The correlation between place and politics was especially strong for this 2016 election cycle. In fact, one's address was
likely a better predictor of how one voted than one's racial or ethnic
identity, religious affiliation, gender, income, or education level.

Prioritizing Geography

What is the significance of this observation about the priority of
geography when analyzing the Asian American vote? This means
that we must understand race as a factor that is not independent
from, but rather inextricably intertwined with, geographical context. The economic concerns, cultural trends, and social values of
urban dwellers differ measurably from those of rural residents for
people of all races and ethnicities, religions, and economic class.
Focusing on race, in other words, is a less effective political strategy—at least when it comes to presidential elections—than focusing on geography. Like the vast majority of other Americans, Asian
Americans vote like their neighbors.

Although nearly 80 percent of Asian Americans cast their vote
for the Democratic Party in this last presidential election, our
political consensus belied our tremendous ethnic, religious, and
economic diversity. The U.S. Census Bureau counts at least twenty
different ethnic Asian subgroups.[1] Asian Americans have no clear
majority religion; the largest subgroup, Christians, make up 42
percent of the population. More than a quarter of Asian Americans claim no religious affiliation at all. In terms of socioeconomic
diversity, Asian Americans include some of the wealthiest, well-
educated ethnic groups as well as ethnic groups with some of the
lowest high-school graduation rates and highest poverty rates in
the nation. The "model minority" myth does not hold up when
looking at the entirety of the Asian American population. In spite
of these differences, Asian Americans overwhelmingly voted for
Hillary Clinton over Donald Trump. We voted like one another
not because we are a homogenous group with shared religious and

---

1. Pew Research Center, "Demographics of Asian Americans," April 4,
2103, http://www.pewsocialtrends.org.

economic interests, but rather because Asian Americans reflect the values found in the liberal, metropolitan areas in which the majority of us reside. The few Asian Americans who live in rural areas tended to vote—like their neighbors—for Trump.

For this past presidential election, we Democrats woefully underestimated the increasingly important role of geography in determining voting patterns. We assumed that Michigan and Wisconsin would remain "blue" despite their Midwestern identity and regional economic concerns. We also lost Ohio and Pennsylvania—states that geographically straddle the East Coast and the Midwest, but whose voters found their economic and cultural identity more aligned with their red neighbors. The urban-rural divide is widening, and the Democratic Party found itself losing rural voters who had voted Democratic in previous elections but shared increasingly little common ground between themselves and coastal city dwellers. Looking at the red and blue electoral map depicting the results of the presidential election, the most striking visual pattern was the uniformly red central and rural parts of the country, and the uniformly blue urban coastal cities. Unfortunately, this graphic made all too clear that we are a divided nation—not just politically, but geographically.

Urban Asian Americans

Well over 90% of Asian Americans live in or near a metropolitan area.[2] Representing approximately 5% of the American population, 79% of Asian Americans voters favored Clinton, 17% Trump, and 3% some other candidate.[3] Clinton actually outperformed Obama by 3% when it came to the Asian American vote. A number of theories have been suggested as to why Asian Americans voted overwhelmingly for Clinton, including, but not limited to their soli-

---

2. Jeff Guo, "The Asian American 'Advantage' That Is Actually an Illusion," *Washington Post*, December 29, 2016.

3. Asian American Legal Defense and Education Fund, "In AALDEF's Election Day Exit Poll of Close to 14,000 Asian American Voters, Clinton Favored over Trump by Wide Margin," November 9, 2016, https://goo.gl/xPJBy9.

darity with other minorities; shared concern with the Black Lives Matter movement; the proposed registration of Muslims, which has parallels to the internment of Japanese Americans during the Second World War; and generally liberal political views toward gay marriage and abortion.

The best way to understand the Asian American vote, however, is not primarily or solely through the lens of race, religion, or economic status. Rather, it is by understanding how much cities and large metro areas tie into Asian American history, politics, and culture. Although the first documented Asians in the United States were Spanish-speaking Filipinos, the first large wave of Asian immigrants were probably Chinese men who arrived in the nineteenth century on the West Coast of the United States to build railroads and work in gold mines. After the gold rush and the completion of the railroads, Chinese men moved to cities to capitalize, literally, upon the economic opportunities made possible in densely populated areas. Businesses such as laundries and restaurants—both of which provided much-needed services, but required minimal language skills for owners and employees—succeeded in places like bustling downtowns where one could develop a steady clientele to provide constant revenue.

Historically, Asian Americans like other immigrant groups tended to settle in areas where previous generations of the same ethnic group lived. Because commercial businesses tended to cluster in major coastal cities, newly arrived Asian immigrants were likely to find both social and economic benefits by living in these urban areas. Until immigrants were able to master the English language, living near those who shared the same mother tongue provided a safety net and access to information about how to navigate life in their newly adopted country. One could more easily learn about housing, schools, jobs, medical care, and other life necessities from those who spoke the same language by settling in an urban center. For well-educated Asian immigrants, who arrived in large waves with the passage of the 1965 Immigration and Nationality Act, career opportunities were often found in cities that were home to major corporations, medical centers, and universities.

Once Asian American communities started to develop around

these coastal cities beyond "Chinatowns," Asian Americans tended to stay in cities. Today, the largest numbers of Asian Americans can be found in or near Los Angeles, San Francisco, and New York City—all cities with populations that voted in large numbers for Clinton. There are a number of factors that likely influenced the continued concentration of Asian Americans near urban areas. First, urban (and close-in suburban) areas tend to attract highly educated populations, and as a whole, Asian Americans tend to have higher education levels compared to other racial groups.[4] A 2016 Brookings Institution report suggests that Asian Americans prioritize access to good schools for their children, regardless of their economic status.[5] While this may be a given for wealthier Asian Americans who can afford to live in neighborhoods with good schools, this is also the case for low-income Asian Americans. Second, for many Asian American families, living close to older generations (e.g., parents and grandparents) remains a priority. Nearly 30 percent of Asian Americans live in multigenerational households, a higher percentage than any other ethnic group in the United States.[6] Children of first- and second-generation Asian immigrants to the United States may be less likely to move away from cities where their ancestors settled. Third, Asian Americans want to live in diverse areas, which typically means in or near metro areas.[7] Asian Americans are more likely than any other race or ethnicity to live in mixed neighborhoods.

4. As noted earlier in the essay, some Asian American ethnic sub-groups, such as the Hmong, have among the lowest high school graduation rates in the country. However, larger ethnic sub-groups, such as the Chinese and Indian communities, have among the highest rates of postgraduate education.

5. Edward Rodrigue, Nathan Joo, and Richard V. Reeves, "Asian American Successes and the Pitfalls of Generalization," Brookings Institution, April 20, 2016, http://brook.gs.

6. D'Vera Cohn and Jeffrey Passel, "A Record 60.6 Million Americans Live in Multi-generational Households," Pew Research Center, August 11, 2016, http://pewrsr.ch.

7. Pew Research Center, "The Rise of Asian Americans," updated April 4, 2013, http://pewrsr.ch.

The Polarization of Places

While it is not clear whether cities turn its residents more liberal, or whether liberals move to cities, cities clearly tend to be more liberal than rural parts of the United States. In their landmark 2008 book, *The Big Sort,* Bill Bishop and sociologist Robert Cushing show how Americans are increasingly moving into like-minded parts of the country with liberal Democrats moving into major cities and conservative Republicans moving into rural areas.[8] This geographic sorting out, they presciently warned, would further polarize our nation culturally, economically, and politically. Over the last several decades, people with college and graduate degrees moved away from more rural areas and into cities; this shift has fueled the economic growth of major cities and the demise of rural economies.

Because cities are far more racially and religiously diverse than rural areas, city dwellers need, at minimum, to be tolerant of others who come from different backgrounds. This is especially true when we examine diversity not just as a black-white issue, but also consider Asian and Hispanic populations. In rural areas, we find greater homogeneity of race and religion. A 2014 Pew Research Center study on political polarization found that "conservatives would rather live in large houses in small towns and rural areas—ideally among people of the same religious faith—while liberals opt for smaller houses and walkable communities in cities, preferably with a mix of different races and ethnicities."[9] This means, unfortunately, that rural conservatives have fewer and fewer opportunities to understand people from different religious and ethnic backgrounds.

Given that our society is becoming more diverse, rather than less, rural citizens of the United States are heading into the future by retreating and insulating themselves from difference. Not surprisingly, the economic ramifications of turning away from dif-

---

8. Bill Bishop and Robert Cushing, *The Big Sort* (Boston MA: Mariner Books, 2009).

9. Drew Desliver, "How the Most Ideologically Polarized Americans Live Different Lives," Pew Research Center, June 13, 2014, http://pewrsr.ch.

ference in our globalized economy are proving to be disastrous. The demise of the rural economy, compounded by the shunning of nonwhite, non-Christian persons, allows white Americans to more easily scapegoat Mexicans, Chinese, Indians, and nonwhite foreigners for economic losses. This perception unfortunately leads to a circular pattern of thought that reinforces the desire of rural Americans to remove themselves from people of color, while cities are able to draw on diversity and to benefit from the growth of the world economy.

Karthick Ramakrishnan argues in *The American Prospect* that Asian Americans became a Democratic bloc beginning in the early 1990s when the party began to make "symbolic appeals and outreach efforts" to the community.[10] These outreach efforts resulted not just in the alignment of Asian Americans with the Democratic Party, but also with their policies. Over the next two decades, party affiliation and agreement with Democratic political platforms reinforced one another with the upshot of Asian Americans becoming reliable supporters of the Democratic Party.

While Ramakrishnan's analysis offers valuable insights into the Asian American vote, the development of Democratic political strategy also coincides with the historic polarization of urban and rural areas. In this most recent election, geography mattered more than how well the Democratic Party played to the Asian American vote. My home city of Washington, DC, exemplifies this trend. In November, 97% of DC voters chose Clinton. That is a remarkably unifying statistic for a city that is extraordinarily diverse: 46% black, 40% white, 10% Hispanic, and 3% Asian. Similarly, when you look at the diversity of Asian Americans across sub-ethnic groups, across religious identification, and across income, which correlates strongly with education levels, there is nonetheless the remarkably unifying factor of urbanness.

For those Asian Americans who voted for Trump, the reasons offered in various interviews seem to mirror those offered by other

---

10. Karthick Ramakrishnan, "How Asian Americans Became Democrats," *American Prospect*, July 26, 2016, http://prospect.org.

Trump supporters. They like his straight talk, want to "drain the swamp" that is DC, and believe that an outsider will shake things up. Also, there are likely Asian American voters who are pro-life and voted for Trump because of his selection of conservative Supreme Court justices. In Louisiana, for example, where the majority of Asian Americans are Vietnamese Catholics, 49 percent of Asian Americans voted for Trump, over the 46 percent that voted for Clinton. Also, notably, Asian Americans who are largely here as legal immigrants draw a distinction between themselves and illegal immigrants, and so have no qualms supporting the building of a wall.

Moving Forward

The larger takeaway here is to consider the relative weight of different factors that go into analyzing voting behavior. The genesis of this essay was a query about how Asian American Christians voted, but after looking at the data, it became clear that race and religion were not the most significant factors in understanding what happened this past November. As we move forward, we can use these insights to turn the tide against Trump and his brand of conservatism. Specifically, we need to prioritize the concerns of those living in rural areas, in the Midwest, and in the exurbs of major cities. We cannot simply assume that the priorities and values of those living in New York City, Washington, DC, San Francisco, and Los Angeles are agreeable to those living in the South or the Midwest. Second, we need to focus on local and state-level races. Sadly, because Democrats have neither the House nor the Senate, and because we will likely face a conservative Supreme Court, we have no effective means for challenging the president. Third, if we are to focus on Asian Americans, an emphasis ought to be made on getting Asian Americans to become more politically active. Although Asian Americans are reliable Democrats, not enough Asian Americans vote. In fact, Asian Americans have the lowest voter turnout of all the minority races in the United States; less than a third of eligible Asian American voters actually show up at the polls.[11] If voter turnout is a measure of political engagement, Asian Americans are among the most politically apathetic in the United States. Needless to say, getting Asian Americans into elected office at local, state, and national levels is another key step in diversifying the political landscape of this country.

As I write this essay just three weeks into the tenure of Donald Trump, we have already witnessed too much incompetence and harm. Yesterday, his National Security Advisor, Michael Flynn, resigned amid allegations of inappropriate conduct with Russian officials. Trump's travel ban, the appointment of clearly inappropriate cabinet members, and the daily assertion of "alternative facts" by the White House have dire consequences for our democracy. We must not allow the energy and momentum of the Women's March and other movements to fade or allow ourselves to become jaded in the long days ahead. Instead, let us focus on the hard work ahead of us and remain clear-eyed as we forge strategies to reclaim our nation.

---

11. Jens Manuel Krogstad, "Asian American Voter Turnout Lags behind Other Groups," Pew Research Center, April 9, 2014, http://pewrsr.ch.

CHAPTER 23

Adelante *in Difference*
Latinxs in the Age of Trump

JACQUELINE M. HIDALGO

In the days after the election of Donald J. Trump, various media and scholars reeled, trying to make sense of the varying threads that led to his election in the early hours of November 9. One particular area of fascination was the polling data surrounding Latinxs.[1] Did Trump really win 29 percent of the Latinx vote as most mainstream media exit polls contended? Or did Trump capture only 18 percent of the Latinx electorate as the Latino Decisions poll suggests?[2]

Besides the limits of polling in 2016, the confusion over the Latinx electorate signals two tensions relevant for this essay. First, whether the number is 18 percent or 29 percent, that any sizeable proportion of Latinxs voted for Trump at all requires some discussion. Second, Latinxs, like the rest of the United States, are a racially, ethnically, linguistically, and religiously diverse population, and it can be hard to identify of whom we speak when we discuss "Latinxs." Thus no brief essay can fully address Latinx complicity in and resistance to Trump's politics. I suggest that the extent to which Latinxs have refused to embrace our own internal differ-

---

1. The "x" is an attempt to include diverse genders when supplying the broader term for the loose conglomeration of peoples of Latin American descent incorporated under the term "Latino."

2. Latino Decisions, "Lies, Damn Lies, and Exit Polls," *Latino Decisions: Everything Latino Politics*, November 11, 2016, http://www.latinodecisions.com.

ences, we have contributed to the rise of Trumpist politics. Latinx histories that have embraced intersectionality and difference, a practice of *acompañamiento* (accompaniment that is more than an ideal of solidarity) among *nosotrxs* understood as "we others," must be the models through which we cultivate a politics for justice.

The Challenge of Immigration and the Limits of Citizenship

Donald Trump launched his campaign by first attacking Mexican immigrants as "not . . . their best," claiming that they bring "drugs," "crime," and "rapists," though "some, [he] assume[s], are good people." While those remarks and the promise to build a border wall signal a specific attack on people in the United States of Mexican descent, even in that speech, Trump signaled little ability to differentiate between Mexicans and other Latinx populations (as well as Middle Eastern populations) because he further claimed, "It's coming from more than Mexico. It's coming from all over South and Latin America, and it's coming probably—probably—from the Middle East."[3] While Mexicans, as the largest ethnic group among U.S. Latinxs, are particularly the target of right-wing vitriol—and specific attention to Mexican histories and struggles should be maintained—all Latinxs are implicated in this rhetoric. Ironically, the U.S. War on Drugs has fueled rising violent crime in much of Latin America, which increased migration in the earlier part of the twenty-first century (overall unauthorized migration from Latin America has decreased in the past few years).[4] Latinxs are mostly in the United States because of histories of U.S. imperial intervention in this hemisphere.

---

3. Donald J. Trump, "Presidential Announcement Speech," *Time*, June 16, 2015.

4. See discussion in any number of essays, including Roque Planas and Ryan Grimm, "Here's How the U.S. Sparked a Refugee Crisis on the Border in Eight Simple Steps," *Huffington Post*, July 18, 2014. A recent decline in immigration has also been documented; see, for instance, Ana González-Barrera, "More Mexicans Leaving Than Coming to the U.S.," *Pew Research Center: Hispanic Trends*, November 19, 2015.

A 2014 U.S. Census estimate placed the "Hispanic" population, referring to people of Mexican, Puerto Rican, Dominican, Cuban, Central or South American, or Spanish heritage, at 55 million people, or 17 percent of the U.S. population.[5] Among this population are people who identify with indigenous, African, Asian, European, or mixed racial heritage; they include practitioners of all religions and no religion. In popular media, including Spanish language media, Latinxs are often imagined as immigrants, and current popular U.S. imagination depicts most immigrants, especially unauthorized residents, as Latinxs. Such depictions reinscribe a sense that people of Latin American descent in the United States are always foreign to this land. These depictions also erase other unauthorized residents, such as those from Asia and Africa, who are in need of sanctuary and *acompañamiento* under Trump.

Although many Latinxs in the United States are the descendants of immigrants, two significant populations are not: ethnic Mexicans whose ancestors dwelled in several Western states from Texas to California prior to 1848, and those whose ancestral home is the island of Puerto Rico. Both of these populations had U.S. citizenship imposed on them. The United States' practices of imperialism, conquest, and settler colonialism necessarily cast these populations as ever foreign to the United States. A southern border wall symbolically blocks unauthorized migrants crossing from Latin America to the United States, but it also re-invigorates the claims of conquest, trying to clarify again that the United States is distinct from Latin America and the lands of Mexico and Puerto Rico taken through conquest.

Perhaps some Latinxs contributed to Trump's rise by supporting too rigorously the fiction of U.S. inclusion encoded into notions of citizenship. The Latino Decisions poll argued that only 18 percent, rather than 29 percent, of Latinxs voted for Trump based on a couple of significant factors: that mainstream polls rarely survey populations voting in high-density Latinx and African American neighborhoods; additionally, the polls rarely interview Spanish-

---

5. CNN Library, "Hispanics in the U.S.: Fast Facts," *CNN*, March 5, 2016.

dominant Latinxs. Since 30 percent of Latinx voters were not born in the United States, and even though many among that 30 percent are fluent in English, English-dominant polls miss a large chunk of the Latinx vote. Additionally, the imprecise, mainstream polling data also suggest that English-dominant Latinxs were more likely to vote for Trump (still not in majority numbers, just at higher rates) than their Spanish-dominant co-ethnics. While we can only speculate about the myriad reasons different Latinxs voted for different candidates, that English-dominants were more likely to vote for Trump also raises questions. Spanish, Portuguese, and Native language loss is the product of more than a century of U.S. governmental and public educational efforts to eradicate Latinx bilinguality. Yet English-language dominance can also indicate a loss of connection to the transnational imagination that connects Latinxs in the United States to Latin America and the Caribbean, an imagination that can serve as an important corrective to U.S. nativism and exceptionalism.

The challenge might be, however, that citizenship itself is a construct dependent on uneven power relations. Media studies scholar Hector Amaya "theorizes that citizenship is inherently a process of uneven political capital accumulation"; citizenship is an unjust arbiter of "rights" because, rather than assuring equal "human rights," citizenship only allocates rights based on hierarchical differentiation.[6] United States' history has evidenced this most starkly in its highly racialized and violent mistreatment of Native Americans, African Americans, women, and the property-less within its founding texts (the Declaration of Independence and the Constitution). Although the space of this essay is too limited to articulate it fully, Latinxs in our present are called to draw upon, remember, and share the lessons of "non-innocent histories."[7] We inherit diverse histories of violence, colonialism, and enslavement; we must fight against our own internalized logics of white supremacy that have historically valorized

---

6. Hector Amaya, "Introduction: Latinas/os and Citizenship Excess," *Citizenship Excess: Latino/as, Media, and the Nation* (New York: New York University Press, 2013), loc. 114 of 6129, Kindle edition.

7. Neomi De Anda, "Jesus the Christ," in *The Wiley Blackwell Companion to Latino/a Theology*, ed. Orlando O. Espín (Hoboken, NJ: John Wiley & Sons, 2015), 166.

mestizaje as a way of eradicating Native Latinxs and erasing African and Asian Latinx populations.[8] We must resist imaginations of citizenship as the inclusive remedy to our lived injustices because citizenship, for all its promises, fundamentally relies on the construction of a justly protected self in relationship to a justly cast aside other.

Logics of white supremacy are bound up with constructions of U.S. citizenship, where citizenship itself works to "discriminat[e]" (to "push down") and to "balkanize[e]" (to "push away") minoritized populations through projects of differential inclusion and exclusion.[9] Under Trump's administration, this tension manifested itself rapidly in his executive order excluding migrants and refugees from seven predominantly Muslim countries. To the extent that Latinxs have bought into the assumption that some people deserve more rights because they are citizens, they participate in the politics of domination that is citizenship excess. The logics of citizenship excess are part of the reason that ethicist Miguel A. De La Torre and others find religious rhetorics of "hospitality" problematic.[10] When we claim that we should be hospitable to immigrants as "strangers" in our land, we reproduce settler colonial violence by acting as if U.S. citizens rather than Native North Americans have a proper ability to be hospitable in this land. Moreover, rhetorics of hospitality, rather than *acompañamiento*, still presume the uneven power dynamics of citizenship excess, that citizens are entitled to hold greater rights than migrants, and thus citizens are able to offer up some of these rights as an act of generosity.

Citizenship excess and its violence had already targeted Latinx bodies before Trump; indeed Latinxs struggling for justice identified President Barack Obama as the "deporter-in-chief." More than two million migrants were deported during his presidency.[11] Never-

---

8. See fuller critique in Néstor Medina, *Mestizaje: Remapping Race, Culture, and Faith in Latina/o Catholicism* (Maryknoll, NY: Orbis Books, 2009).

9. Amaya, "Introduction," 143/6129.

10. See, for instance, the discussion in Miguel A. De La Torre, *The U.S. Immigration Crisis: Toward an Ethics of Place* (Eugene, OR: Cascade Books, 2016), 150–60.

11. Miriam Valverde, "Trump Right on Obama's Deportation Numbers, Wrong about Nobody Talking about It," *Politifact*, October 21, 2016.

theless, early on-the-ground reports suggest that ICE raids seeking to further criminalize and deport immigrants have increased since Trump assumed the presidency.[12] Whether as citizens or as immigrants, Latinxs easily find themselves on the losing side of U.S. citizenship excess, which is probably part of why there is only one Latinx in Trump's cabinet.

Learning from Past Struggles: *Nosotrxs* as Our Path Onward (*Adelante*)

Citizenship and its excesses have divided Latinx communities before; even in California of the 1960s and 1970s, which is remembered as an iconic time of Latinx activism, activists in the Chicano movement concerned themselves more with citizens than with the struggles of unauthorized residents. Historian Jimmy Patiño describes how Chicanx and Mexican nationals worked together to seek justice for Martha Elena Parra López. On May 31, 1972, only fifteen miles north and just across the U.S. border from her home in Tijuana, Parra López was detained, interrogated, harassed, and ultimately sexually violated by a Border Patrol agent. Though Parra López's assailant was only fired rather than prosecuted, her clamor for justice from the U.S. Border Patrol brought together communities who were not necessarily always easy allies in the 1960s: ethnic Mexican citizens in the United States, unauthorized Mexican residents in the United States, and Mexican nationals in Tijuana. Patiño exposes how these communities came together specifically through the rhetoric of *la familia* Chicana, a family whose patriarchal leadership was violated when the women of *la familia* were assaulted.[13]

---

12. Guadalupe García de Rayos, an unauthorized resident who lived here for twenty years and annually checked in with ICE, was suddenly deported despite significant public protests in February 2017. On-the-ground reports about actions in other cities have communities on edge. See Nicholas Kulisch, Caitlin Dickerson, and Liz Robbins, "Reports of Raids Have Immigrants Bracing for Enforcement Surge," *New York Times*, February 10, 2017.

13. Jimmy Patiño, "'All I Want Is That He Be Punished': Border Patrol Violence, Women's Voices, and Chicano Activism in Early 1970s San Diego," in *The Chicano Movement: Perspectives from the Twenty-First Century*, ed. Mario T. García (New York: Routledge, 2014), 21–22, 33.

On the one hand, this moment of shared struggle enabled Latinx communities to forge an alliance across differences of citizenship. Yet, this incident reveals that Parra López's full humanity—and its violation—was not respected on its own terms in the fullness of her intersectional location.

In the 1980s, black feminist Kimberlé Crenshaw outlined the import of "intersectionality," an attention to class, race, and gender as identities that cannot be separated because they operate in concert.[14] The attack on Parra López was about her ethnicity, citizenship status, and gender altogether; unity came by acting as if her violation was an affront to Mexican and Chicano masculinity alone. Chicana feminists such as playwright Cherríe Moraga have previously argued that patriarchy and heterosexism divided the movement as much as U.S. governmental COINTELPRO infiltration did.[15] Yet, some Chicanxs and Latinxs learned from these limits and have advocated for intersectional recognition. In Moraga's essay, "Queer Aztlán: The Re-formation of Chicano Tribe," she renegotiates Aztlán, the mythical Aztec homeland that was a central utopian vision of the Chicano movement, around "queer *familia*," in an attempt to redefine Aztlán as embracing of Chicana feminists and queer Chicanxs, where no one is a "freak," but neither is it necessarily a "safe space." Rather, "it is unequivocally the original familial place from which I am compelled to write, which I reach toward in my audiences, and which serves as my source of inspiration, voice, and lucha [struggle]."[16] She depicts the struggle for sovereignty as one where "our freedom as a people is mutually dependent and cannot be parceled out—class before race before sex before sexuality," a struggle that "requires a serious reckoning with the weaknesses in our mestizo culture, and a

---

14. See, for instance, Kimberlé Crenshaw, "Mapping the Margins: Intersectionality, Identity Politics, and Violence against Women of Color," *Stanford Law Review* 43, no. 6 (1991): 1241–99.

15. Cherríe Moraga, "Queer Aztlán: The Re-Formation of Chicano Tribe," *The Last Generation: Prose and Poetry* (Boston, MA: South End Press, 1993), 149.

16. Ibid., 147.

reaffirmation of what has preserved and sustained us as a people."[17] Not unlike *mujerista* theologian Ada María Isasi-Díaz, Moraga depicts *la lucha*, the struggle, as sacred, and daily life as the locus from which divine revelations for a better world may be sought. Moraga imagines these revelations as demanding an ambivalent embrace of our heritage, a reckoning with the full violence of our histories even as we find in those same histories the strategies for survival that have made Latinx lives possible.

In Latinx theologies, daily life has long been a resource for revelation, and many have seen within daily Latinx lives an ethics of accompaniment, a practice in the struggle for justice that works to subvert, refuse, and undo unjust hierarchical relations. Many Latinx theologians have drawn attention to the way that Spanish fundamentally encodes intersectional allegiance in the term *nosotrxs*, a term that constructs "we" as "a community of *otros*, or others."[18] Affirming a radical intersectional praxis, Latina feminist theologian Neomi De Anda argues that a complex and messy sense of nosotrxs properly reflects the notion of *imago dei*, that we are made in the image of God because we are made in relationship with God and in relationship with one another. In recognizing the divine call of relationality, we necessarily challenge hierarchies of domination that have created our present struggles because we understand that "we" are a collection of "others." We struggle together in difference. De Anda underscores that daily realities of struggle are not romantic; in fact, they are complex and painful, but in truly living together in our differences—not our sameness—we must all attend to one another as equals.[19] Precisely because Latinxs are so diverse and yet struggle together anyway, we can demonstrate how otherness is fundamental to community. In the era of Trump where some in the United States want to wall themselves off from the rest of the world, the United States needs Latinx lessons in the messy realities of living as "we others" more than ever.

---

17. Ibid., 174.

18. Roberto S. Goizueta, "Nosotros: Toward a US Hispanic Anthropology," *Listening* 27, no. 1 (1992): 57.

19. De Anda, "Jesus the Christ," 165–68.

CHAPTER 24

Is Peace in the Time of Trump Possible?

MARIE DENNIS

Peace is a work of justice. Here too: not a justice proclaimed, imagined, planned . . . but rather a justice put into practice, lived out. . . . Peacemaking calls for courage, much more so than warfare. It calls for the courage to say yes to encounter and no to conflict: yes to dialogue and no to violence; yes to negotiations and no to hostilities; yes to respect for agreements and no to acts of provocation; yes to sincerity and no to duplicity. All of this takes courage, it takes strength and tenacity.[1]

—Pope Francis

A combination of factors shortly before and immediately following the end of the Cold War in 1989 created a wave of hope that the world would move into an era of peace, with a dividend comprised of financial resources and human ingenuity made available to meet human needs, to eliminate misery and exclusion, and to address environmental concerns. Successful struggles for independence in Africa, the People Power revolution in the Philippines, the ouster of

---

1. Pope Francis, "Homily of the Holy Father at Holy Mass, Koševo Stadium, June 6, 2015," http://w2.vatican.va; and Pope Francis, "Invocation for Peace, Vatican Gardens, Sunday, June 8, 2014, http://w2.vatican.va.

repressive military regimes in South America, the end of civil wars in Central America, and the victory over apartheid in South Africa, to name a few, suggested that the world was about to become more just and peaceful.

Sadly, that has not been the case. The number of interstate wars has decreased, but war and violence have shifted in character dramatically, and generalized insecurity has risen. Fed by fear that is both real and orchestrated, by the proliferation and aggressive trafficking of weapons, sometimes by deep-seated social, economic, or political injustices, and often by the geopolitical interests of powerful nations, too many wars have raged for years, even decades. Now extremist groups, nonstate actors, street gangs, drug cartels, and even official security forces perpetrate a kind of violence that seems unstoppable.

Since the end of World War II, one U.S. president after another, with some significant differences, has pursued a kind of *pax americana*, projecting U.S. military strength in the service of U.S. economic power and prosperity. From the foundation of the Bretton Woods institutions, which cemented U.S. global economic dominance, to development of the military-industrial-intelligence complex, peace on earth has been strikingly elusive. Always, the lack of peace was felt most painfully by people in other countries—Korea, Vietnam, Laos and Cambodia, Nicaragua and El Salvador, Iraq and Afghanistan, Pakistan and Syria, Yemen and Somalia—and by our own military. But terrible violence has been perpetrated on U.S. soil as well—especially in African American and Native American communities, where the toll of racism, deep economic injustice, and outright repression are painfully visible.

Since the end of the Cold War, the United States has shifted from one national security strategy to another—from a general emphasis on hard power and peace through strength (Ronald Reagan and George W. Bush) to softer power, diplomacy, and trade (Bill Clinton and Barack Obama), and to something "in between" (George H. W. Bush). Consistently, however, U.S. presidents have galvanized support for national security policy by identifying an "enemy" to fear, have promoted free market capitalism, and have consciously or unconsciously supported the integration of militarism and tremendous private sector profit. It is not likely the Trump administration will be very different.

Most administrations also have embraced more positive social, political, and cultural values essential to establishing sustainable peace. These include respect for human rights, including of women and minorities; pursuit of the global common good through international cooperation and the rule of law; good governance and freedom from repression; respect for cultural diversity; and care for the earth. What impact is a Trump presidency likely to have on possibilities for peace?

Beyond the immediate crises Mr. Trump will face during his term in office, a few areas of grave general concern come to mind. First, some of Mr. Trump's personal characteristics are troubling, particularly his unpredictability, his volatility, his extreme self-assuredness, his off-the-cuff way of communicating, and the capacity he demonstrated during the long campaign to denigrate others, especially vulnerable groups and people with special needs. We live in a complex world, where differences of culture and language exacerbate the possibility of misunderstandings and where violence can erupt over a perceived insult or a culturally insensitive remark.

The president of the United States lives under intense international scrutiny. Every word and every action has the potential to trigger an international incident or violence. It is often impossible to identify the specific event that sparks violent conflict, war, even genocide. The world does not need any additional excuses for violence, including ill-advised words or actions by the U.S. president.

Peace through Strength

Mr. Trump apparently shares former President Reagan's belief in peace through strength. His campaign promised he would repeal the defense sequester and submit a new budget to rebuild the "depleted U.S. military."[2] Already U.S. defense-related expenditures each year are well over $500 billion, not counting war spend-

---

2. Trump-Pence campaign website, "Fact Sheet: Key Policies Proposed in Mr. Trump's Military Readiness Speech," https://www.donaldjtrump.com.

ing.[3] The new administration plans to increase the size of the U.S. Army, rebuild the U.S. Navy, provide the U.S. Air Force with 1,200 fighter aircraft, grow the U.S. Marine Corps to thirty-six battalions, invest in a missile defense system to meet growing threats from Iran and North Korea, and create a state-of-the-art cyber defense and offense.

Mr. Trump has said he will pay for the expanded military by conducting a full audit of the Pentagon, eliminating incorrect payments, reducing duplicative bureaucracy, collecting unpaid taxes, and ending unwanted and unauthorized federal programs. Some of these steps should be taken anyway, but resources saved should not go to increased military spending when a more just and sustainable peace could be achieved through nonviolent means. These include diplomacy, atrocity-prevention mechanisms, peace-building strategies, and programs to meet crucial social and environmental needs in our own country and around the world.

Multilateral Noncooperation

In a major foreign policy speech six months before his election, candidate Donald Trump said the following: "Our goal is peace and prosperity, not war and destruction. The best way to achieve those goals is through a disciplined, deliberate and consistent foreign policy. . . . Our friends and enemies must know that if I draw a line in the sand, I will enforce it. However, . . . war and aggression will not be my first instinct. You cannot have a foreign policy without diplomacy. A superpower understands that caution and restraint are signs of strength. . . ."[4]

Time will tell to what extent the Trump administration will invest in diplomacy or multilateral cooperation. In the same speech, Mr. Trump added, "I am skeptical of international unions that tie us up and bring America down, and will never enter America into any agreement that reduces our ability to control our own affairs. . . ."[5]

---

3. Friends Committee on National Legislation, "Pentagon Spending," https://www.fcnl.org.

4. Donald J. Trump Foreign Policy Speech, April 27, 2016.

5. Ibid.

His inaugural address strongly reinforced this idea: "from this day forward: a new vision will govern our land, from this day forward, it's going to be only America first. America first. . . ."[6]

"America First" seems to be the bedrock of President Trump's approach to international relations. He has threatened to reduce drastically the U.S. role in the United Nations and to review internationally agreed UN conventions or multilateral agreements—including the 1951 UN Convention on Refugees, the 1981 Convention on the Elimination of All Forms of Discrimination against Women, and the Climate Change Agreement that came into force November 4, 2016. He also threatened to dismantle the nuclear agreement signed by Iran and six of the world's major powers,[7] calling the Iran deal "stupid," a "lopsided disgrace," and the "worst deal ever negotiated."[8] Finally, he has repeatedly made it clear U.S. participation in defense alliances, including with NATO, Japan, and South Korea, will depend on other countries sharing more of the costs of defense.

John Feffer, director of Foreign Policy in Focus for the Institute of Policy Studies comments on some possible consequences of such a strong U.S. turn inward:

> Once the anchor of the international community, the United States under Trump will become its chief adversary. The United States will not by itself deconstruct the international community. A number of hyper-nationalist leaders will help Trump in this effort. . . . Racist and anti-immigrant sentiment is on the rise throughout the world. The international community is a fragile construct. It doesn't require a lot to shake it up. A relentless, four-year onslaught by Donald Trump and his allies will have a terrible effect.[9]

---

6. Donald Trump's Inaugural Speech, January 20, 2017.

7. Thalif Deen, "Trump's Threat on Multilateral Treaties Keeps Us Guessing," *IPS News*, November 15, 2016.

8. Jim Cason, "Questions for Trump's New Foreign Policy Team," *Friends Committee on National Legislation*, December 22, 2016.

9. John Feffer, "Under Trump, the U.S. Will Become an Enemy of the International Community," *Institute for Policy Studies*, November 14, 2016, www.ips-dc.org.

Anti-Muslim Bigotry

As a candidate, Donald Trump called for "a total and complete shutdown of Muslims entering the United States until our country's representatives can figure out what is going on."[10] He regularly refers to the danger of "radical Islam" and "Islamic terrorism." His (original) National Security Advisor, Lt. Gen. Michael T. Flynn, painted Islam, a religion with 1.6 billion adherents worldwide, as "a cancer" and called Islam a political ideology "hiding behind the notion of being a religion."[11]

In reaction, retired U.S. Army General David Petraeus warned, "politicians here and abroad who toy with anti-Muslim bigotry must consider the effects of their rhetoric. Demonizing a religious faith and its adherents not only runs contrary to our most cherished and fundamental values as a country; it is also corrosive to our vital national security interests. . . ."[12] The offensive implication that Islam as a religion promotes violence undercuts critical efforts to address the root causes of extreme violence in our world.

Nuclear Weapons

Although during the campaign he called nuclear proliferation "the single biggest problem that our country faces right now," Donald Trump seems concerned only about nuclear weapons in the "wrong hands." He suggested it would be fine for Japan, South Korea, and even Saudi Arabia to acquire nuclear weapons: "The United States must greatly strengthen and expand its nuclear capability until such time as the world comes to its senses regarding nukes"[13] and that, if necessary, the United States would participate in a renewed nuclear arms race.

---

10. Trump-Pence campaign website, "Donald J. Trump statement on Preventing Muslim Immigration," December 7, 2016, https://www.donaldj trump.com.

11. ACT! for America, Dallas speech of Lt. Gen. Michael T. Flynn, August 13, 2016, https://www.youtube.com.

12. *Washington Post*, May 13, 2016.

13. Donald Trump tweet, 8:50 am, December 22, 2016, https://twitter. com/realdonaldtrump/status/811977223326625792?lang=en.

It is deeply troubling that the United States would, by implication or action, do so. No moral justification exists for impeding the already painfully slow steps to nuclear abolition, undercutting existing nuclear-arms-control agreements, or encouraging the proliferation of nuclear weapons, including among so-called "friendly" countries. The United States should abandon plans to modernize its nuclear weapons arsenal, investing billions to ensure these deadly weapons remain ready for use. These funds and tremendous human talent are diverted from meeting true human security goals and from protecting the integrity of creation. The Trump administration should actively support negotiations at the United Nations on a treaty that would not only make it illegal for nations to use or possess nuclear weapons, but would also help pave the way to their complete elimination, strengthening existing nonproliferation and disarmament efforts.

Russia

President Trump's relationship with Russian President Putin has been the topic of significant speculation. A more amicable relationship with the Russian Federation would be positive, especially if it enabled fruitful steps toward peace in Syria and Ukraine or more serious steps toward nuclear disarmament. What impact the appointment of former chairman and chief executive officer (CEO) of ExxonMobil, Rex Tillerson, as secretary of state will have on U.S.-Russian ties is to be determined.

China

The Trump administration's relationship with China could be troubling. Most dangerous is the ongoing dispute over control of the South China Sea where China has been converting into military bases small islands that are also claimed by Brunei, Malaysia, Vietnam, and the Philippines. The United States has a defense treaty with the Philippines and relies on free passage through the South China Sea for its warships heading to the Middle East.[14] As a can-

---

14. Michael Klare, "Escalation Watch: Four Looming Flashpoints Facing President Trump," TomDispatch (Common Dreams), January 17, 2017.

didate, Trump said that China has no respect for our country or for our president. Asked if he was prepared to use military force in response to the Chinese buildup, he responded, "Maybe."[15]

Analyst Michael Klare asserts that

> a U.S. effort to deny China access to the islands could involve anything from a naval blockade to air and missile attacks on the military installations built there to the sinking of Chinese warships. It's hard to imagine Beijing would refrain from taking retaliatory steps in response, and as one move tumbled onto the next, the two nuclear-armed countries might suddenly find themselves at the brink of full-scale war.[16]

North Korea

On January 1, North Korea's Kim Jong-un reiterated his commitment to future preemptive nuclear action, adding that his country would soon test-fire an ICBM.[17] This will present the Trump administration with another huge international challenge. Of the three options seemingly available, the most hopeful would be to negotiate a disarmament deal directly with Kim Jong-un. Trump has indicated his willingness to do so. However, in a recent tweet, he also appears to have implicitly countenanced a preemptive strike.[18]

Iran

Despite his promises, President Trump may be hard pressed to "scrap or renegotiate" the Iran deal, but he could counter the Iranians on other fronts. Michael Klare:

> This could take a variety of forms, including stepped-up sanctions, increased aid to Saudi Arabia in its war against

---

15. Ibid.

16. Ibid.

17. Tony Munroe and Jack Kim, "North Korea's Kim Says Close to Test Launch of ICBM," *Reuters*, January 1, 2017.

18. Donald Trump tweet, 3:05 pm, January 2, 2017, https://twitter.com/realDonaldTrump/status/816057920223846400?lang=en.

the Iranian-backed Houthis in Yemen, or attacks on Iranian proxies in the Middle East. Any of these would no doubt prompt countermoves by Tehran, and from there a cycle of escalation could lead in numerous directions, all dangerous, including military action by the U.S., Israel, or Saudi Arabia.[19]

Israel and Palestine

While any of the above situations could become a flashpoint for violence, President Trump's policy direction on Israel and Palestine is possibly the most ominous in terms of peace. His appointments of unabashed Israel-supporters Jared Kushner as a special advisor and David Friedman as U.S. ambassador to Israel confirm Trump's commitment to ensure that Israel "receives maximum military, strategic and tactical cooperation from the United States." He has promised to "oppose any efforts to delegitimize Israel, impose discriminatory double standards against Israel, or impose special labeling requirements on Israeli products or boycotts on Israeli goods."[20] President Trump is committed to supporting the expansion of Israeli settlements in East Jerusalem, which may well be the death knell for a two-state solution, and intends to move the U.S. embassy from Tel Aviv to Jerusalem, a move almost guaranteed to inflame tensions in the region.

Peace in the Time of Trump?

Is peace in the time of Trump possible? Possible, but not probable. Little, if any, evidence points in that direction.

---

19. Klare, "Escalation Watch."

20. Jason Dov Greenblatt and David Friedman, "Joint Statement from Jason Dov Greenblatt and David Friedman, Co-Chairmen of the Israel Advisory Committee to Donald J. Trump," https://medium.com/@jgreenblatt.

CHAPTER 25

Trump's America
What Will We Do about It?

KELLY BROWN DOUGLAS

There are those who have advised that we all should take a breath and give Donald Trump a chance, to see what he will do as president. They have suggested that the bigoted, misogynistic, Islamo-phobic, and xenophobic hatred that accompanied his presidential campaign was nothing more than rhetorical bluster to serve his election and not a signal of policies to come. The fact of the matter, however, is that with that rhetoric he was elected. Moreover, it is not about what he will do; it is about what he has already done. He has unmasked a disturbing truth about America—a truth that got him elected. Furthermore, during his first ten days in office he has unleashed executive orders implementing travel bans and law-and-order procedures that reflect the bigoted rhetoric of his campaign.[1] And so, one thing is clear: Donald Trump's ascendancy to the presidency brings us to a point of decision in this nation and hence a particular challenge to religious scholars and leaders.

The warring soul of the black American, which W. E. B. Du Bois so poignantly described in his 1903 book *Souls of Black Folks*, provides an apt description of America itself. Drawing on Du Bois's

---

1. See Aidan Quigley, "All of Trump's Executive Actions So Far," *Politico*, January 25, 2017, http://www.politico.com. Note especially orders referring to immigrants, refugees, and crime.

prescient words, America is a nation defined by "two thoughts, two warring ideas."[2] What America must decide is whether it wants to be a nation defined by its Anglo-Saxon myth of exceptionalism or one defined by its democratic rhetoric of being a nation of liberty and justice for all. This question is more poignant for people of faith. For we must decide if we are a people committed to a divine vision that reflects an Anglo-Saxon God or a divine vision that reflects a God whose image is revealed through a racially, religiously, and culturally diverse humanity? If we are in fact committed to building a nation and being a people that reflects a vision of justice and freedom for all who are children of God (and that is everybody who has breath), then the work we do as theologians, religious scholars, and leaders must be defined by at least three things: moral memory, moral identity. and moral participation.

Moral Memory

We continue to arrive at these "Make America Great Again" moments of Anglo-Saxon chauvinistic backlash where whiteness continues to stand its ground because of America's utter refusal to face the hard truths of it own story. As we have just seen, it is a story about the various vicissitudes of America's defining Anglo-Saxon narrative and the culture of whiteness that accompanies it. We as a people and as a nation will certainly continue to be held captive to and defined by this narrative until we as a people and a nation confront it and the history it has created. That is what a moral memory is all about.

Moral memory is a memory defined by telling the truth—even the harsh truths about who we are as a nation and a people—and then taking responsibility for the truth that is told. For moral memory is not about facile apologies meant to exonerate white Americans from the past. Rather, it is about holding oneself accountable to the truth of a past that continues to enact itself in the present. This is something that this country, particularly white America,

---

2. See W. E. B Du Bois, *Souls of Black Folks* (New York: W. W. Norton, 1903).

has simply refused to do—to tell the truth. Instead, it would rather maintain a comfortable "racial amnesia" and ignore the unrelenting realities of whiteness that indeed compromise the possibilities of this nation ever being a place where there is justice and liberty for all.[3] In this regard, William Faulkner was right: "The past is never dead. It is not even past." As long as the truth of our past is not confronted it will not be dead; rather it will continue to control our present realities and shape our future.

We must make clear that it is only in employing a moral memory that we will ever be able to be honest about the very real racial contract on which this country was built and on which it continues to be enacted. It is only with a moral memory that the relationship between the slavocracy and the Prison Industrial Complex can begin to come to light. Such a memory will also expose "stop and frisk" and voter ID laws as the twenty-first-century versions of the Jim Crow laws and poll taxes that they are. It will also compel the nation to confront what happened to the Trayvons, Renishas, Tamiras, Sandras, and Philandros and continues to happen and to understand that these are nothing less than twenty-first-century lynchings. Essentially, a moral memory will force this nation to confront the truth that the 1857 Dred Scott decision, though overturned, has remained the de facto law of the land: at any given moment in time, black people have "no rights that the white man is bound to respect," and hence black lives in this Anglo-Saxon exceptionalist country have never really mattered.

James Baldwin once spoke of the necessity of what I am calling a moral memory this way. He said that the fact that Americans—and by this he meant white Americans—have "not been able to face their history . . . hideously menaces this country." He went on to say, "it menaces the entire world."[4] If indeed we are to live into a professed commitment to social justice as a people of faith,

---

3. For reference to "racial amnesia," see John Blake and Tawanda Scott Sambou, "How Trump's Victory Turns into Another 'Lost Cause,'" *CNN*, December 28, 2016.

4. James Baldwin, "White Man's Guilt," *The Price of the Ticket* (New York: St. Martin's/Marek, 1985), 410.

then our work as theologians, religious scholars, and leaders, must engage and reflect a moral memory even as we demand that of this nation.

Moral Identity

My son was seven or eight years old. He and his best buddy at the time (I will call him James) were sitting in the back seat of the car as I was driving them home from school. James was white. It was during Black History Month, so they were learning about "famous" black people. That day, Arthur Ashe was the focus of the black history lesson. As my son and James were discussing Ashe James said, "Good thing we [meaning white people] decided to share our stuff with you guys [meaning black people] or Arthur Ashe would have never been champion." Already implanted within James's young consciousness was the awareness that with his white skin came certain privileges that were not given to black people. The only way for black people to attain these privileges was for white people to confer them upon black people. Otherwise, these privileges were off limits to black people—like the privilege of playing tennis and becoming a champion.

To claim a moral identity in a society shaped by a kind of stand-your-ground culture that privileges whiteness even as it penalizes—sometimes unto death—those who are the nonwhite other, is to name and denounce white privilege. There is a certain paradox of white privilege illustrated in the story about my son and James. Even as white privilege ascribes a false sense of superiority to white Americans at the peril of the nonwhite other, it is not the nonwhite other—that is, those without the benefits of white privilege—that are the most dehumanized. Rather, it is the humanity of those who live out of and into the privileges of whiteness that is compromised and denigrated. The fact of the matter is, the only way "white" people can be who they are is by claiming a privilege that belittles the humanity of nonwhite others. Baldwin rightly observed that white people's sense of self for far too long has depended on the lie that black people are inferior to them; and tragically, what white people have not realized is that in "this debasement and definition they have debased and defined themselves."[5] In this way, it was actually James's very humanity that was being compromised and debased, even as he viewed himself as superior to my son.

In order to claim a moral identity there is one thing that must be understood: to be white is an immoral choice. It is the choice to see oneself as better than another and, thus, it is the choice to betray the sacredness of our common humanity—the fact that everyone who has breath or has ever had breath is a sacred child of God, reflecting God's own image, nothing more and nothing less. (In the words of James Cone, just because one looks like a white American does not mean that one has to act like one.[6]) To understand this makes it clear that whiteness is a sinful choice, and likewise the culture that privileges whiteness is a sinful culture, for they both separate human beings from God. To reiterate, they both distort the very integrity of our human being as sacred children of God.

In short, to live into the privileges of whiteness, that is to be white—whether one does so innocently or guilefully—is to live into a sinful identity. Therefore, there is an ethical responsibility to claim and call others to a moral identity. Borrowing from the words of theologian Paul Tillich, our work as religious thinkers and leaders must exemplify the "courage to be oneself," that is, the courage to be ourselves—children of God, nothing more and nothing less.[7] Such courage requires letting go of and certainly not striving for what it means to be white in America. A moral identity is one that lets go of those spoken and unspoken privileges of whiteness such as the privilege to claim space, the privilege of voice and perspective, the privilege of innocence—and the privilege of being protected from the "nonwhite" other. It is this last privilege of whiteness that has much to do with the deep divides of race in the United States, and thus merits closer examination.

---

5. James Baldwin, "On Being White and Other Lies," *Essence*, April 1984.

6. James H. Cone, *A Black Theology of Liberation* (Maryknoll, NY: Orbis Books, 2010), 156.

7. Paul Tillich, *The Courage to Be*, 2nd ed. (New Haven: Yale Nota Bene, 2000 [Yale University Press, 1952]), 87.

Recent studies have revealed that the core social networks of most white Americans are 91 percent white and only 5 percent some other race, with only 1 percent of that being black. Worse yet, fully three-quarters (75 percent) of white Americans report that the network of people with whom they discuss important matters is entirely white, with no minority presence.[8] With this being the case, it is no wonder that white and black people have grossly different perspectives on the reality of racial injustice in America, such as whether or not the criminal justice system is fair or whether or not incidents like the killings of Trayvon, Tamir, Freddy, or Philandro are incidental or a part of a pattern where black males are disproportionately brutalized if not killed by police.[9] Notwithstanding the issue of skewed perspectives, there is an even more costly implication stemming from the white privilege of social segregation: the inability to empathize with, let alone enter into solidarity with, those who are victimized by the violent and sometimes deadly realities of systemic, structural, social, and culture whiteness itself. This inability to enter into solidarity with those victimized by whiteness is even more consequential for those who claim to be followers of Jesus, the one who was crucified.

That Jesus was crucified, a fate that he refused to escape, shows that he emptied himself of any sense of exceptionalism and privilege that might be bestowed upon him because of his maleness, Jewishness, or even divinity. In short, he "let go" of that which would set him apart from humanity, especially the crucified classes of humanity—those victims of the deadly cultural, political, and religious privilege of his time. In this regard, central to those who would follow Jesus is the requirement to let go of white privilege.[10]

---

8. See Daniel Cox, Juhem Navarro-Rivera, Robert P. Jones, "Race, Religion, and Political Affiliation of American's Core Social Network," *PRRI*, August, 3, 2016.

9. Ibid.

10. I take this concept of "letting go" from Rosemary Radford Ruether, who suggests that those of privilege in any context must develop a "theology of letting-go." See Ruether, "A U.S. Theology of Letting Go," in *The Reemergence of Liberation Theologies: Models for the Twenty-First Century*, ed. Thia Cooper (New York: Palgrave Macmillan, 2013).

Put bluntly, it is impossible to be at once white and Christian. To reiterate, whiteness is a sinful reality, for it means that one is not able to be where the God of Jesus is—in solidarity with those who are victimized by the crucifying realities of white privilege. Worse yet, one is not able to see Jesus in the face of the Trayvons and Renishas of our world. To be Christian therefore requires a moral identity—one free from the pretensions of Anglo-Saxon exceptionalism and the privileges of whiteness.

One thing that the 2016 presidential election revealed, given the high percentage of white Christians who voted for Donald Trump, is that there were many whose whiteness seemed to "trump" what it means to be Christian. As one commentator pointed out, if in voting for Trump one was able to overlook his racism, his sexism, Islamophobia, and other forms of bigotry, then one was clearly voting from a place of white privilege—since it is only from the standpoint of white privilege that these things would not matter.[11] And so, borrowing from the platform of Black Lives Matter in response to Trump's election, giving up the privilege of whiteness requires white people "to organize their communities, to courageously help their loved ones understand the importance of solidarity and to show up for us, for themselves, and democracy."[12]

This brings us to the final aspect of what is required if we are in fact committed to building a nation and being a people reflective of a God with a vision of justice and freedom.

Moral Participation

If faith is about partnering with God to help "mend the world," then faith communities are compelled to join God in mending the world of its injustice and thus building a world where everyone is cherished for who they are. This is a world and a society where the peace of God that is justice and freedom flourishes. Practically speaking, this means that our work as religious thinkers and leaders as well as our lives should be a place of sanctuary and witness.

---

11. Blake and Sambou, "How Trump's Victory."

12. Monique Judge, "Black Lives Matter Issues Official Statement on Donald Trump's Election," *The Root*, November 15, 2016.

To be a sanctuary means that in our work and presence no one should feel diminished or unsafe because of who they are or are not. It also means that we must work to make our communities safe spaces for all who are made to feel unsafe by the various narratives of exceptionalism and privilege in our society and our world, especially as they are exhibited through the various policies of Donald Trump. More specifically, it means creating spaces free of bigotry or intolerance of any kind and resisting at every level of our society any efforts to reinstate twenty-first-century versions of Jim Crow laws like "stop and frisk," or poll taxes in the form of voter ID laws, or versions of McCarthyism with "House Un-American Committees," or ethnically and religiously driven "travel bans" and immigration policies. In short, that aspect of moral participation that is sanctuary means that, drawing on the words of Mahatma Gandhi, we must be and work for the "change we want to see." This leads to what it means to be a witness for the vision of a God for freedom and justice for all.

At the least it means calling out racism, xenophobia, and any other ism or bigotry for what it is, even when it masks itself in the patriotic language of "greatness." It further requires calling out the ways in which our socioeconomic policies, laws, systems, structures, and criminal-justice complex privilege whiteness and refusing to be silent until they are dismantled. Audre Lorde has reminded us that "our silence will not save us," and she is right.[13] Our silence has not and will not save us from the crucifying death that is Anglo-Saxon exceptionalism. We must stand as witnesses against it.

In the final analysis, moral participation, for those who claim to be followers of Jesus, is about nothing less than remembering Jesus—as in *anamnesis,* the Greek word for the remembering that

---

13. Paraphrased from Audre Lorde, "The Transformation of Silence into Language and Action," paper delivered at the Modern Language Association's "Lesbian and Literature Panel," Chicago, IL, December 28, 1977. First published in *Sinister Wisdom* 6 (1978). Also, Audre Lorde, *Sister Outsider: Essays and Speeches,* Crossing Press Feminist Series (Trumansburg, NY: Crossing Press, 1984), 40.

Jesus called his disciples to during the Last Supper. Such remembering is about more than a mental recollection of events. Rather, it is about bringing the past into the present through our bodies, our lives, and our very work. In this regard, moral participation is about bringing the past that was Jesus' ministry into our very present. This, then, is a past defined by a ministry of sanctuary, especially for those who are most marginalized by the power and privilege of whiteness; it is a past that empowers us to witness against the forces of oppression and the perpetrators of unjust privilege.

In 1961 James Baldwin declared, "The time has come, God knows, for us to examine ourselves, but we can do this only if we are willing to free ourselves of the myth of America and try to find out what is really happening here."[14] The time has come in this era of a Trump presidency for us to be a people with moral memory, moral identity, and moral participation. And therefore, in the words of #BlackLivesMatter,

> We must reckon with the anti-blackness of America's history that led to this political moment [and] operate from a place of love for our people and a deep yearning for real freedom. . . . In our work, we center the most marginalized, and look to them for leadership. We must fight for our collective liberation because we are clear that until black people are free, no one is free. [And so] we must remain committed to practicing empathy for one another in this struggle—[while not] negotiating with racists, fascists or anyone who demands we compromise our existence.[15]

Yes, we know who Trump is and what Trump's election has done. The question remains, who are we, and what we will do?

---

14. Quoted in James Baldwin, "The Discovery of What It Means to Be an American," *The Price of the Ticket: Collected Nonfiction 1948–1985* (New York: St. Martin's/Marek, 1985), 175.

15. Judge, "Black Lives Matter."

Conclusion

MIGUEL A. DE LA TORRE

When the purpose of politics is to change a country merely in form without changing the conditions of injustice endured by its people, when the purpose of politics, in the name of liberty, is to replace contented authoritarians with hungry ones, then the duty of honest persons can never be to excuse themselves by stepping aside, and allow parasites to infest public life.

—*José Martí*

For marginalized communities in the United States, especially racial and ethnic communities, Donald J. Trump is the true face of America. It is the face we have confronted throughout most of our interactions with societal authorities, though it remained masked to those in the dominant culture who embraced the illusion of a postracial society. On election night, that mask was ripped aside, revealing that face to society at large, and leaving many of us terrified.

Whether by those on the right or the left of the political spectrum, intolerance and demonizing of the other have become the normative *modus operandi* of U.S. political discourse. Simply to characterize Trump's supporters as a "basket of deplorables" would be a simplistic way of understanding what occurred on November 8, 2016. And yet, there is no doubt that some of Trump's supporters did resonate with the misogynist, racist, homophobic, xenophobic, and Islamophobic comments he continuously made. We cannot ignore those on the alt-right extreme who specifically

226

voted for Trump because they agreed, shared, and cheered his more egregious rants and tweets. But for a significant "moveable middle" who voted for Trump, many of whom previously supported and voted for Obama, their motivation remains baffling.

Maybe the Democratic candidate's promises of more-of-the-same failed to resonate with members of a downwardly mobile middle class who are losing jobs and homes due to the consequences of global neoliberal policies? Maybe Trump voters were able to compartmentalize between the character of the man and his promise to "make America great again"? Maybe the barrage of media attention focused on outrageous tweets rather than the feasibility of policies swayed voters looking for change? Or maybe the alleged influence of foreign entities or the fallacious insinuations of wrongdoing by the FBI changed the minds of last minute voters?

In their minds, they are the "forgotten Americans" economically struggling to survive. We face the realization that the reasons for Trump's support remain complex.

Many of those who voted for Trump assure us that misogynist, racist, homophobic, xenophobic, and Islamophobic motives were not the reason they cast their votes. But underneath their reasons it is impossible to ignore the element of white privilege among this moveable middle. If it was not *because* of his racist, misogynistic, xenophobic, Islamophobic positions that they supported it, they nevertheless found it possible to support him *despite* these positions, because he did not threaten their existence.

On the morning of Trump's inauguration, two Latinx women visited our home. Their eyes were puffy and red. All night long, they told my wife, they had attended Mass with *la comunidad*. All night long they had wept about the trials and tribulation they fear will befall members of their community. Children made offerings—coins from their piggy banks—to *la virgencita* in hopes that God would soften Trump's heart. They, and many communities like theirs, lack the white middle-class privilege that can shield them from Trump's xenophobic pronouncements.

This is a candidate who began his campaign by calling Latinxs rapists and thieves and promised to respond by building a wall. This is a candidate who made it clear that black lives do not matter, emboldening those for whom they never did. This is a candidate who has consistently demeaned women's bodies and excused predatory sexual behavior, heartening a new generation of misogynists. This is a candidate who made Islamophobia central to his campaign.

The reality of a Trump presidency means greater hatred, as was demonstrated during the first forty-eight hours after his election. For example, a woman at San Diego State University was confronted by two white men who targeted her because of her Muslim faith, signified by the hijab she wore.[1] Children (hatred is taught early) from Royal Oak Middle School in Michigan chanted in the cafeteria: "Build the wall! Build the wall!"[2] On busy intersections in Durham, North Carolina, the expression "Black lives don't matter and neither does your vote" was spray painted on two walls.[3] On the seventy-eighth anniversary of Kristallnacht, Philadelphia police reported several incidents in which walls and vehicles were defaced. On the main city throughway, Broad Street, graffiti appeared with phrases like, "Sieg Heil 2016," and a swastika substituted for the T in Trump.[4] And a transgender veteran from Cookeville, Tennessee, had her truck vandalized with graffiti reading "Trump," then set on fire.[5] So many incidents occurred in the first forty-eight hours after this election that insufficient space exists to document them all.

And while a person should not be held responsible for the hate crimes conducted in his or her name, nevertheless, the deafening

---

1. CNN Wire, "Reports of Hate Crimes and Racist Graffiti, Including in California, Following Trump's Election Win," *Los Angeles KTLA 5*, November 10, 2016.

2. James David Dickson and Candice Williams, "Royal Oak Middle School Student's Chant 'Build That Wall,'" *Detroit News*, November 10, 2016.

3. Al Janavel, "Downtown Durham Graffiti Takes Aim at Black Voters," *CBS North Carolina*, November 9, 2016.

4. "'Sieg Heil,' Swastikas, Racist Trump Graffiti Appear in South Philly," *Philadelphia Inquirer*, November 9, 2016.

5. Ariana Sawyer, "Cookeville Transgender Veteran's Truck Painted 'Trump,' Lit on Fire," *Tennessean*, November 9, 2016.

silence from the president-elect repudiating these incidents and chastising perpetrators of violence spoke volumes. Furthermore, this form of overt violence seemed an extension of what we saw during the Trump campaign rallies where, from the podium, he incited physical violence against protestors with comments like: "I'll beat the crap out of you"; "I'd like to punch him in the face"; "Try not to hurt him. If you do, I'll defend you in court"; or "Knock the crap out of them."[6] Why then should we be surprised by the threats, intimidation, and physical violence that occurred within hours of the election? Mark Potok, of the Southern Poverty Law Center (which tracks hate crimes), stated that he was "seeing a rash of hate crimes, of hate rhetoric, racist graffiti in campuses around the country. We have seen [Ku Klux] Klan literature drops, we have seen that suicide hotlines are ringing off the hook, and we are hearing of very extensive bullying in and around schools."[7]

Yes, we can dismiss those perpetrating hate crimes as ignoramuses, but the fingerprints of the president-elect, along with all those responsible for stroking fear to win votes, were also all over these incidents.

But while it is easy to identify explicit physical violence, the more insidious violence is normalized in social structures designed to exploit one group of people (usually along race, ethnic, and gender lines) so the minority can live a life of power and privilege. The lack of physical violence does not mean a culture of death is not created. While not dismissing the viciousness of physical violence, the entirety of this book has mainly focused on what liberative theologians call institutionalized violence.

When a police officer pulls over an unarmed person of color and ends up shooting him or her, that is a vivid example of physical violence. Redefining violence to encompass its institutional manifestations shifts the emphasis from an individual act that can be dismissed as some unfortunate outlier (a bad apple) toward collective

---

6. Ainara Tiefenthäler, "Trump's History of Encouraging Violence," *New York Times*, March 14, 2016.

7. Asher Klein, "Rash of Hate Crimes Reported Day after Trump's Election," *New York Channel 4, NBC*, November 10, 2016.

and social phenomena with which society as a whole—its political administration, governmental agencies, corporations, financial institutions, and a militarized police apparatus—is complicit.

Institutional violence is not some random, isolated act committed by a single perpetrator; rather, it is part of a societal structure operating within a legal framework designed to sustain and maintain unjust relationships responsible for human alienation, economic devastation, and early death. Such violence is seldom immediate, as in the case of police brutality; instead violence is drawn out over years, if not decades, making it no less violent or deadly. Trump's election only magnified the institutional violence already too familiar to the world's marginalized.

As we face the next four or eight years of this regime, it is hard to be hopeful. In the face of the enormity of white supremacy, and a global economy designed to channel the world's resources to a Eurocentric minority, the prospect of dismantling these structures may seem truly hopeless. Faced with these odds, no doubt some will turn to some form of escapism.

The question is how are we going to resist? Perhaps one answer is in what I call an ethics or praxis of *joder*. *Joder* is a Spanish word never used in polite company; it can be translated as "to screw with." An *ethics para joder* is an ethics that screws with the prevailing institutional violence. An *ethics para joder* fosters an effective response to the consequences of a Trump regime. To *joder* is to resist. A *joderon* is one who strategically becomes a royal pain in the rear end, purposely causing trouble, constantly disrupting the established norm, shouting from the mountaintops what is supposed to be kept silent, audaciously refusing to stay in one's assigned place. To *joder* is to create instability, upsetting the prevailing social order designed to maintain the law and order of the privileged. Think of Jesus cleansing the Temple, the liberative praxis of literally overturning the established tables of order and oppression (Matthew 21:12-13). To *joder* is to overturn established tables. Political and social change requires going beyond the rules created by the dominant culture, moving beyond what is expected, pushing beyond universalized experiences.

History demonstrates the futility of simply denouncing unjust social structures, for those whom the structures privilege will never willingly abdicate what they consider to be their birthright. The trickster act of overturning tables might lead to new possibilities, unavailable while established tables remain stable. Within a Trump era that legitimizes and normalizes the privileges of the few at the expense of the many, *joderones* become tricksters who unmask deeper truths. *Joderones* are consummate survivors, offering ways for the disenfranchised to endure and prevail over the reality of a Trump presidency. Disrupting the equilibrium of the dominant culture creates compromising situations for those in power, revealing their weaknesses, exposing what they prefer to remain hidden, and removing their artificial masks of superiority.

Even following a Trump presidency, it would be naïve to assume that oppressive structures will cease to exist. An *ethics para joder* is a liberative praxis by which we learn to transform society for the better, even though the ultimate utopian goal will not and may never be realized. Nonetheless, we strive forward not because we expect to succeed; we strive toward justice because we have no other choice if we wish to maintain our humanity. We strive forward because it is in the crucible of struggle that we construct our identity and define our purpose in life. Faced with the insurmountable task of constructing justice in an age of Trump makes screwing with the social structures responsible for institutional violence the only ethical response in the *hope* of creating new opportunities through disorder and chaos.

In the praxis of *joder* the disenfranchised are not motivated by a desire for vengeance. To *joder* is an act of love toward the oppressors, forcing them to confront their complicity with oppressive structures, and thereby leading them toward their own salvation. To *joder* is thus a nonviolent survival strategy based on love designed to liberate both the abused from death-dealing social structures that deny their humanity, as well as the abuser whose own humanity is lost through complicity with these same structures.

Immediately after the election, there were calls for all Americans to come together and support our new president. But can we really expect marginalized groups to come together with apologists for the hatred they continue to experience? What we witnessed on election night was a great *whitelash* against the audacity of the historically disenfranchised for hoping they could be equal; a *whitelash* against the gall of a nation having elected a black man to the highest office. (Oh, how dreadful it is to remember yesteryear's hopeful, yet naïve chants of "yes, we can" turn to today's haunting dirge.)

We refuse to hold hands and sing "Kumbaya." Let this book be a small step toward unmasking the injustice of a Trump age. Seekers of justice, especially whites, are invited to join us in solidarity in singing a different song—*¡Basta!* And part of saying Enough! is to hold accountable those who traded their public profession to Divinity for a triumphant profession to Trump. The success of Trump is partially due to the complicity of religious leaders who failed to hold Trump accountable to the standards of justice they profess to follow.

So what happens when clergy who align with structures responsible for institutional violence choose to be profiteers rather than prophets? They sell the poor for a pair of sandals, exchanging what they claim to believe for an opportunity to have a say as to who sits on the Supreme Court, or, as an expression of a more self-serving vanity, for an opportunity to preach a prosperity gospel during the inauguration.

In contrast, those who have contributed to this book have done so to contribute to a praxis of resistance against institutionalized violence and as a profession of faith. We write as an outward expression of an inward belief. In seeking to be prophetic, we unapologetically resist the normalization of Trump and hold accountable the beneficiaries of the institutional violence that Trump initiates, expands, and/or sustains. Faith and resistance become our spiritual response in an age of Trump.

Index